PLAYING
WITH
PURPOSE:
RACING

PLAYING WITH PURPOSE: *RACING*

INSIDE THE LIVES AND FAITH OF AUTO RACING'S MOST INTRIGUING DRIVERS—

MARK MARTIN, TREVOR BAYNE, JAMIE MCMURRAY AND OTHERS

MIKE YORKEY

WITH MARCUS BROTHERTON AND MATTHEW WEEDA

BARBOUR
PUBLISHING

Print ISBN 978-1-62416-618-1

eBook Editions:
Adobe Digital Edition (.epub) 978-1-62836-982-3
Kindle and MobiPocket Edition (.prc) 978-1-62836-983-0

The author is represented by WordServe Literary Group, Ltd., Greg Johnson, Literary Agent, 10152 S. Knoll Circle, Highlands Ranch, CO 80130

Published by Barbour Publishing, Inc., P.O. Box 719, Uhrichsville, Ohio 44683, www.barbourbooks.com

Our mission is to publish and distribute inspirational products offering exceptional value and biblical encouragement to the masses.

Member of the
Evangelical Christian
Publishers Association

Printed in the United States of America.

CONTENTS

INTRODUCTION

NASCAR'S ALLURE,
SEEN THROUGH FRESH EYES

Just shy of a hundred years ago now, somewhere deep in the Appalachian region of the United States, one man developed a powerful thirst. We don't know who this man was, nor is his identity particularly relevant to this story. What's significant is that he wasn't just thirsty for any old beverage, no sir. He had a particular hankering for moonshine whiskey. But the trouble—for him at least—was that obtaining a stiff drink in the Prohibition era proved no simple matter.

They say necessity is the mother of invention, so, as the legend goes, that man talked to a friend, and his friend talked to a friend, and that friend talked to a friend, and soon an entire system was constructed and coordinated to cook up moonshine, hide moonshine, sell moonshine, buy moonshine, and—most crucial to this story—*transport* moonshine.

Enter the professional bootlegging car driver.

He was no ordinary driver. Not in 1920. Considering that moonshine was often concocted up in the hills far from the prying eyes of prohibitionists and policemen, that meant that the driver needed to control a big-engined, highly maneuverable car to haul 'shine around the slippery twists and turns of the gravelly Appalachian back roads. If we set aside the obvious illegalities for a moment and examine the craft of evasive, high-speed driving itself, we see it took skill to drive that way. Real skill.

Prohibition dried up in 1933, and soon there was no need for moonshine runners. But that didn't sit well with many of the drivers. See, these drivers had come to enjoy much of what they were doing. They liked the speed and the engine tunings, the suspension modifications, and the more honorable codes of their craft. Not just any-ole-body could do what they did. Soon enough, they began to organize races among themselves, mostly for bragging rights, occasionally for prizes—

and that is how stock car racing was birthed.

It took awhile longer before the sport became officially known as the National Association for Stock Car Auto Racing, Inc. (NASCAR). World War II factored into history's mix from 1939 to 1945, when the nation's attention focused squarely on the fight for liberty. Then, two weeks before Christmas in 1947, an enterprising auto mechanic named Bill France struck up a conversation with his buddies at the Ebony Bar in Daytona Beach, Florida.

France had an idea to turn the sport into a formal affair. Nah, he didn't want to impose any of that hoity-toity European auto racing flavor into the mix. He just wanted things official. You know—standardize the rules. Make a regular schedule. Organize a series leading up to a grand championship. Bill and his buddies scratched out a points system on the back of a bar room napkin, as the story goes, and ordered another round.

A SPORT IS BORN

Two months later, France's wish came to fruition. France was a savvy promoter at heart and a serious auto racing enthusiast to boot. His leadership led to the official creation of NASCAR on February 21, 1948, with France named president, ex-vaudeville-performer-turned-motorcycle-racer Erwin "Cannonball" Baker hired as the first commissioner, and the city of Daytona Beach, Florida, christened the unofficial Mecca of the sport. The city held a 150-mile race that same month with more than 14,000 fans turning out to cheer on the drivers. A plethora of fans and drivers flocked down from the other Southern states, too—from Mississippi, Alabama, Georgia, and South Carolina, and a particularly vocal contingent came from North Carolina. They'd been driving and racing stock cars up there for years, and another big hub of racing grew up around the city of Charlotte.

Even though the sport of stock car racing began in the backwoods, over the years it grew into a mighty oak. By 1956, NASCAR sanctioned 56 official races held everywhere from Florida to New York state. Time passed, more races were held, and by the early 1970s big-name sponsors began to get involved, which grew the sport's influence even more.

One of the earliest big-time sponsors, like it or not, was the R.J. Reynolds Tobacco Company. Even back in the heyday of smoking, Big Tobacco wasn't allowed to run commercials on TV. Company officials noticed there were a lot of smokers wherever the bulk of the NASCAR races were being run, particularly in the tobacco-friendly Southern states, and that meant a prime advertising opportunity. Deep-pocketed sponsors dropped an infusion of big money into the sport. Other sponsors jumped on board, and soon the top drivers were getting big cash rewards for winning NASCAR races.

More time passed, and the sport grew and grew. Legends were born—the stuff of real sports greatness. Who could forget February 19, 1979, the first time the entire Daytona 500 race was televised? With thousands of eyes glued to their TV screens, Cale Yarborough and Donnie Allison duked it out neck and neck for most of the race. Right down to the wire, it looked too close to call, but then, on the very last lap, they crashed into each other. They weren't hurt—in fact, they both jumped out of their cars and started a fistfight with each other. Donny's brother, Bobby, screeched his car to a halt and joined the fray.

Meanwhile, a cool middle-aged upstart named Richard Petty sped past the fight, claimed his sixth Daytona 500 win, and proved once again the veracity of his nickname—The King. Petty had long since established his reputation as the undisputed champion of the sport. Back in 1967, he had won an amazing 27 of 48 regular-season races—with 10 of those wins coming right in a row. He'd go on to win a staggering 200 races in his career before retiring in 1984.

Today, NASCAR has grown to become the biggest professional auto racing sport in the country—both in popularity and in number of races. Fans today can cheer for their favorite drivers at more than 1,500 NASCAR-sanctioned races each year. Those races are held in 39 states and Canada with exhibition races held in Japan, Australia, and Mexico. NASCAR is an American sport at heart—with strong emphasis placed on patriotism, supporting the country's troops, and respect for God and country.

Even then, viewers from some 150 countries around the world

regularly watch NASCAR races, with some $3 billion being spent annually in NASCAR-licensed products alone. Compared with other sports, NASCAR's national appeal in the United States is second only to professional football, and security experts say that of the 20 biggest single-day sporting events ever held in America, 17 of those are NASCAR races.

RACESIDE AT THE TRACK

Like many Americans, I (Mike Yorkey) am a big NASCAR fan, and while I wanted to gear this book toward the sport's fans, I also wanted to make it accessible to people who may be newcomers to NASCAR. There's a certain familiarity bred whenever a fan becomes deeply immersed in a sport, a certain insider lingo that's picked up and tossed about, so I wanted to add into the mix a rawness that comes from viewing the sport with a fresh set of eyes.

First up, since so many people are only able to watch NASCAR on TV (compared with how many can go to an actual race), I wanted to capture the observations and reactions of someone viewing a NASCAR race from the bleachers for the first time. So I sent my research assistant, Matt Weeda, to Charlotte, North Carolina, for the 2013 All-Stars race, asked him to keep his eyes and ears open, and expect to be debriefed when he got back.

Matt flew cross-country from his home in Washington state and arrived at the Charlotte Motor Speedway for the big two-day event. Immediately after landing, he drove out to the track to get his bearings and pick up his tickets. It was late on a Thursday afternoon. The event didn't officially begin until the next day, but the Speedway was already in full swing.

Matt's first reaction was shock at the sheer size of the place. The Speedway is far bigger than a regular city stadium. Acres and acres of land are devoted to the massive professional complex, and there's nothing backwoods about it at all. The Charlotte Speedway is a huge corporate identity with a big high-rise (called Smith Tower) built on site where business is housed for a myriad of NASCAR-related entities.

From a bird's-eye view, on the very outside of the complex are acres of parking lots, campgrounds, and rolling fields filled with campers, trucks, and trailers. Several campgrounds already looked to be full, Matt said. The atmosphere on the outside was like a state fair, with barbecues set up and tailgate parties well underway. Coolers and lawn chairs abounded. Everywhere, everyone seemed to be playing a beanbag toss game. Large tents and tall flags crowded the road, and semitrucks lined up end-to-end behind the tents. Stages for local rock bands were set up for entertainment.

Parking proved easy, convenient, and surprisingly cheap—free for that day at least—and it was only a five-minute walk to the gate. Matt described the immediate mood of the areas surrounding the complex as highly fan oriented, family friendly, and celebrative. Everybody seemed in a good mood. NASCAR's All-Star weekend is a big party, after all—and the entire country was invited.

SENSORY OVERLOAD AT THE SPEEDWAY

As evening fell, Matt left the grounds for a quick night's sleep, then came back to the speedway early on Friday for the official start of the racing weekend. Again, he described how the overall complex was an immediate overwhelming spectacle of lights and logos and signs and smells and sounds, and how sensory overload went right along with taking in his first NASCAR race.

This day, he parked and went inside the complex. Inside the gate were the grandstands with box seating above them and buildings for concession areas. The race track, with its high-banked sides, encircled a strip of logo-festooned turf. (Tracks vary in length; the Charlotte Motor Speedway is 1.5 miles long.) Pit road flanked one side of the infield with row after row of brightly colored pit stalls. Seven-member pit crews were in action setting up equipment. The middle of the Speedway was filled with row after row of trucks and trailers belonging to the various racing teams, and a camping area for the diehard fans could also be found in the infield.

One ticket for Friday's truck races cost $25. A ticket for the next day's All-Star race cost $79. Matt also purchased a pit pass for $50, which meant he was able to walk underneath the track via a tunnel to access the infield area. Once in the infield, he could walk around and see the cars lined up before the races. He could tour the pit areas but wasn't allowed to go into the actual garage areas, and the pass was good for a limited amount of time. Shortly before racing started, all pedestrians who weren't members of the media, sponsors, or racing teams needed to clear out.

The pit area was awesome, Matt said. Cars were already out on the track, practicing for the next day's event. It was the first time Matt had ever seen or heard a race car up close. "You keep hearing a roar and a zip," Matt said. "The cars just fly around the track."

The infield area, particularly the campgrounds, seemed to be mostly populated with diehard fans. An eclectic array of fan transportation was found in the infield, undoubtedly reflective of a wide swath of socioeconomic fan base. Converted school busses sat next to huge RVs with custom overhead scaffolding set up so people could better watch the action on the track. Rich or poor, the love for the sport didn't waver—vehicles everywhere were decked out with driver numbers and NASCAR flags. There were also a lot of American flags, military, and POW flags flying. Part of the infield was sectioned off for the tour buses of the team owners, pit crews, and drivers.

Matt toured the infield for about two hours. It was hot as the sun beat down, so about three o'clock in the afternoon, he made his way back through the tunnel to the grandstand and concession area. The tunnel itself is narrow, and golf carts ferried people back and forth. When race cars passed overhead, nothing shook or vibrated, but the sound of cars roaring overhead could definitely be heard. Everything was loud, loud, loud.

At the concession area, nothing was cheap but everything looked and smelled delicious. Available was everything from a foot-long corndog to a raspberry funnel cake to a Charlotte-style cheesesteak. Fan favorites included french fries, nachos, pizza, chicken tenders (or chicken thunders with barbecue sauce), regular hotdogs, and good old-fashioned cheeseburgers. The specialty of the Speedway was the "Behemoth Burger," costing a hefty $35 and consisting of six-and-a-half pounds of grilled meat plus toppings sandwiched between two huge buns. (Dieters beware: the Behemoth puts 6,500 calories in your system and equals eating about 14 regular hamburgers.)

DIGESTING A TRUCK RACE

As evening fell, the grandstands filled up with fans. Matt found his seat and met his neighbors. Sitting next to him was a military man with his five-year-old son, who would be enjoying his first NASCAR race. On the other side sat 70-year-old twins both decked out in Jeff Gordon gear. The brothers hadn't missed an All-Star race weekend together in a decade. Nearby was a couple from California who'd been saving for seven years to fly out and attend the race.

The big race of the night was the Camping World Trucks, the third tier of NASCAR. In NASCAR, trucks don't go as fast as cars. The bodies of the trucks look like vehicles you'd see on the street, like Ford F-Series or Chevy Silverados, but they have modified engines, souped-up suspensions, and colorful paint jobs. (A race truck's horsepower is 750 compared with a regular passenger truck of about 160 horsepower.) Trucks race in fewer events each year (only 25, compared with 36 for cars), and truck races last about half as long.

Qualifying began at 4 p.m. Each truck rolled out of pit road one at a time, drove around the track to the start/finish line, and hit the line going full speed. At that point, the lap time began. Each driver had one timed lap, which was recorded to determine where he would start in the race. All told, qualifying took about an hour, with the fabulous Jeb Burton clocking the fastest qualifying speed at 181.3 miles per hour.

One of the first things you'll notice whenever vehicles are raced on the track is the noise. Matt wore earplugs, but even so, the noise level was like "putting your head next to a chainsaw revving up," Matt said with a wry grin. "Everything at a NASCAR speedway is loud. The concession area is loud. The track is loud. There's a volume switch on everything, and it's always set to loud."

After the trucks qualified, race officials ran the qualifying heats for the Sprint Showdown race scheduled for the next day, which meant all the cars lined up and did the same thing as the trucks had just done.

It was cool to see the cars qualify, Matt said, but seeing a qualifying heat was nothing compared to an actual race. The overall intensity of the spectacle ramped up considerably when the trucks came back next for the actual competition—134 laps total, which equaled 201 miles. The first sensation a fan feels is speed—a speed unlike anything he or she has experienced anywhere but at the race track.

When vehicles are qualifying, only one vehicle is on the track at a time. A vehicle passes, and then about ten seconds later, a huge gust of wind rushes by. Mixed into the wind is the smell of rubber and oil and burnt motor fuel. Between the fans and the track is a chain-link fence that shakes like mad whenever a car passes. When vehicles are racing, an entire row of vehicles passes by and creates a roaring channel of wind, sound, turbulence, and rattling. As the race progresses, the trucks get spread out, and the turbulence isn't always felt. Sometimes a few seconds will pass where things in front quiet down momentarily. Then they come around with a roar again, and you can't help but hold on to your seat and cheer.

Truck racing fans are truly unique, Matt added. A lot of people that night were cheering for a particular driver, or, conversely, booing a driver they didn't like. For instance, Kyle Busch, who's won 17 NASCAR races in the Sprint Car series, was racing a truck that night, and oh, the distain heard from diehard truck race fans! The ubiquitous idea seemed to be that Busch belonged in a car, not a truck, and that by being somewhere he didn't belong, he was ruining the fans' favorite truck racers' chances of winning. Kyle won the race that night, much to the displeasure of virtually everyone around Matt.

The truck race lasted two hours, and the sky was dark when the race ended. The truck race didn't bring out as many fans as the car race, so it wasn't as crowded as it could have been when Matt was leaving the seating area, but it was still shoulder to shoulder out of the grandstands and bumper-to-bumper getting out of the parking lot. "You need to shower after a race," Matt said. "You feel grimy from all the dust, particles of rubber, and fuel in the air." Once he was back in his room, Matt fell asleep quickly, still hearing the sounds of engines in his head.

THE GRAND FINALE

The next afternoon, Saturday, Matt returned to the track. Today was the big All-Star race, the event made up of drivers who'd won a regular series race in the time since last year's All-Star race. The racers on the track this day were the best of the best, and the second day definitely felt like the grand finale of the weekend.

Before the race, Matt explored some of the vendor booths outside the grounds. The atmosphere again felt like a state fair, except this time the volume was cranked up to eleven. Musicians rocked out in small stage shows. Campers everywhere had grills fired up and smoking. Every driver's team has a souvenir truck lined up with hats, shirts, and stickers to hawk.

Matt had made contact earlier with Lonnie Clouse, a chaplain for Motor Racing Outreach (MRO). Lonnie invited Matt to attend MRO's pre-race chapel service that Saturday. The service followed the mandatory drivers' meeting, which is held before each race. It's where drivers get updates on info and rules from NASCAR officials.

That Saturday, an open garage space served as the meeting place and then became the chapel space. Inside the building, the furnishings were barebones and consisted of a portable sound system and a small stage in front of 15 rows of chairs. Matt sat in the back and found it difficult to recognize most of the more familiar drivers, dressed in their street clothes as they were, but he recognized Mark Martin and David Reutimann a few rows in front of him. NASCAR legend Ned Jarrett and team owner Joe Gibbs took chairs on the other side of the aisle.

Chapel began with a single hymn, led by a worship leader strumming a guitar. There were no printed words available, but everyone seemed to know the words by heart, and the congregation of crew members, drivers, family, and friends all joined to sing "Jesus Paid It All." A time of prayer immediately followed the song, and after that a few announcements were made, one about a special child dedication service coming up the next week. Pouches for giving were passed around unannounced and unassumingly, and then everyone listened to a short message from James 4 about drawing closer to God. A closing prayer and a benediction concluded the service.

Matt noted how the overall tone of the chapel service was solemn. The drivers, many of whom have wives and children, were about to literally risk their lives while engaged in a sport they love.

Think about it: NASCAR is the only sport in which there's a very real chance that this day could be your last. Though no drivers have died in the 2010s, eight perished in the 2000s, 10 died in the 1990s, and 13 drivers lost their lives in the 1980s. Each and every member of the driving brethren understands and accepts the inherent risk and danger of the sport they love.

But no one likes to dwell on his mortality at a time like this. Even though the setting was subdued, Matt was encouraged to see world-class drivers worship Almighty God in a heartfelt manner. As the exciting race action was about to begin, Matt found he didn't want chapel to end. He wanted to know more about these men's faith and about how they live for Christ.

To make the All-Stars day even more of a big event, NASCAR holds the Sprint Showdown race first. The showdown race is shorter than a regular race—only 40 laps—and it's held as one last chance for all the teams and drivers who haven't qualified for All-Stars to earn a spot in the race. Since the first- and second-place finishers of the Showdown race earn coveted spots in the All-Stars, hope runs high. Additionally, fans are given the opportunity to vote one single driver into the All-Stars. For 2013, the fans voted in Danica Patrick, the lone female racer in the Sprint Cup circuit, as the fan favorite.

With the Showdown race over, a truck and trailer pulled up mid-track with a big stage on back. Driver introductions were made. Next up was the singing of the national anthem and an invocation. Then it was showtime.

Twenty-two racers lined up for the start of the 2013 Spring All-Star race. Racing began at 9 p.m. Compared to the truck race, the cars ran faster. Everything seemed more intense. Matt struggled to describe the sensation in the stands. "It's like some unseen force follows the cars," he said. "Each car is not only amazingly loud—it contains a complex combination of smells, and the air moves right along with it. A race is a total assault on your senses. You don't just see and hear each car, you smell it, taste the air, and feel the fine debris pelting you as it streaks past you like the tail of a comet."

Unlike a regular series race, the All-Star race isn't about points. It's completely an exhibition for the fans, and it's run in four segments of 20 laps each, with a final fifth segment of 10 laps being the one that counts for the win. Kurt Busch won the first and fourth segments, while his little brother Kyle won the second and third. For the final segment, Jimmie Johnson battled the Busch brothers, as well as top driver Jamie McMurray, for most of the race but was able to dash to the finish 1.226 seconds ahead of his next closest contender and clinch the win.

For his efforts (a record fourth All-Star win), Jimmie Johnson took home a purse worth slightly more than a million dollars. Second-place finisher Joey Logano received $244,175, and Danica Patrick finished twentieth and took home $89,150.

AN AWESOME PROMISE IN VIEW

So, from a newcomer's perspective, why does America love NASCAR as much as she does?

"To begin with, the cars are familiar," Matt said. "We all have a relationship with a car and with driving, so we see these drivers and what they drive, and that's what pulls us into the sport. We can't drive as fast as they drive . . . but we'd like to. We're limited. The drivers aren't. So in a way we can experience the thrill of speed vicariously through this sport. There's also an incredible family atmosphere at a NASCAR event. You see fathers attending with their sons and it's clear they've bonded over cars, or you see a whole family attending, and they're all enjoying the event together. NASCAR isn't a solitary sport. It bonds people."

Did you catch that last line? That's why we wrote this book.

There's a definite inspirational quality about NASCAR, a tone imbedded within the sport that points people to the stuff of life that really matters—community and being with people you love. If we let them, those relationships have an uncanny way of pointing us toward spiritual matters. When we're in true community, we see we're not alone in the world. In addition to the relationships we enjoy here on earth, we also see that there's a God in heaven who loves us and cares for us deeply.

A good number of NASCAR drivers subscribe to this worldview. In this book, Matt, Marcus Brotherton, and I explore their stories, their statistics, their climb up the ranks of the sport they love most, and the often-precarious position they occupy at the top of the game.

In the pages ahead, you'll meet Bobby Labonte, Mark Martin, Jeff Gordon, Michael Waltrip, and more. The drivers featured in this book are all Christians. They're far from perfect, and they'd be the first to tell you they've made more than their share of mistakes. But they all have two big things in common: they're dedicated to NASCAR, and they all follow Jesus Christ.

What holds our featured drivers together through the rough times as well as the good?

It's faith in Jesus, pure and simple. It's belief in a God who so loved the world that He gave His Son to die on a cross. This same Jesus, after dying on that cross for our sins, rose from the grave on the third day, as He said He would, and lives today. The Bible says that anyone who believes in this Son will have eternal life.

With that awesome promise in view, these drivers are racing with more in mind than the checkered flag. They're playing with purpose, running a race, in the words of the apostle Paul, "to get a crown that will last forever."

Their invitation—as well as ours as authors—is for you to run that good race, too.

UNDERSTANDING THE THREE NATIONAL SERIES OF NASCAR

"NASCAR consists of three national series . . . four regional series, and one local grassroots series, as well as three international series. Also part of NASCAR is GRAND-AM Road Racing . . . NASCAR sanctions more than 1,200 races [each year] at 100 tracks in more than thirty U.S. states, Canada, Mexico and Europe."

—FROM THE NASCAR WEBSITE

This book primarily features drivers associated with the three national NASCAR-sanctioned series. Here's a brief explanation of how the three series work:

NASCAR SPRINT CUP SERIES

Sprint Cup is the top series of NASCAR, the highest-profile series with the most recognized drivers, and is considered the premier racing series in the world. With 36 races each year at 23 different tracks across the United States, Sprint Cup is the second most popular regular-season sport on television. Some 100,000 fans attend each Cup race, with many travelling great distances for the exhilarating race and speedway experience.

The Sprint Cup Series has had different sponsorships over the years. During the 1970s through 2003, the R.J. Reynolds Tobacco Company sponsored the series known as the Winston Cup. In 2004, the wireless telecommunications company Nextel took over title sponsorship duties for the Nextel Cup Series. When Nextel and Sprint merged in 2008, the name was changed to the Sprint Cup Series.

NASCAR NATIONWIDE SERIES

Nationwide is NASCAR's second-tier series, North America's second most popular racing series, and where many Cup drivers began their careers. Compared with the Cup Series, there are slight differences in car height, weight, and wheelbase. There is a significant difference in horsepower, however; Sprint Cup cars generate 850 horsepower, versus the 750 horsepower produced by Nationwide cars.

There are 34 Nationwide races a year, allowing up-and-coming drivers to hone their skills in hopes of racing full-time in the premier series. Veteran drivers also race in Nationwide. Some 70,000 fans attend each race, where the young guns race door-to-door with crafty old-timers. NASCAR calls the Nationwide Series the "final proving ground."

The Nationwide Series was sponsored by the Anheuser-Busch brewing company during the 1980s and was called the Busch Series through 2007, when Nationwide Insurance took over the sponsorship role for the 2008 season.

NASCAR CAMPING WORLD TRUCK SERIES

The Truck Series debuted in 1995 as a third tier in NASCAR and quickly became a favorite for truck enthusiasts. The series has NASCAR's most brand-loyal supporters. In 25 events each season, full-sized, American-made, 750-horsepower trucks vie for dominance in front of 20,000 to 50,000 impassioned fans. Fast trucks, in shorter races, usually run under Friday night lights, providing a racing experience the Sprint Cup and Nationwide cannot match. Many younger drivers get their big break driving in this developmental series.

The Camping World Truck Series was sponsored by Craftsman Tools from 1995 through 2008, when NASCAR announced that Camping World would be the new title sponsor, beginning in 2009.

A LIST OF NASCAR TERMS

Aerodynamics: Refers to the tendencies and motion of air flowing over, under, and around the race car, interacting with a car's surfaces and affecting a car's efficiency and handling.

Apron: The paved portion of the track that separates the racing surface from the infield.

Back marker: A car at or near the back of the pack.

Backstretch: The straight section of the track located opposite the start/finish line and usually between turns 2 and 3.

Banking: The slope of a track, specifically at a curve or a turn, from the apron to the outside wall, and recorded by degrees at the height of the outside edge.

Black flag: This flag tells a driver to pit or move to the back of the pack, usually for a rules violation.

Caution flag: This flag warns drivers of trouble on the track, most commonly due to an accident, oil debris on the track, or a weather-related issue.

Chassis: The steel skeleton or frame of a car.

Checkered flag: This flag signals the winning car and driver have crossed the finish line.

Chute: A race track straightaway.

Crew chief: The leader of a race team who oversees employees, decides race strategies, makes necessary changes to fine-tune car, and talks with driver over radio during the race.

Deck lid: The rear trunk lid of a race car.

Dirty air: Aerodynamic term for the turbulent air currents caused by fast-moving cars that can cause another car to lose control.

Down force: The air pressure and downward force that holds a car to the track and keeps it from losing control, especially in the turns.

Drafting: The strategy of cars running nose-to-tail on large speedways. Cars cut through the air much faster together when the first car creates a vacuum effect that pulls along the second car behind it.

Fabricator: A person who specializes in creating the sheet metal body of a stock car.

Frontstretch: The straight section of the track located between the first and last turns.

Fuel cell: A holding tank for a race car's supply of fuel.

Green flag: This flag starts the race.

Green-White-Checkered sequence: Used near the end of the race in an attempt to keep it from finishing under a caution flag.

Groove: A slang term for the best route around the track. Grooves are known to change throughout a race depending on track and weather conditions.

Handling: How a car performs on the track while racing, qualifying, and practicing. Factors that determine handling include tires, suspension, and aerodynamics.

Horsepower: A unit of measurement for mechanical or engine power. Measured in the amount of power it takes to move 33,000 pounds one foot in a minute.

Loose: Term for when the rear tires have trouble gripping the track and the back end of the car slides or fishtails, possibly causing the driver to lose control.

Modern era: From 1972 to present day, when corporate sponsorships began and when a new points system and a more structured schedule were introduced for NASCAR.

Motor home lot: The area designated in the infield where drivers and team owners park their motor homes during race weekend.

Motor Racing Outreach (MRO): A Christian organization that provides chapel services for drivers and their families, events for team members' children, and outreach to fans during race weekends.

Pit road: The area usually located along the frontstretch where pit crews service cars with gas, tires, or repairs.

Pit stall: The area along pit road teams use during pit stops and where they watch the race and keep their equipment.

Pole position: Term for the inside position of the two-car front row. It is the best position on the starting grid and awarded to the fastest qualifier.

Red flag: This flag tells all drivers they must stop because racing conditions are unsafe.

Restart: The waving of the green flag following a caution period.

Roll cage: The protective steel frame surrounding a driver and strictly designed to protect them during an accident.

RPM: Short for revolutions per minute, a measurement of the speed of the engine's crank shaft.

Tight: Term for when the front tires lose traction before the rear tires do going through a turn and making the car tough to steer, which could cause loss of control and a wreck.

Trading paint: Term used to describe aggressive driving involving a lot of bumping and rubbing.

Tri-oval: A race track with a "fifth turn." Looks like a hump on a standard four-cornered oval track.

Victory Lane: The roped-off or fenced-in area located in the infield where drivers, crews, owners, sponsors, and their families celebrate a victory. (Also called Victory Circle.)

White flag: This flag means the lead car has one lap to go.

Yellow flag: This flag means caution. All drivers must slow down.

1

BOBBY LABONTE:
A BROTHERHOOD OF CHAMPIONS

If you're a NASCAR fan, you may have heard of the driver who helps customers taste test new frozen yogurt flavors at the Red Mango yogurt and smoothie shop in High Point, North Carolina—the store he owns.

If you're a NASCAR fan and a cyclist, you may know that this driver loves to take long rides on his bike and has lent his name to the annual "Share the Road Memorial Ride."

If you're a NASCAR fan and a computer nerd, you may have heard that this driver loves hanging out at the Apple Store for hours on end, shopping and asking questions.

If you're a NASCAR fan and a hunter or angler, then you'll love hearing that this driver loves the great outdoors and has shot gobblers in Georgia, bagged big bull elk in Wyoming, and fished for salmon in Alaska.

But what you may not know, because it's not greatly publicized, is that this driver sits on the board of directors for Motor Racing Outreach (MRO), a Christian ministry that serves as a spiritual resource for NASCAR drivers, and that he often sits behind the boardroom doors at MRO, praying with eleven other men who love Jesus and NASCAR.

Do you know this man?

If you've been a NASCAR fan for the past 15 or 20 years, chances are pretty good that you know we're talking about veteran driver Bobby Labonte.

Longtime NASCAR fans still like talking about Labonte's championship season in 2000, which was the result of years of steady progress in the sport—start after start, season after season.

In a way, the analogy of the tortoise beating the hare doesn't quite seem to fit a successful career in NASCAR—a sport where you need to be rabbit-fast every time you come to the track. But it works for Bobby Labonte because, in a very real way, he plodded along in the sport . . . just like the tortoise who wouldn't give up until he tasted victory.

To better understand what it took for Bobby to reach championship form, back up in time to 1990, when he first started racing in NASCAR. Year after year, he finished well, sometimes near the top, but that ultimate goal of the championship win always eluded him.

In 1998, Bobby finished sixth for the season—not a poor showing, but not exactly great, either. The following year, he finished second to Dale Jarrett. Victory was so close, Bobby could almost taste it. Then, in 2000, he finally reached his goal and emerged as NASCAR champion.

Two significant things happened to Bobby during those years along the road to victory. First, he earned a reputation as a NASCAR iron man, a racer who always showed up faithfully to do his job—the veritable Cal Ripken of stock car racing. In 2000, when he finally hoisted the championship trophy over his head, he had already amassed 256 consecutive starts in the Winston Cup Series, as the series was known back then. The other significant thing is that Bobby emerged from his famous brother's shadow.

Bobby's older brother, Terry Labonte, known among racing colleagues and fans alike as "Texas Terry," was already a 20-year veteran who had won two NASCAR Series championships by the time his younger brother reached the top. Of course, Bobby had some NASCAR stock of his own by then, too. But when you have such an accomplished older sibling, you have to win big yourself in order to escape from your brother's big shadow.

Bobby's championship proved blockbuster big. Once he reached the top, his accomplishments came to light as journalists filed back through a decade of racing achievements during his long climb to NASCAR's summit. In addition to his championship, Bobby's legacy included a Busch Series (as the Nationwide Series was called back then), Most

Popular Driver award in 1990, a Busch championship in 1991, a Winston Cup Rookie of the Year Runner-Up award in 1993, the long starting streak, and his 21 Victory Lane appearances in the Winston Cup.

Bobby's fans already knew how he accomplished the things he did. They understood that he had a solid foundation of knowledge when it came to race cars. They knew that he started every race with uncommon resolve. And they were aware that he drove his Interstate Batteries #18 car to more and more Top-10 and Top-5 finishes as the years went by, always with his eyes on the prize.

Bobby's legacy today includes another hallmark, one that unites him and his brother once again. You see, the Labontes are the only pair of brothers to each win NASCAR's premier series championship.

Let's take a closer look at how Bobby Labonte's legacy formed.

BROTHERS BORN TO RACE

NASCAR lore is replete with brothers who race—both as rivals and as comrades. Stories include such famous brother combos as Tim, Fonty, and Bob Flock; Herb and Donald Thomas; Jeff and Ward Burton; Kurt and Kyle Busch; Darrell and Michael Waltrip; and Bobby and Donnie Allison, who have more combined wins—94—than any other brother combo.

The Labonte brothers have a combined 43 wins—22 for Terry and 21 for Bobby—which places them sixth on NASCAR's lists of most wins by brother combos. Their combined wins are unusual in that with every other brother combo except one other—Kurt and Kyle Busch, who each have 24—the younger brother has earned significantly fewer wins than the older. For instance, Herb and Donald Thomas combined for 49 wins, but Herb has 48 of them. Darrell and Michael Waltrip have a combined 88 wins, with Darrell owning 84.

The Labontes' brotherly bond is American steel strong. They're not bitter rivals or weighed down with jealousy. On the contrary, each welcomes the other's involvement in his career, and they are proud to share in each other's successes.

After Bobby won in 2000, many in the media floated speculation about Terry's influence on his career. Bobby was forthcoming with praise for his brother's involvement, crediting Terry for helping him over the many hurdles and through the many challenges young drivers face. "[My older brother] showed me what being a champion is all about," Bobby said. "I just hope I can be the same kind of champion he has been in the past."

Terry took the first of his two Winston Cup championships in 1984. Bobby, then 20 years old, worked for his brother's team that year, doing whatever needed to be done around the garage. Terry's second championship came in 1996, a remarkable 12 years later.

Why did it take so long for Terry to win again after his 1984 championship? Some speculated he was waiting for his little brother to catch up to him. The way Terry won his 1996 title, that scenario is not unimaginable. It's a NASCAR story for the ages.

It was November 10, 1996. Bobby was 32 years old with a fast car of his own. It was the last race of the season—the NAPA 500 at the Atlanta Motor Speedway. Bobby was about to begin his dominance of the NAPA 500. On that day, Bobby finished first and Terry took *fifth* place—but Terry's finish meant he had collected enough points to clinch the season title. Other championship contenders had waited all season long for Terry to falter, but it didn't happen. Terry knew he needed to finish strong, and he did just that.

In an enduring show of family unity, the brothers took their victory lap driving side-by-side. Terry wiped tears off his face as he climbed out of his car, and Bobby led with his heart during a post-race interview: "Goldang, this is so cool, Terry winning the championship, me winning the race. This is the coolest thing I've ever done in my life."

THE LABONTE BROTHERS' SECOND-COOLEST EXPERIENCE

If the result of the '96 NAPA 500 was the coolest thing Bobby ever experienced, what was next on the list? How about shoot up their dad's truck with a .44 magnum?

The story goes that one day his father called to tell the boys to take his old truck to the junkyard. Before they did, they thought they'd have some fun. Bobby and Terry both hated the truck because it had a habit of breaking down on them, so this was payback. They even gave their mom a bullet if she wanted to join in.

Mom couldn't pull the trigger, but the boys took out their frustration and riddled the broken-down truck with bullet holes. Then they hauled the carcass to the local junkyard.

It turns out that dear ol' Dad got the last laugh. He stopped by the junkyard and saw the bullet holes. When he got home, he told Bobby he had a buyer for the truck.

The brothers panicked. Terry blamed Bobby for shooting up the defenseless truck, and Bobby blamed Terry. Dad had a good laugh.

FORGED IN THE TEXAS HEAT

Bobby is not sure what he would be doing if he weren't a NASCAR driver. He passively says he would probably be "a construction guy" because he likes building things. Then he chuckles and says, "or a destruction guy" because he likes taking things apart just as much.

Bobby's musing is not mere conjecture. He learned solid construction *and* destruction skills—especially as they relate to cars, engines, and racing—from his father, Bob Labonte, who grew up around racing and fell in love with the sport as a teenager.

When Bob Labonte was 15 years old, he went to Oxford Plains Speedway in his native state of Maine and began working on his friends' race cars. His enlistment in the Navy provided him a brief hiatus from his favorite pastime, but he got right back to working on cars after he was discharged in 1953. He settled in Corpus Christi, Texas, where his wife, Martha, gave birth to their first son, Terry, on November 16, 1956.

In the early 1960s, the Naval Air Station in Corpus Christi became home for a much-needed Army depot-level maintenance facility. The depot was a Department of Defense facility where Army aircraft engines were overhauled, repaired, modified, or modernized. It proved the perfect place for Bob to work at a job that actually paid the bills. But Bob never left behind his hobby of working on engines. Many evenings after work, he'd head to the garage unit he kept off Old Brownsville Road and tinker with and fine-tune his engines until the wee hours of the morning.

On May 8, 1964, Bob and Martha welcomed their second son into the world. The child's full name: Robert Alan Labonte—Bobby for short.

Bobby sometimes jokes that he was born at a race track, and that isn't too far from the truth, considering that his brother was already actively racing and that his father was trucking around his older brother to make it happen. The Labontes were a racing family, and Bobby was born right into the thick of the sport.

Growing up, the climactic event for Bobby each weekend was going to the races. Even Martha Labonte was an active participant, working at the ticket booth before the race. It was in this setting—where everybody he knew was involved in racing—that Bobby's love for the sport began to form. He was 12 years younger than Terry, so he had a special opportunity to see how much work went into getting his brother to the track each weekend. During those growing-up years, Bobby became his brother's biggest fan. And as Bobby watched Terry race, he dreamed about how much fun it would be to start races against him someday.

Bobby was the kind of kid who wanted to learn everything he could about cars and racing. He would watch his father work on something and then ask if he could give it a try himself. He wanted to learn as many of the ins and outs of the sport of racing as he could, which would prove important for his future success. So if Bobby had not succeeded in NASCAR, he might well have been a construction or destruction guy.

GO-KARTS AND QUARTER MIDGETS

Before Bobby Labonte was even five years old, long before he would compete in front of thousands of NASCAR fans, he stretched out his little-boy hands to clinch his go-kart's steering wheel. From the steel seat of his go-kart, he took turns his father had marked out for him with milk jugs on a makeshift short oval track around Yeager Elementary

School's parking lot. He wasn't yet racing for the applause of huge crowds, only for the thrill of the sport and the smiles of his parents. His father also constructed the track Bobby would race on when he entered kindergarten and began racing Quarter Midgets.

Bobby's first racing championship came in 1971. He was seven years old, and it was his first national Quarter Midget race. The sport, which is for kids between five and 16 years old, was already popular in the early '70s, and it is even more popular now, thanks in part to NASCAR greats like Jeff Gordon, who got his start racing in Quarter Midgets and still supports the sport today.

Quarter Midgets of America is the national organization behind 4,000 young drivers. Boys and girls race full throttle around small oval tracks. Sitting behind the wheel in a fiberglass car body, the youths are protected by a roll cage of foam-padded bars as well as protective gear. The open-wheeled cars have single-cylinder engines that can propel them at up to 40 miles per hour.

Bobby's boyhood days were full of racing exploits. He started traveling around the country for races when he was only nine years old. In the driver's seat of his Quarter Midget car, he raced on tracks across his home state of Texas, but also in California, Ohio, Alabama, Colorado, and Washington.

FROM TEXAN TO TAR HEEL

If you're going to be serious about a career in racing, it means travel. That's especially true if you want to race against bigger and faster cars. There are only so many municipalities that can support serious racing. And the Labontes raced seriously—and fast. In fact, Terry and Bobby are still remembered around Corpus Christi as "two youths who loved fast cars."

Corpus Christi had its own speedway. Other major cities in Texas did, too, even though the hub of all automobile racing was arguably North Carolina. But Terry's success was growing. He was popular among local racing fans, but he was also winning in every Texas town that had a track. That would turn out to be to his good fortune, as he met his future NASCAR team's owner, Billy Hagan, in Houston.

Bobby was 13 years old when Terry met Hagan, an oil industry businessman, auto racing fan, and race team owner. Terry had raced at Meyer Speedway in Houston, but there came a now-infamous weekend when the family didn't have the money to travel to Houston so Terry could race. They were flat out of cash and couldn't make the trip.

Well, the Meyer Speedway owner wasn't going to let a crowd favorite sit out a race, so he put Terry in touch with Hagan, who thereafter made racing possible for the Labonte family. In 1978, Hagan's NASCAR team needed a new driver, so he invited Terry to move to North Carolina to run some races. Terry accepted the invitation, and his NASCAR career took off.

A year later, Bob and Martha made the big decision to follow their oldest son's career and move to the Tar Heel State as a family. That proved one of the biggest disappointments of Bobby's youth. He was a year away from getting his regular driver's license and longed to drive out on the beaches of Corpus Christi. He had lived all his life in Corpus Christi, and all of his friends lived there. And now racing—not his, but his brother's—would take him on a one-way trip away from the Corpus Christi Speedway and the garage unit on Old Brownsville Road.

Bobby describes the event in briefest terms: "I went to Tom Browne Junior High on Friday, and I was in North Carolina on Saturday."

Fortunately, the big move to North Carolina turned out for Bobby's best—although it took some time for him to realize it. He enrolled at Trinity High School and excelled in the classes he liked most—wood shop, small engines, and study hall.

Terry found a good groove racing with Hagan's team. And right there in the team garage was Bobby, doing what he could to help his brother, even sweeping up at the end of the day.

After graduating from high school, Bobby went to work for Hagan as a mechanic and fabricator on the cars Terry raced. He began to feel more and more comfortable with his new surroundings.

Bobby had grown up at last. His Texas years were miles behind him. He was settled on being a Tar Heel and living in racing country. And though he didn't know what his future held, he knew he was in the right place.

HUMBLE FROM THE START

At the same time Bobby worked for Hagan's racing team, and thereby helped his brother's career, he pursued his own racing career. He raced late models on tracks throughout North Carolina and began building his own car for a future NASCAR Busch Series race.

The skills Bobby possessed and put to use for his own career are virtually unheard of in NASCAR these days. Bobby not only owned his first car but also worked on it so he could race. In 1982, he made his first official NASCAR start, at Martinsville Speedway. He started in the 15th position in a field of 30 cars. He finished in 26th place and won $220, which covered his fuel costs and not much else. A humble beginning for sure, but it was a start.

Throughout the 1980s, Bobby continued honing his driving skills. For the most part, he raced near home. He burned up tires at Caraway Speedway in Asheboro, North Carolina, and at nearby Concord Motorsports Park in Concord. Toward the end of the decade, in 1987, he won the late-model championship. At Concord Motorsports Park the next year, he finished first in six different races.

THE NEW DECADE

NASCAR, like most professional sports, has its own proving grounds. Today, a driver needs to compete well at lower levels, like the Nationwide Series, to keep his hopes for a full-time Sprint Cup ride alive. He must also compete for sponsorships, and to get sponsored, he must prove himself on and off the track.

Bobby, like most young drivers, dealt with the challenges of getting sponsors and holding on to them. Many sponsors are business owners who know success in racing is difficult, and some are corporate executives who watch bottom lines closely. If sponsors don't see the car sporting their logo out in front of the pack, or if the car isn't being talked about, then they often pull their support. It's a business decision that tends to affect young drivers personally. Yet without sponsorship, there is no start on race day, period.

Penrose Firecracker, a meat snack company, took a chance on Bobby in 1990, and Bobby immediately put his sponsor's dollars to good use. He lit up the competition and wasn't embarrassed to pose for a picture with a guy in a spicy sausage costume. Bobby's reliability secured his sponsor for the next three seasons in NASCAR's Busch Series, which ignited his career and turned into a streak of 93 consecutive races—31 races each year in 1990, 1991, and 1992.

Bobby padded his racing résumé with 29 Top-5 and 57 Top-10 finishes, but being fast and grabbing the checkered flag five times during the streak was purely groundwork for the construction of his career. The capstone looked different each season. In 1990, he was deemed the fan favorite and named the Busch Series' Most Popular Driver. He came out blazing in 1991, winning his first and second NASCAR races and finishing as series champion. And in 1992, Bobby and Joe Nemechek wrote racing history by giving fans a whirling points race to watch—the closest finish ever.

During this exciting time, Bobby married the love of his life, Donna Slate, in the spring of 1991. They formed a terrific team. The two had known each other for eight years, so Donna was fully aware of Bobby's racing lifestyle. There were no wild surprises after they tied the knot. She expected that in the coming years Bobby would take on NASCAR's best drivers, and she firmly decided to be the race car wife who supported her husband. Bobby called her "my rock."

In the early years of Bobby and Donna's marriage, she came to every race. She would cheer on her husband from the pits and keep lap times and track fuel mileage. If she needed to share driving responsibilities to or from a race, then she would do that, too. Donna supported Bobby by helping out in any way she could.

Bobby thought his wife would never miss a race. Then they had their son, Tyler, and later a daughter, Madison. The time came when Donna realized she needed to stay home to care for the kids. Together, Bobby and Donna made it work. They always figured life out—including how to spend 45 minutes having a family dinner together, even though Bobby was home for just an hour.

Bobby's big break came in 1993, when Bill Davis Racing put him behind the wheel of a Ford Thunderbird full-time. During the Winston Cup season, he started 30 of 30 races in his Maxwell House Coffee-sponsored car.

But did Bobby know he was only beginning a streak of consecutive starts that would extend to more than 700 over the next twenty years?

Doubtful.

Rather, he was fully aware that racing offered no guarantees and never would. Bobby finished his rookie season with one Top-5 and two Top-10 finishes. He also earned his first pole position, in a race at Richmond International Speedway. The pole position is the No. 1 position at the starting grid—where the cars line up to begin racing. It's the position given to the fastest car during qualifying.

THE 180-DEGREE TURN

When a person turns his life over to Christ, it's sometimes referred to as making a 180-degree turn. That's what happened when Bobby became a believer in Jesus Christ.

Bobby was 30 years old at the time and had made it to the pinnacle of stock car racing. He'd won many close battles along the way, and he was still winning. But at the same time, Bobby was battling the anxious thoughts that tend to go along with trying to control your own destiny—or thinking you need to because no one else will.

It's not an uncommon way of thinking. Uncertainty grips the lives of nearly every man and woman on earth, and fear of the unknown becomes problematic for people in all kinds of work. There are few certainties in this world, and Bobby sought to control what he could. What he couldn't control, he worried about.

What Bobby lacked was peace that things would be all right—if not today, then someday. Then Bobby heard the gospel message, confessed his sins, and turned his life over to his Creator—the One who knew him best. After Bobby's conversion, he found peace in reflecting on Jesus' words from the Sermon on the Mount (Matthew 6:34 NASB):

> *"Do not worry about tomorrow; for tomorrow will care for itself.
> Each day has enough trouble of its own."*

In 1995, just after the grace of God had won over Bobby's life, he began the first of his eventual eleven seasons with Joe Gibbs Racing (JGR). His sponsor, Interstate Batteries, gave him full support along the way.

Joe Gibbs, today the head of a network behind a NASCAR racing team, already knew something about winning. Before he got involved with NASCAR, he was a National Football League head coach who won three Super Bowl Championships with the Washington Redskins.

Bobby had also experienced winning at a high level, and he and Gibbs committed themselves to becoming champions together. Over Bobby's eleven seasons in the #18 Interstate Batteries car, he earned 21 wins. In fact, all of his career wins to date have come while driving for JGR.

During this time, Bobby also became grounded as a young Christian. Gibbs, himself a strong believer, applied Christian principles as he led his team. Being around JGR, Bobby applied his desire for understanding the ins and outs of his new faith. This time, the subject wasn't as much cars as it was about being a Christian. Bobby learned all he could from the JGR team chaplain and from Gibbs himself. He recalls that he was like a sponge, soaking up spiritual truths he could apply in his life.

Some of Bobby's thoughts when he signed a contract extension with JGR in 2003 brought his relationship with Gibbs into full light:

> *They have made me feel like part of the family since day one. I
> am very blessed to have been able to drive for Joe and be part of
> such a great organization. He has taught me a lot over the nine
> years I have been here, not only about myself, but also more
> importantly about being a good Christian, a good husband and
> a good father.*

Bobby's first win with JGR came on May 28, 1995, at Charlotte Motor Speedway in the Coca-Cola 600. Right behind Bobby in second place was his brother Terry. Three months later, at the Michigan International Speedway in the GM Goodwrench Dealer 400, the brothers finished with the same one-two Labonte punch. The very next weekend, Terry took the checkered flag at the Goody's 500 at Bristol International Raceway. By winning that race, the Labonte brothers gained an elite position on a short list of brother duos to win back-to-back Winston Cup Series races.

Bobby won just one race in 1996, the same race in which Terry won the Winston Cup championship. They took a victory lap together.

Back at the Atlanta Motor Speedway in November 1997, for another NAPA 500, Bobby once again grabbed the checkered flag with an average lap speed of 159.904 miles per hour. After Bobby accomplished this remarkable feat—winning the same race in back-to-back years—the high-banked Atlanta track became known as "Bobby's House."

RISING STAR

The Daytona 500 is the first race of each NASCAR season, and in 1998, NASCAR celebrated its 50th anniversary by honoring members of the All-Time Great list during the race's opening ceremonies. The crowd in Daytona exploded in cheers when Dale Earnhardt Sr. won the race. Earnhardt, already a member of the All-Time Great list, had never won the illustrious Daytona 500.

Bobby finished second that day, and some commentators believe he was positioned to pass Earnhardt on the last lap until a caution flag came out with two laps to go. During a caution, drivers stay in the positions they were in when the flag came out. In some instances, the drivers finish under a caution flag.

That February day in 1998, 16 drivers were in contention with five laps to go, bringing fans to their feet. But of those 16 drivers, only Bobby Labonte was muscling his car to the front of the pack, moving aggressively toward what he hoped would be a Daytona 500 win. But it wasn't to be, as the caution flag effectively awarded the race to Earnhardt.

That was okay. The '98 season would prove to be a great one for Bobby. With every green flag he lined up for, he was becoming more of a prominent NASCAR driver.

Three weeks after his second-place finish at Daytona, Bobby was back in Atlanta for the Primestar 500. Since his NASCAR debut, he was steadily becoming a household name, and now he was back at the Atlanta Motor Speedway for the first time since his last victory.

The headlines queried how Bobby Labonte would finish. Was the speedway really "Bobby's House?"

Well, Bobby showed that he had taken up residence and was all moved in. He led 47 of the 325 laps and finished first under the flapping checkered flag. In April, he won his second race of the season, the Diehard 500 at Talladega Superspeedway. It was a dream-come-true kind of race in which Bobby and Terry battled through 188 laps. Terry led 88 laps compared with Bobby's 60. In the end, though, Bobby tasted sweet victory while Terry finished fourth.

With Bobby in the driver's seat, everyone at JGR was looking forward to 1999. Norm Miller, the chairman of Interstate Batteries, made sure his company continued as the primary sponsor of the #18 car, fully believing that Bobby was about to enter an exciting phase of his career.

Miller was right. Bobby became one of NASCAR's elite drivers, and he also proved to be one of the most consistent. Not only did he regularly place in the Top 10 and even Top 5, but he also hoisted trophies over his head more frequently. Bobby crossed the finish line first five times in 1999, confirming his star status within the NASCAR constellation.

THE *OTHER* STREAK AND THE CHAMPIONSHIP

At Richmond International Raceway on September 11, 1999, Bobby began what would become a streak of 14 consecutive Top-10 finishes. Those 14 races zoomed Bobby into the Top 10 overall and made him one of only four drivers since 1990 to have reached or surpassed that mark. During this amazing streak, he never finished worse than eighth and won twice, including his third career win at the NAPA 500 in Atlanta, the last race of 1999.

The last race of Bobby's streak also took place in Atlanta. It was March 12, 2000, and the race was the Cracker Barrel Old Country Store 500. The thrilling finish to this race is the greater story. With Bobby racing just inches from the rear spoiler of Dale Earnhardt's car (at over 180 miles per hour), the two drivers came around the final turn when Earnhardt took a high track position, giving Bobby a chance on the lower track. In a blur of speed, the two drivers raced door-to-door down the stretch, crossing the finish line just inches apart. NASCAR's electronic timing system recorded Earnhardt as the winner by .01 seconds.

On his way to the championship in 2000, Bobby won his first race at Indianapolis Motor Speedway, also known as "The Brickyard." But Bobby didn't just win; he set the track record for average lap speed at 156 miles per hour—a record that still stands today.

Every driver and every team competing in NASCAR covets the cup championship. Bobby and Joe Gibbs Racing had been working together for the championship since 1995. It finally became reality for them when they clinched the win with two weeks remaining in the 2000 season. Bobby gave credit to his dad and brother. Afterward, Gibbs spoke about God's blessings:

> We'd been building toward this. When Bobby came here, he hadn't won a race. Then he won. Then we built a new building. Then we added another team and built another new building. Then we started our own engine program. We kept putting the pieces together, and last year, we could finally say we were capable of being a challenger. And all along the way, I'm not saying God favored us, but He blessed us at different times.

When the 2001 season began, the defending champion was in the spotlight. Like it did every year, the season's opening race, the Daytona 500, brought NASCAR's electric atmosphere to Florida. JGR and Bobby were ready to defend their title.

But they didn't have a strong qualifying round, and Bobby started in the 37th position in a field of 43 cars. The day only got worse for Bobby when he became involved in a wreck on lap 176. In this wreck, Tony Stewart's car flipped upside down and landed—of all places—on the windshield of Bobby's car. Half of the field was wiped out in the wreck, but, thankfully, no one was seriously injured.

THE END OF AN ERA

On November 7, 2005, Joe Gibbs Racing announced that, after eleven years with the team, Bobby would be leaving at the end of the season. Bobby's career had taken another turn. The wins he'd grown accustomed to had become scarce. In 2002, Bobby won just one race. In 2003, he doubled his previous year's record with two wins. But in 2004 and 2005, he was skunked.

"A dry well," says an old Texas proverb, "teaches us the worth of water." Bobby didn't know it at the time, but he would experience the analogy of a dry well in his NASCAR career. His faith was not shaken, though. Rather he learned through his struggles to lean on God and on other believers, including his wife, for support in the midst of trials.

During Bobby's drought, Donna encouraged her husband to reach out to NASCAR chaplains for guidance. Bobby heeded his wife's counsel and found encouragement from the chaplains.

Donna is still Bobby's rock today. She has been his encouragement and guide while the two have enjoyed gentle conversations or taken late-summer walks. She has cheered him by inviting special friends— friends who encourage him to count his blessings—over for a meal.

DRIVING WITH PURPOSE

In his last four years with Joe Gibbs Racing (2002–05), Bobby may have struggled to finish first, but he still had numerous Top-5 and Top-10 finishes, and he was still racing with purpose—a purpose he shared with Gibbs and the chairman of Interstate Batteries, Norm Miller. Gibbs and Miller have testified about their enthusiasm for Christ and the gospel by using the #18 Chevy Monte Carlo that Bobby raced.

Over the years, many drivers who found themselves behind Bobby

Labonte took notice of the paint job on the back of his car, including the evangelistic Bible reference—John 3:16. The paint scheme had been there for all of Bobby's years. Gibbs and Miller thought it was the proper verse to be on the back of the car. Bobby was happy to have it there because John 3:16 is the foundational scripture that shares the Good News of salvation through Jesus Christ.

Bobby's car has displayed other impactful gospel messages. In 2004, Miller saw the movie *The Passion of the Christ* at a screening in California and decided to team up with director Mel Gibson to put an ad for the film on the race car. Since the movie was to be released in late February of that year, they decided to run the car with the ad at the Daytona 500.

Bobby started his 12th straight Daytona 500 in 13th position; he raced the car into sixth place before he had to pit with trouble. Back on the track, he was running 40th but worked back to 30th, then 12th. It was another thrilling exhibit of Bobby's skilled driving. He almost cracked the Top 10, finishing 11th.

The movie ad brought up some controversial questions, but Bobby answered them the way he always answered tough questions—with straight-up honesty. He told media outlets he was a true believer and a Christian. He told them he hoped the hood logo would prompt people to see *The Passion of the Christ*. "It's a chance to get the word out . . . maybe someone who is curious about Jesus and has never been saved sees the race . . . maybe we can change their minds."

Change.

That's something Bobby knows personally, both in his faith and in his career. The grace of God is at work in his life, and his faith is maturing. That's why Bobby is able to say, "Whatever God wants me to do, He will lead me. And it'll be for the right reasons, and it'll be what He wants for me."

Today, Bobby is still racing fast cars at a high level—and for a purpose much greater than trophies and money. The race wins may not be there like before, but Bobby is steadily driving with purpose. As a Christian, his purpose for racing goes far beyond the car, the driver, and the track.

In 2013, Bobby showed his fans once again the impact his relationship with Christ has made on his life, on his racing, and on others around NASCAR.

Just a couple of weeks after Bobby and his family celebrated his 700th consecutive career start (at Talladega), he received the news that his streak would most likely end at 704. His car owner, JTG Daugherty Racing, decide to turn the car over to another driver for a couple weeks.

Bobby was shocked. He had no control over his tomorrow, but he said, gracefully, "You know, the streak was going to end at some point in time, but I was really looking forward to going to Kentucky. I don't want to say, 'No big deal,' because it is a big deal, but you can't make a big deal of it either because at the end of the day, it's really not that big of a deal."

Bobby ended up picking up a ride for start number 705. He was back with his team for number 706. And that's where it ended. His next start came two weeks later.

The day of the news was surely troubling, but Bobby took Jesus' words to heart and showed the power of racing with purposes beyond glory and streaks.

These days, the big question is, "How much longer will Bobby race?"

"I don't know," he says. "That's a question I can't really answer."

True enough, Bobby. Tomorrow will care for itself.

2

MARK MARTIN:
FROM BACKWOODS BOY
TO LIVING LEGEND

There was *no* Plan B.

None. Zero. Zilch. Yep, there was absolutely no backup plan, says legendary NASCAR driver Mark Martin, if racing didn't work out.

That might sound a little crazy to those of us raised in today's security-holic culture. Most of us believe that not having a Plan B could be embarrassing, even disastrous. But Mark comes from tough stock.

Mark Martin was born in January 1959 to Julian and Jackie Martin of Batesville, Arkansas. Julian died in 1998, and those who knew him best remember Mark's father as a driven, determined, and tough businessman.

Mark possesses some of the best of his father's traits.

No one around NASCAR was surprised at Mark's reply when author and Speed Channel personality John Roberts asked him what he would be doing if he weren't a race car driver. No firefighting, photography, or factory work would suit Mark. Nor have his attempted retirements been right. God made him a racer and has held him fast to the track.

As it turns out, Mark never needed a Plan B anyway. Today he is considered one of the 50 greatest drivers in NASCAR history. His story is one by which legends are made.

The rugged terrain of the Arkansas back roads soaks through Mark's pores. He learned to grip those slippery gravel grades, which, in turn, helped make his footing on NASCAR's pavement sure. Passing through dust clouds cleared his vision for future billows of fire, smoke, and exhaust. The one-lane wooden bridges Mark took at 80 miles per hour over cavities his father called "death" made NASCAR's eight-foot-wide gaps between a concrete wall and another steel car possible, even when he roared through them doing 160.

The independence of country life helped shape Mark's racing mind. He knows that a ruffian is not truly free, so respect for others flows from him. The Golden Rule is his standard. He puts 100 percent of everything he has into every day. Most importantly, the God of the universe calms his soul, gives him a resting place, and is his source of strength.

Mark lives life like a steady stream, and while it has been turbulent at times, when he smiles, his face lights up like the sparkling White River near his home in Batesville.

Don't ask Mark to give up racing. In fact, don't even ask him if he is retiring. NASCAR needs this living legend.

TELLING THE OLD, OLD STORY

Mark is currently in his fourth decade of NASCAR racing, but his career is *still* a roller coaster. He started his vocation in 1981, lost his independence and went broke in 1982, choked and sputtered in 1983, disappeared in 1984, then began a comeback in 1987. He has been rocking the premier Sprint Cup Series ever since he joined up with Jack Roush in 1988. But the whole legendary tale begins in 1964 on those Arkansas back roads.

Time and again the story has been told about how a five-year-old Mark learned to handle a car under his father's tutelage. Here is Mark's own account of that part of his life:

> My dad used to prop me up on his lap while he was in the driver's seat of the car, and without taking no for an answer, would make me take the steering wheel. Then he'd slam his foot on the accelerator and off we'd go. It scared me to death, but I was stuck steering that car sometimes at speeds over 80 mph on gravel roads around our hometown. The more we drove, the more I got used to it—and the more I fell in love with the sensation of going fast and taking the car to the edge.

So how strong was a five-year-old boy from Arkansas? Well, about as strong as any five-year-old from any state—not very. And we're talking about controlling a car without the luxury of power steering. But there was Mark, thundering down the crooked back roads around Batesville, learning how NASCAR's old-school drivers—moonshine runners like Bob Flock and Junior Johnson—learned to race by outrunning the law. Except Mark's family heritage wasn't moonshining but trucking.

What possessed Julian Martin to prop Mark up behind a steering wheel and fly him around like he did? A combination of two things: first, Julian was fond of fast driving, so his trucking company sponsored races that were taking place at the local tracks. Second, it was family tradition to learn to handle a fast car at a young age.

At his 100th birthday party, Clyde Martin (Mark's grandfather) told parts of his life story. He recalled a time when his son Julian, who was eight years old at the time, sat in his lap steering a truck loaded with logs down the rugged roads. Four years later, Julian was driving a truck by himself. Clyde himself had been put in charge of hauling lumber as a 13-year-old. His own father, a self-made man since the age of 14, gave him the reins to a team of mules and sent him down the steep and rugged Brock Mountain, back when the road was little more than a trail.

Evidently, when Mark's dad let him take the wheel, he was just doing what seemed to come natural to a family of drivers.

A 1955 CHEVY BEL AIR

In the fall of 1973, Julian, Mark, and a good friend named Larry Shaw got to work building Mark's first race car. Another friend, Wayne Brooks, supplied the engine. "Martin Trucking" was emblazoned across the front panel.

By the next racing season, 1974, the car was ready, and Mark began his first year of stock car racing. His first race took place in April, just four months after he turned 15, "at a small dirt track in Locust Grove." Mark got his first win in just his third start, and he won the Arkansas State Championship in his division that year.

In 1975, Shaw produced another car for Mark—a 1955 Chevy Bel

Air. Mark raced the car on the dirt tracks around Arkansas, learning the ways of "rubbing racing"—the all-important skill of moving someone out of your way with your bumper or with "rub rails" along the car's sides. It was just one of the many skills Mark would need before he moved into the V-8 division and onto asphalt, which he did in 1976. (Years later, Shaw found and restored the old '55, and it was put on display at the Mark Martin Museum at Mark's Ford dealership in Batesville, located 85 miles northeast of Arkansas' capitol, Little Rock.)

Mark tested his skills further in 1977. His chance of qualifying for the 24-car field at the National Short Track Championship was merely one in eight when more than 200 cars lined up bumper-to-bumper in an attempt to qualify for the open invite at Rockford Speedway in northern Illinois. Oblivious to chance, Mark, with his dad serving as crew chief and sponsor, made the 600-mile trip from Batesville to Rockford, where he set the second-quickest qualifying time. There was no question anymore about his chance of making the field. He was in.

The championship event is also dubbed "One Great Racing Weekend," and that certainly was the case for Mark. He won the 400-lap, 100-mile race and became the National Short Track Champion.

Mark kept racing. He won on the dirt tracks, and he won on the short asphalt tracks, too. He always faced good competition, but he knew that NASCAR provided the best competition in the sport of stock car racing. Mark hadn't yet won at that level, and for three more years—until winning his third American Speed Association (ASA) championship in a row in 1980—he would continue racing at the lower levels of stock car.

And then in 1981 . . . they started calling him "The Kid." He was just 22 years old at the time, and his shaggy hair and smooth face revealed his youthfulness. Yet he was destined to be like "them."

But who are *they*?

"They" are some of NASCAR's all-time greatest drivers:

- Richard Petty
- Bobby Allison
- Darrell Waltrip

- Harry Gant
- Ricky Rudd

Since Mark is today in his fourth decade of NASCAR racing, it's possible that even longtime racing fans can't remember his days as "The Kid." It's likely that younger fans can't imagine Mark as ever being young at all, simply because his presence around NASCAR has been defined as that of the steely veteran. Mark is as strong as an iron girder, and his 55-year-old body is chiseled and has been since the late '80s, when he got hardcore into weightlifting. Today, his strawberry hair, now tinged with gray sideburns, is cropped short. His rugged face, craggy from years of sun and pressure, is better described as epic or wizened.

"Is not wisdom found among the aged?" asked Job. Mark has that wisdom. His mind is as sharp as a tack. Nobody overlooks him when he is in the garage, even though he stands only 5 feet, 6 inches tall. And at the track, well, everyone looks up to him. In the race car, he's positioned like an old hand in complete control of a richly oiled glove; he reacts with learned precision.

What makes Mark Martin so legendary today? For one thing, he has never failed to qualify for a race. He's always ready to take on the field and race with the best the day offers, even if "the best" are half his age. Mark has raced with NASCAR's best more than 1,100 times.

Mark's first NASCAR competition took place on April 5, 1981, at North Wilkesboro Speedway (NWS). And to understand the full significance of why it is important that Mark Martin first raced at the NWS as a 22-two-year-old, a short lesson in NASCAR history is needed.

HAVE YOU HEARD OF THE NWS?

The NWS doesn't get much attention these days. It's old and unpreserved. It's got its historical highway marker with 20 words describing its history, but it hasn't received a lot of other press or print in the past 15 years.

There are still some faithful NWS fans today. A few write online about the once-popular short track and try to raise funds for the abandoned speedway in hopes of bringing it back to life.

Some old-timers still remember NWS' heyday, when it had the

reputation as one of the fastest short tracks in racing. They recognize a name or two and try to piece together some NASCAR lore about an infield fight or a finish that came down to a few feet. These days, a hundredth of a second might decide a winner, but before the aid of computers, back when the North Wilkesboro Speedway was crowning victors, the old language of *feet* and *yards* was used. Consequently, when a finish came down to *inches*, the old measurements would sometimes lend to a fight breaking out. Petty, Earnhardt, and other greats have gone to blows at the NWS. Fans would get two sporting events for the price of one—a car race *and* a boxing match.

The town of North Wilkesboro, North Carolina, is the resting place for the old speedway built in 1946. It was built one year before Martinsville Speedway in Martinsville, Virginia. For decades, both proud towns came roaring to life while hosting two races a year. Both dirt tracks sat as the eye of the dusty storm orbiting their respective towns.

These days, however, the two short tracks could be compared to two race cars. One was maintained as NASCAR rolled through the years and is still in the race, while the other track wasn't maintained so it couldn't keep up. Martinsville Speedway continues in a 65-year tradition of running two NASCAR races a year, while North Wilkesboro Speedway lost the continuity of historic racing when the last NASCAR race was held there in 1996.

But don't think the little town of North Wilkesboro doesn't keep a little NASCAR lore for itself. Some folks are fond of reciting the old adage: "If walls could talk . . . ." Well, if that were so, then one could wonder what the walls in Hotel Wilkes might say.

In the fall of 1947, in the North Wilkesboro downtown hotel, Bill France, who could rightly be called the father of NASCAR, joined with the racing minds of his day, most of whom were leveling acre upon acre around their hometowns to construct race tracks. In the meeting, these early promoters of sanctioned racing laid another kind of groundwork that would in a few short months be organized as NASCAR.

The *end* of the story about NASCAR's founding is the most familiar part. In December 1947, most of these pioneering men who first met at Hotel Wilkes gathered together again at the Streamline Hotel in Daytona Beach, Florida. There were 35 men at the meeting— "young racers, older veterans, car owners, whiskey trippers, and car dealers." It was then and there that the National Association of Stock Car Racing was born. After that meeting, NASCAR had its list of standardized rules. The association's new president, Bill France Sr., also known as "Big Bill," took charge of promoting the new sport.

In June 1949, NASCAR held its first-ever "strictly stock car" race in Charlotte, North Carolina. Eighteen thousand people attended. Seven more NASCAR races were held that first year. Any guesses as to where the first season's champion was crowned on October 16, 1949? That's correct: at North Wilkesboro Speedway. Moonshine runner Bob Flock won the race that day by 100 yards. Lee Petty finished second. Red Byron was crowned the 1949 champion.

North Wilkesboro's current population is just under 5,000. Folks hope their track will someday roar to life again with the latest generation of cars, drivers, and fans. But the old oval needs help. In 1999, NWS supporters may have seen their last hope look away from them and toward their neighbors just ninety minutes to the south. That's how far Concord is from North Wilkesboro. Concord is home to a superspeedway—the Charlotte Motor Speedway.

In 1999, Lowe's, the home improvement and hardware superstore, bought the naming rights to the track in Concord. For the next decade, the superspeedway, with its corporate backing, would cast long summer shadows over old NWS. This may not have meant as much to the people of North Wilkesboro if it weren't for the fact that Lowe's own history is so intimately linked to the small town. The retail giant got its humble start in 1946 as North Wilkesboro Hardware Company. That was the same year the town's speedway was built. In a way, the home improvement retailer turned its back on its hometown track in favor of the track down the road in Concord.

So by 1999, three years after it held its last main event (in which Jeff

Gordon finished first and Mark Martin ninth), the old NWS had lost its traction—its *platform*. Call what it lost any number of things, but the venerable track was no longer suitable for the NASCAR brand. There were some moments of hope every now and then, such as when local events were held at the historic oval. But the fury wasn't the same.

In 2004, the Roush Racing Team brought one of those rays of light to town when it held a driver tryout at NWS, which stirred up excitement and memories as well as a small crowd.

Mark was driving for Roush Racing in 2004, but he wasn't trying out. He didn't need to because he'd already been with Jack Roush for 16 years. In fact, in 2004 it had been 23 years since Mark debuted at NWS. He had 15 years of NWS racing memories to recall while looking out over the old track. Each year, the No. 7 race on the schedule was at NWS, followed in late September or early October by another race. Mark ran a total of 22 races at NWS.

Twenty-two.

That's how old Mark was when the storied NWS first gripped his attention.

START BRASH . . .

It was the seventh race of the 1981 season—the Northwestern Bank 400. Each lap at NWS was five-eighths of a mile long, so the 400-lap race went 250 miles. The field of drivers had been at Bristol Motor Speedway the weekend before. Darrell Waltrip won the race for his third of twelve victories of the season. Bobby Allison, Ricky Rudd, Dale Earnhardt, Benny Parsons, and other greats were all trying to keep up with Waltrip, but in the end none could. Waltrip went on to win the 1981 championship.

Mark joined the elite field of racers on April 5, 1981. He wouldn't have a shot at the title in '81 because he wasn't yet racing full-time, but he was going to race against the best the sport offered.

Mark, today a frequent Twitter user, once tweeted: "When I was twelve, Richard Petty was my favorite NASCAR driver. When I was twenty-two, I got to race with him." That was a dream come true, but

Mark wasn't focusing on boyhood dreams.

On the day of Mark's first race, he lined up in the starting grid four rows in front of his boyhood favorite—"The King." Mark had qualified his Pontiac in the number five spot. Petty started 13th with Dave Marcis lined up on the pole. Earnhardt idled beside him. Allison was behind Marcis, and Rudd was behind Earnhardt. Next to Mark was 14-year NASCAR veteran Benny Parsons.

Mark raced behind the veterans for 166 laps before gears started clashing on his #2 Pontiac. The car's rear end went out, ending his day.

There's another "22" in this story: twenty-two thousand fans swarmed North Wilkesboro's hive of a track that day. Mark wasn't the hot item on the ticket—not in those days. He later became "The Kid," but at this stage in his career, he could have been in the ticket booth selling the tickets and still be unrecognized as a bonafide NASCAR racer.

By lap 267, Petty had taken the lead. He held on for 27 laps until Allison swept by him. Then Marcis and Waltrip joined Allison and Petty for 44 laps of veteran racing—each battling to the front but then getting passed by the next contender. With 62 laps to go, Petty willed and skilled his way into the lead and then hung on until the checkered flag dropped. In Mark's NASCAR debut, he had a front-row seat to watch his favorite driver win.

Four weeks later, in May, Mark took his Pontiac to Nashville, Tennessee, for his second race. Eighteen thousand fans saw Mark race a grand total of 1.192 miles—exactly two laps around the Nashville Speedway track. This time, it was a camshaft failure that sent him to the garage early.

Mark was having some tough luck in NASCAR. Two races, one fifth- and one sixth-place start in the books, but 27th-place finishes both times—last and almost last.

In July, back in Nashville, Mark had the opportunity to see if starting in the pole position would change his finishing position. This was his first NASCAR pole. He was already making a name for himself as a good qualifier, but it was time to finish a race.

It's hot in Nashville in July. Expect temperatures in the upper 80s and low 90s. In that kind of heat, fatigue easily sets in as the temperature in a race car, with its 850 horsepower engine revved to 9000 rpm for three hours, reaches up to 150 degrees.

Mark led for 36 laps before Waltrip screamed by him on lap 37. By race's end, Waltrip and nine others had passed Mark. But he finished, and finished well—just outside of the Top 10 at 11th. Waltrip led for 303 of the 420 laps and was first to the checkered flag.

Five weeks went by before Mark raced again.

On September 13, Mark was in Richmond, Virginia, for his fourth NASCAR race. His reputation as a great qualifier spread to another raceway when he sat at the pole for the second straight race.

With 27,000 fans in attendance, the wily veteran Darrell Waltrip, poised in his Buick, lined up beside him. It was set up as a good old-fashioned duel at the start, the sage veteran and the young gun—a little like Doc Hudson and Lightning McQueen in the movie *Cars*.

Waltrip, nicknamed "Jaws" for his endless chatter and arrogance back in his younger days, probably knew what "The Kid" beside him was thinking. Just nine years earlier, Waltrip had been in the same position: a young gun making his fourth career start in a field of veterans, just trying to earn enough money to stay racing another week.

The race began with the pace car leading the way while car engines and tires warmed up to the track. The pace car peeled off onto pit road, the flagman waved the green flag, "Jaws" stepped hard on the gas, and "The Kid" was not in the picture. But that day Mark accomplished what every racer remembers forever: his first Top-10 finish, in seventh place.

After a week off, Mark was feeling pretty good about himself as he made his way to Martinsville Speedway. He was steadily improving his performances week by week. But this was his last running for the 1981 season. Six more races would take place, but Mark wouldn't be competing in any of them. This was his last chance for improvement.

That's how it is for many racers early in their careers. Oftentimes, limited resources and other obstacles prohibit them from getting into all the races.

Mark would learn a couple of lessons about limits over the course of his career, but in his last race of 1981 he would chase after the checkered flag like a moonshine runner bent on escape.

In Martinsville, he started fifth on the grid Ahead of him once again were the all-time greats: Parsons, Gant, Rudd, and, of course, Waltrip. To get past them at the tiny Martinsville track, Mark would have to use his ability to grip the wheel and bump and bang through little created space. The confident 22-two-year-old kid hung around the front of the pack before making his move and taking the lead, which he would hold for 40 laps.

After the 40 laps, Gant took over. Mark wouldn't pass Gant for the remainder of the race, but he would finish in third place for his best finish. Waltrip took first for his ninth win of the year and the first of four in a row. It was his race, and 1981 was his year.

As it would turn out, 1982 would also be Waltrip's year. He once again recorded 12 wins on his way to the NASCAR Winston Cup Series championship.

So can we just take Darrell Waltrip out of the story? Not quite yet. He would give Mark some advice, which, unfortunately, Mark didn't heed.

... AND FINISH BANKRUPT

Mark began his official rookie season in 1982. (He wasn't officially considered a rookie in 1981 because he didn't run a full schedule.) He would start all 30 races but finish with mixed results. By the end of the season, he had earned two Top 5s and eight Top 10s. But he also failed to finish 12 races—not because he wrecked a lot (he only wrecked in one) but because of engine problems and other mechanical failures.

The cost of repairing those mechanical problems further taxed Mark's trickling revenue stream. Breakdowns can bankrupt an underfunded team quickly. That's why the young drivers these days often sprint toward opportunities to race better equipment if and when those opportunities arise.

Mark had those opportunities, but he turned them down. Why? He told ESPN journalist David Newton: "If [in 1981] I sat on the pole twice in five races in my own car, why would I want to drive theirs? I didn't think their car was as good as the one I could build." That's the veteran Mark talking about his youthful cockiness. Then he humbly added, "I didn't know nothing."

Brashness sometimes blinds a man to the reality of his situation. Mark had decided to run a full schedule in 1982, but by the end of the season he'd learn how much 30 weeks of racing costs.

Mark, a cocky rookie at the time, also ignored Waltrip's attempt to persuade him to "run a limited schedule and save money." Waltrip wasn't looking to get rid of the competition; he genuinely cared about Mark. But Mark continued with the full schedule. In the end, his know-it-all attitude would cost him everything.

In Mark's first-ever Daytona 500, he raced his Buick 75 laps before taking it to the garage with engine problems. That would be the first of 12 races he would fail to finish in 1982. His season began on the wrong note, but there were several highlights over the long haul. One of those was beating Waltrip to the finish line for the first time.

By season's end, Mark's decision to race a full-time schedule made him eligible for the Rookie of the Year award. His performance on the track was good enough for a runner-up finish for the award. He also finished 14th in total points. He would have placed higher if not for the six DNFs (Did Not Finish) in his last ten races. His reasons for not finishing look like a scrap yard inventory: rear end, steering, ball joint, valves, engine, and con arm. That adds up to a long and expensive list.

One word describes Mark's situation by the end of the season: bankrupt. The revenue stream dried up. He had spent all his own money, as well as the money from his father and his sponsor. He was deep in debt and needed to find another way than his own if his career was going to go forward. Mark's answer to his situation was "to auction off all his equipment and look for a ride."

In 1983, Mark raced a part-time schedule. He raced for four different car owners in a total of 16 races, eight of which he did not finish. Furthermore, owner Jim Stacy fired "The Kid" after the first seven races. But Mark picked up rides irregularly for nine more races and three different owners. The season was far from successful. Mark told ESPN's David Newton, "If '82 wasn't humiliating enough, '83 was incredibly devastating." Any of the early success he had gained as "The Kid" who was a good qualifier, a future star, and someone destined for greatness, became a distant memory.

GOING HOME

During those early years, Mark's church involvement resembled the racing schedule of his young NASCAR career—in and out. Overall, he had a low level of commitment to God. This was partly due to his racing lifestyle, which didn't allow for regular church attendance. But Mark says he wasn't really seeking spiritual growth back then. The in-and-out approach wasn't enough to grow him spiritually, but it was where Mark was with God when his young career went bankrupt.

Maybe Mark's next decisions would have been different if he had been more committed to God—or if he had decided after disappearing from the NASCAR scene to seek the spiritual growth he had lacked. But it would be a full decade before Mark would get serious about his relationship with God.

Instead, Mark decided to go "home"—home being back to the American Speed Association (ASA), where he raced on tracks throughout the Midwest during the late 1970s, where he won the Rookie of the Year in 1977, where he won the series championship back-to-back-to-back from 1978 to 1980, and where he was racing successfully before he made his jump to NASCAR.

Mark could have gone home to Batesville in 1983. He could have worked for his father's successful trucking business. But "home" for Mark was defined by a race car on a track. Of course, Mark knew something about the family business, but racing is all he really wanted to do. So even after the roller coaster ride called NASCAR, Mark was not going to give up on his racing career. He may have been bankrupt and back where he started, but he had no other plan in life than to be a racer.

What Mark didn't plan on at this time in his life was meeting his future wife.

On his way to Wisconsin, where he expected to revive his racing career, he stopped at Batesville for Christmas in 1983. During this visit, his sister Glenda introduced him to Arlene Everett. Less than a year later, Mark and Arlene were married. Arlene had four daughters from a previous marriage, and she and Mark had a son, Matt.

Mark did successfully revive his career. In 1986, he won his fourth ASA Series championship. His plan was moving forward.

However, something else was happening that Mark hadn't planned on.

Mark didn't plan to become an alcoholic. But at the time of the 1986 championship, he was two years into an addiction that would last another two years. We're talking heavy drinking—late at night, after work was done. It was the addiction that also gripped his father. Mark, like many drivers, would simply have a few beers after a race. It progressed from there to going from the track to the bar and having a few more drinks. When his NASCAR career disappeared in 1983, Mark started drinking more heavily.

Still, the heavy drinking didn't impact Mark's on-track performance. After Mark's success in 1986, Bruce Lawmaster hired him to drive in the 1987 NASCAR Nationwide Series (at the time, the Busch Grand National Series). Mark drove Lawmaster's Ford for the entire 27-race schedule. He won three races and recorded five Top 5s and thirteen Top 10s. He also started on the pole six times.

THE COMEBACK KID

Once again, Mark Martin was being watched and talked about.

Late in the 1987 season, when word got around that automotive engineer Jack Roush was looking to start up a NASCAR Sprint Cup team for 1988, one of Mark's old friends, Bobby Allison, dropped Mark's name to Roush.

Roush vetted Mark and discovered his addiction in the process. When it came time to make a deal, he didn't ignore Mark's alcoholism, but Mark got the job anyway. That was the first marvelous thing that happened to Mark as a result of meeting Jack. The second was that Mark quit drinking altogether.

Roush made it a nonnegotiable part of the deal—"the boozing had to stop"—and Mark shook his hand and gave him his word that he would quit drinking. Mark had his last drink in 1988. True to his promise, Mark recently celebrated 25 years of sobriety.

When Jack Roush celebrated his induction into the Texas Motorsports Hall of Fame in 2013, Mark was there with the kindest of words for his former boss and lifelong friend.

Before one of Mark's last races for Jack Roush Racing, a fan asked him what his fondest memory was. Mark's answer: "My most memorable was sitting in Jack's little office talking about driving his car and at the end of the conversation standing up and shaking hands. That meant I had a ride in NASCAR."

What happened over the next 19 seasons has been called "one of the greatest pairings in Cup history." Forty races won. Top-10 finishes in season points 16 times—twelve of those in succession and four of them second-place finishes.

Sometimes people make a big deal of Mark's second-place finishes without mentioning the name of the season champion. But consider that Mark finished second to Dale Earnhardt twice. Then to Jeff Gordon. Then to Tony Stewart. These are first-ballot racing Hall of Famers, just like Mark will most likely be.

On October 22, 1989, while driving one of Jack Roush's Fords, Mark got his first NASCAR Sprint Cup Series win. Right behind him were the familiar foes—Rusty Wallace and Darrell Waltrip. Mark finally knew the thrill of victory at the highest level and racing against the absolute best in his sport.

VICTORY IN JESUS

Faith came out of personal tragedy for Mark, as his renewed commitment to his relationship with God came in the wake of a close friend's death.

The death of Clifford Allison occurred while he was on a practice run at Michigan International Speedway in 1992. Mark had run a few Nationwide Series races with Clifford, and the two became close friends. Bobby Allison, Clifford's father, was also especially close to Mark.

Clifford was 27 years old and married with three children. Mark was 33 at the time. The reality of Clifford's death shook Mark out of his spiritual lethargy and sent him into action. Just like he has done with racing, just like he has done with pumping iron, and just like he did with the bottle, Mark poured everything he had into his renewed relationship with Jesus.

Part of Mark's testimony is the relevance he finds in the teachings of the Bible. He says, "The cool thing about the Bible is that even though it's a very old book, it is still up to date and teaches you how to handle things today." That shows that Mark has come a long way from his up-and-down level of commitment to God in the early '80s.

Mark is regularly present at chapel services held by Motor Racing Outreach on race days. And he and Arlene generously give to ministries like Kyle Petty's Victory Junction, which serves children with serious illnesses, and John 3:16 Ministries, which reaches out to those with addictions—something Mark knows about since he and his father were both alcoholics.

Mark's father died in a 1998 plane crash that also killed his stepmother and the couple's daughter. After the next race Mark won, he was provided with a platform to share his thoughts. He dedicated the win to his father, saying, "He was my hero. He was a man's man, with everything that represents."

Mark is likewise a hero to many.

THERE IS NO END TO THE STORY

There is no foreseeable end to Mark's story. The 2013 season marked his 31st year in NASCAR.

Mark officially retired from Jack Roush's organization in 2005. But another member of the team wiggled away, and Jack persuaded Mark to stay on for one more year. But then he signed with Bobby Ginn for 2007 and then with Dale Earnhardt, Inc. for 2008 to race part-time schedules. Then Rick Hendrick called and Mark signed up to drive full-time again. That lasted through the 2011 season. For the past two seasons—2012 and 2013—Mark was back to a limited schedule with

MARK MARTIN: FROM BACKWOODS BOY TO LIVING LEGEND 59

Michael Waltrip Racing. Then Tony Stewart broke bones in his right leg in an August sprint car crash. Mark started filling in for Tony, becoming the full-time driver of the No. 14 car for the Stewart-Haas Racing team.

Back in 2006, Mark said, "I don't see myself running Cup races when I'm fifty-something." However, as of this writing, he's 55, and that's five full years of races he's run. But at the end of last season, Mark retired from the driver's seat. Well, he didn't "retire." He won't use that word. Mark's immediate future continues with Stewart-Haas Racing in various advisor roles.

Mark's grandfather, Clyde Martin, once tried to talk him out of getting into the racing business, but he wouldn't listen. NASCAR Nation is thankful. Mark has led a storied and successful career.

3

MICHAEL MCDOWELL:
ALWAYS AIMING HIGHER

Think back to when you were a kid. Can you remember the first wheeled machine you raced? Maybe it was the Big Wheel you rode up and down the driveway. Or perhaps it was a Schwinn Gremlin with training wheels. After that, you may have graduated to the BMX bike you raced around the block. Eventually, you might have moved on to motorized "toys," such as a gas-powered go-kart.

If you were like NASCAR driver Michael McDowell (aka "McFlippin" or "Lucky Dog"), you just had that insatiable desire to go faster. As a young boy, Michael's dream machine was anything bigger, stronger, faster, anything with more torque—whatever was available that he could make go as fast as it would possibly go. He just loved to race.

In that respect, not much has changed for Michael, who is 29 years old as of this writing. He still has a deep desire to go faster and a strong ambition to stay relevant in racing. Any souped-up NASCAR machine that keeps his racing career on the track is his next dream machine. And he is none too ashamed to do whatever it takes—within the rules, of course—to get behind the wheel of a fast ride.

Michael's resolve to become a racer, and now to *stay* a racer, is the golden cord throughout his story. Every mile of his journey is marked with persistence.

Because of where Michael is in his career—with his past successes and current challenges, with his gritty determination to be Sprint Cup–fast week after week, and with his need to prove to sponsors that his talents belong on the track and not buried in the garage—his story is relevant to thousands of fans asking big questions about their own lives.

Michael's story speaks to those who wonder what their own success should look like, those who are prone to ask questions such as:

Why is life really tough right now?

I have the talent, and I'd do just about anything to move forward, so what should I do?

NASCAR IN 1984

Michael's story begins in 1984, the same year NASCAR's king, Richard Petty, duked it out with fellow racing great Cale Yarborough for first place in the Firecracker 400 at Daytona International Raceway.

It's not hard to imagine that Bill and Tracy McDowell watched the *ABC's Wide World of Sports* broadcast of Petty's 200th victory from their home in Glendale, Arizona, a suburb of Phoenix. They were, after all, huge NASCAR fans.

But the McDowells had a lot more on their minds than Richard Petty and NASCAR in 1984. Later that year, on December 21, they welcomed their second son, Michael, into their home. Michael was a "Christmas baby," as children born around the holiday season are often called, and he joined his older brother, Billy McDowell V, in the middle-class McDowell family.

THE GIPPER AND NASCAR

On July 4, 1984, at the Firecracker 400 at Daytona International Speedway, Ronald Reagan became the first sitting U.S. president to witness a NASCAR race.

At 10 a.m., from high above Daytona in Air Force One, Reagan started the race. His mellifluous voice invoked "Gentlemen, start your engines" and boomed through the speakers. Then, like a choir following a great conductor, 43 stock car engines and 80,000 NASCAR fans roared symphoniously to life.

The president's plane landed as the race was in full swing.

President Reagan continued his trip to the track, arriving at the raceway with 35 laps to go, just in time to see NASCAR greats Yarborough and Petty duke it out for first place. In the end Petty was victorious—his record 200th and final victory. The requisite pictures were taken, and a picnic with the president was held in the infield.

President Reagan was invested another way in the Firecracker 400. The #73 car driven by Steve Moore was sponsored by the Republican Party and Reagan's presidential campaign. In classic NASCAR fashion, the car's paint job said it in as few words as possible: "Reagan in '84." The polls don't tell us how Reagan's presence that day contributed to his presidency, or to what extent being around NASCAR for a day impacted the vote of the fans, but it certainly didn't hurt his cause.

In the first week of November, "Reagan in '84" became a landslide victory. The president captured 49 states, received 59 percent of the vote, and collected 525 electoral votes. If Reagan were a race car driver and those numbers could somehow be turned into racing stats, he'd be the guy to beat virtually every week—he'd be Hall of Fame bound. As a twist to the analogy, consider this: if there were an equivalent in racing to Reagan's election numbers in '84, then Richard Petty would be in the White House.

Part of Glendale's sports scene is the Phoenix Kart Racing Association (PKRA), which boasts a three-quarter-mile track. That meant Michael had a *real* race track almost literally in his own backyard. When He was old enough to begin competitive racing—in other words, *three* years old—he traded in his Big Wheel for a BMX bike. He raced BMX for five years before getting into go-karting.

Michael was only seven years old, and not yet racing, when he first visited the kart track in Phoenix. But he still remembers sitting in the seat of a kart that still sat in the bed of a pickup truck. Looking from the back of the truck, he saw the colorful tents and flags flapping in the desert breeze, and he saw the farthest corner of the track and the cones marking it off. He heard engines revving and popping and brakes screeching.

Michael was captivated, and his future was sealed. He just needed to wait one year before he could race in one of the machines he heard and saw that day.

When his first driving day finally arrived, Michael seized it with ready hands. But the fulfillment of his dream wasn't going to be easy, and there were plenty of rough spots in the road ahead.

A WAY OF LIFE

"Karting was a way of life for my family and me," Michael says. "We traveled across the country pursuing my dreams." He lived the kart-racing phase of his dream for the next ten years. For the first couple of years of that phase, he stayed around the Phoenix area. His racing was made possible through the "prolific support" of his mom, dad, and brother. Michael's family even took on a venture of buying and selling karts to help pay for the racing.

Bill and Tracy McDowell loved each other deeply, and they cared for and loved their two boys as well. They made the usual sacrifices involved in raising children, and they laid a firm foundation for their sons' lives. Michael's mom, dad, and brother Billy were the founding force in his racing. To this day, he never hesitates to give his family credit for helping him pursue his early racing dreams.

Michael singles out his brother for special praise: "My brother Billy believed in me and my ability. He sacrificed a good bit to help me a great deal. He could have done other things than help me, but he believed in my ability and he was there for me."

As Michael excelled on the race track, he enjoyed more and more opportunities to race in places beyond Phoenix. Trips across the southwest United States to race became a way of life for Michael.

Michael's racing proved a significant expense for his family. Even junior league racing cost the McDowells thousands of dollars, dollars they just couldn't spare. Crossing the desert into Nevada and southern California drained the family's bank accounts. Though Michael's parents would keep cheering him on, they wouldn't be able to pay the way anymore. Despite the costs, Michael was determined to succeed in racing. To meet this challenge head on, he took off his helmet and came up with a plan. At the age of 12, he sat down and wrote his first sponsorship proposal.

VOLUNTEERISM, RANDOM JOBS, AND TEACHING

As a twelve-year-old facing the possibility of no longer competing in karting due to the costs, Michael didn't just spend his time writing sponsorship proposals; he also went to work. He got his hands dirty working for free in karting shops and also took random jobs, such as selling phone plans to earn money. Michael's do-whatever-it-takes plan worked. He kept racing.

Michael's employers noticed his willingness to do whatever they asked of him. Occasionally, one of his employers would ask him to teach a child or grandchild how to drive a kart. Michael approached those jobs with passion. He eagerly passed on racing techniques, such as recognizing and taking the best racing line or driving under pressure. Over the purr of kart engines, he shared his secrets for race starts, taking a hairpin turn, and passing an opponent. Michael relished his teaching opportunities, and his charisma made him a hit with the younger drivers.

A few years passed, and Michael's charm also made him a hit with a certain teenage girl. His life was already busy, but Jami Horne won his heart and became his steady girlfriend. Michael and Jami were high-school sweethearts even though Michael, because he was so busy with racing, finished school through correspondence courses with the American School Academy. Jami and Michael would eventually marry in 2003.

Michael wasn't what you might call "religious" growing up; in fact, he never even held or opened a Bible until he was 18 years old. In his earlier teen years, Jami's aunt and uncle invited Michael to church, where he was first exposed to the Bible. Around this time, Michael felt God working on him. Jami's family had a huge impact on Michael's spiritual journey.

Backpedal a few years: Michael found that he had a knack for coaching, so he began seeking out a full-time position as a coach. He certainly wasn't giving up his dream of racing—there was no way coaching could replace that goal. He was just adding coaching to his experiences in racing.

As fortune would have it, the Phoenix area is home to arguably the most prestigious driving school in America, the Bob Bondurant School of High Performance Driving. For Michael, applying there was a no-brainer. But there was just one problem: Michael hadn't yet celebrated his 16th birthday. Without a driver's license, how could he teach someone else how to drive?

LIMITATIONS IMPLY POSSIBILITIES
Just about everyone who knew Michael believed he had the ability to coach at a world-class driving school. On December 21, 2000, the door of opportunity to do just that flung open when Michael turned 16 and got his driver's license. He was quickly hired as an instructor at Bondurant.

At 16, Michael didn't fully understand just how many doors his coaching at Bondurant would open. But as he worked at Bondurant, and as he stayed active in racing, he continuously developed relationships that would prove to be pivotal to his racing career.

Between 2002 and 2004, Michael's budding relationship with Bill Mayer of MMI Karting landed him in his first professional races. He started winning, and that led to more opportunities . . . and more wins. He won the '03 Star Mazda Series Rookie of the Year award and then followed that up in '04 with a Star Mazda Series championship.

But before Michael's trophy had made it to the mantel, the racing community was struck with a great loss. His employer, mentor, and friend—Ron Huber—died in a freak accident on an electric Segway Human Transporter. The Segway flipped in a routine trip around the pit area, and Huber suffered a fatal head injury. The tragic irony is that Huber, a man who often raced cars himself and routinely went 150 miles per hour, died in an accident that occurred at only five miles per hour.

TURNING MOURNING INTO DANCING

Following Huber's unlikely and bizarre death, Michael's life was at a crossroads. He had met Ron Huber when he had no money and was working hard to make it in racing. They became friends, making Ron one of the growing number of Christians coming into Michael's life. Ron, a successful businessman and philanthropist, was involved in motorsports ministries. He attended Bondurant because he owned a race car but didn't know much about competitive driving. In the course of his friendship with Ron, Michael started mentoring Ron's grandson Andrew. Consequently, Michael and Ron spent many hours at the track together.

Michael wasn't opposed to Christianity at the time. By now, he and Jami had gone to church with her Aunt Kym and Uncle Deano a few times. He hadn't committed to anything, but he was listening. God seemed to be using a variety of people and circumstances to speak to Michael. Was it possible that God was using the tragic passing of Ron Huber to reach Michael?

At Ron's memorial service, Michael listened closely—not just to what was said during the service but to what a friend of Ron's asked him afterward. Here's how Michael recalls what happened that day:

> Tom Barnett . . . a man of faith, challenged me at Ron's funeral about my life. He asked me if I thought Ron was in heaven, and I obviously said yes and then he asked me if I was to die today would I go to heaven? I paused and really didn't know. I started evaluating my lifestyle, my heart, and who I really wanted to be.

Michael eventually surrendered his life to Christ at a church service in which the preacher spoke about forgiveness and about how to have a new life in Christ. Here is what Michael later said about that day:

> I thought to myself, man, that would be nice, a second chance to have all my sins washed away, to be forgiven and start over, and I did that day, that second.

Michael regularly talks about the joy and peace he has experienced through his faith in Christ. But he's honest, and he doesn't leave out the reality of the struggles he faces as he lives out his faith in his line of work. It's sometimes tempting to think that living the Christian life is easy. But that's not Michael's story any more than it's yours or mine. He still presses on in diverse ways, and he is still working on his dream.

One of Michael's dear friends had died, but that tragedy led to his new life in Christ budding forth. Michael mourned the loss of his mentor, but, as the psalmist put it, God turned mourning into dancing (Psalm 30:11).

DREAMS COME TRUE

Driving education courses at Bondurant's 60-acre campus in Phoenix teach first-timers, semi pros, and pros alike at the level suited for them. Classroom lessons, hours of driving on the track, and even visits to the onsite museum round out a student's education. Instructors teach within the parameters of basic car control and finding *your* limit.

As a renowned and respected driving school, Bondurant attracts a diverse student body. Over the years, men and women have learned accident avoidance, teenagers have learned the fundamentals of defensive driving, and many people, such as Ron Huber, have seen their childhood dreams of racing cars fulfilled.

Michael has guided several thrill seekers who came to Bondurant with the same aim his friend Ron had. But no relationship developed out of the instructor/student bond has proved more valuable to Michael than the one with Rob Finlay.

Rob, a racing enthusiast and successful businessman from New Hampshire, came to Bondurant with very little race car experience. He wanted a better taste of race car driving, and he landed Michael as his instructor when he arrived in Phoenix.

Michael and Rob clicked like two ends of a seatbelt, and it wasn't long before they began talking about working together. After Bondurant, Rob formed Finlay Motorsports, and Michael took the wheel of its Grand American Rolex Series car. For the 2005 season, they ran in 10 races—winning in Mexico City—and finished fourth in the championship standings.

That same year, the Finlay Motorsports team banded together with Rocketsports, a professional Champ Car team. Champ Car racing is the top tier of open-wheeled racing (different from NASCAR, in which fenders cover the wheels). Driving the Champ Car was what Michael had been striving to do for a long time. "I have been focusing my whole career to get to this point," Michael said. "I am lucky that I will get to live my dream and drive a Champ Car."

Sadly, during the off-season that year, Michael lost his mother to cancer. Her battle with the disease ended in January of 2006. Tracy McDowell was never shy in voicing how proud she was of both of her sons, and she often showed her pride in Michael by telling her friends to check out Michael's website so they could follow his latest racing exploits. Michael took much of his gritty determination from his mom, who was the kind of woman who never doubted herself when she decided she wanted to do something.

Michael's parents were married for 25 years and, like Michael and Jami, had known each other since they were teenagers.

FENDERS FOR MICHAEL

After a couple years of success in top-tier open-wheel racing, Michael was introduced to owner Eddie Sharp. It was 2006, and Sharp had just committed to NASCAR team ownership and a 40,000-square-foot race complex in Denver, North Carolina.

At the time of the meeting, Sharp's team was running in the Automobile Racing Club of America series (ARCA). ARCA works a lot like a developmental league for NASCAR. Though ARCA is not officially NASCAR sanctioned, many young ARCA drivers itch for a big-league ride.

In August, Michael took the wheel of his first race car with fenders— an ARCA stock car. He ran five races that year and took three Top-10 finishes. Sharp employed Michael again in 2007, and he made 23 starts that year, nine of them from the pole position. On his way to winning the '07 ARCA Rookie of the Year title (his second such title in two major racing series), he captured the checkered flag four times, recorded fifteen Top-10 and eleven Top-5 finishes, and finished as runner-up in the season standings. Michael was Eddie Sharp's first successful driver. For Michael, the success with Eddie Sharp Racing (ESR) paid off.

Michael completed the '07 ARCA season in October. A week later, he was racing a NASCAR Truck Series truck owned by iconic NASCAR figure Darrell Waltrip. Then, through a series of friends who know friends, Michael became involved with Michael Waltrip. Eddie Sharp, a friend of Michael Waltrip's, passed along a glowing recommendation of McDowell. Waltrip put Michael in the seat of his Nationwide Series car for the last three races of the season.

Michael's 2007 racing year proved a dramatic one, as he shifted between car body styles and horsepower maximums and worked on three different stock car stages. He rightly sensed excitement around every corner. Michael was busy at the end of '07 as he finished off the last three Nationwide Series races, the second of which was back home in Phoenix, where, at Phoenix International Raceway and in front of 42,000 fans, he finished 14th.

By the end of 2007, Michael had good reason to be excited about what God was doing in his racing career. He was, after all, in the running to drive the #00 Aaron's Dream Machine Sprint Cup car for part of 2008.

THAT'S ONE LUCKY DOG

Michael got the call from Waltrip and got the #00 Aaron's Dream Machine ride, beginning with the sixth race of the 2008 season. In late March, Michael made his NASCAR Sprint Cup debut at Martinsville Speedway. His childhood dream had come true: he'd reached the highest level of racing.

Michael was ready. Even though he had spent most of his racing career in open-wheel cars, he was prepared to learn as much as he could from those around him, just as he had done all through his career. Like he said, "I want to do well, but at the same time you have to balance that by not doing anything stupid."

His goal was always the same: "I have dedicated myself to being the hardest working driver anywhere, to winning in every car I step foot in, and to understand the business of motorsports as much as the driving."

Michael's boss said, "I feel real good about where he's at with us. He's tested real well, and I fully expect him to be with us 100 years." Now that's exuding confidence—but maybe Waltrip was giving Michael a bit of a pep talk, too.

Michael started 34th in his debut and finished 26th. But after the race, veteran Jeff Burton lambasted him in the press, claiming Michael had blocked him from catching up to race leader Denny Hamlin. Michael talked with Burton later in the week and later said he learned something from the veteran.

Michael explained that when he got in Burton's way toward the end of the race, he was actually racing for the "free pass" position. It's also called the "Lucky Dog" position, and it happens when the first lapped driver is given a lap back if a caution flag comes out. In Michael's debut, he was racing to be the "Lucky Dog."

That same week, the team traveled to Fort Worth, Texas, home of the "Great American Speedway"—Texas Motor Speedway. It was also the home of Michael's first-ever NASCAR race the year before.

In Fort Worth, thunder struck and a gushing rainstorm followed on Thursday night. But the storm passed relatively quickly, and by Friday, the day teams were going for their qualifying times, the 1.5-mile paved track had dried up.

Qualifying for a race can be a little tricky. Virtually every driver has missed the cut at one time or another. Usually it's the younger, less-established drivers who lose out. Each driver gets a two-lap run around the track. Drivers start from their pit, and by the time they get to the start/finish line, when the computers start calculating their time and speed, they should be at running speed.

Drivers don't have to take both laps in qualifying. If they like their stats from lap one, then they can forego the second. But they have the option of trying to do better if they want to. For most races, qualifying determines drivers' race-day starting position. The fastest driver gets the pole, and they move back from there.

On that Friday in April, Michael took the Aaron's Dream Machine Toyota Camry out of the pits and rounded the track alone. Coming out of turn 4, Michael keyed the mic and said, "Something is not right. I'm going to run another lap."

Earlier in qualifying, a car blew an engine and dropped its load of fluids on the track. A NASCAR crew worked to get it cleaned up before qualifying continued. As Michael came out of the turn, his back end broke loose on him, possibly from picking up some of the residue from the earlier spill. "Loose" means the back of the car is coming around. You don't want to be loose, especially in the corner.

As Michael corrected, his front end rocketed up the bank. He had no brakes because they had been pulled back for more qualifying speed, so the Dream Machine tore off up into the bank of turn 1 and hit the barrier head-on at 170 miles per hour.

Jami, Michael's wife, felt her stomach drop as she watched the wreck on the Jumbotron screen from pit lane.

All of that force hitting the wall needed to go somewhere. The wall took a chunk of that force, but Michael also took a share. The rest of the force came off the wall, flipped the race car on its top, and sent it sliding down the track some 200 feet. Then, like an Olympic gymnast after a long approach bounds off a mat, the car began to bounce. The specialized stock car flipped once or twice, then bounced again, and flipped again. The car flipped a total of eight times.

Miracle upon miracle, Michael was alive and stepped out of the car with a wave to the dead-quiet crowd, which quickly erupted in cheers. You can watch the horrific accident on YouTube by typing in "Michael McDowell crash." Years later, Michael's survival still awes millions of online viewers.

The following day, Saturday, Michael unwrapped a brand-new #00 Aaron's Dream Machine and finished his practice laps. Afterward, he stood with media microphones in his face and thanked NASCAR for the safety devices they had in place, which factored into keeping him alive. He thanked God that he was able to walk away from the crash but said he was upset that he caused so much work for the guys who take care of his car and because he had held up qualifying. Fearful of losing his Sprint Cup ride, he praised his sponsor and team owner for making his dream come true.

Riding on the hood of the Aaron's Dream Machine was the team mascot, a canine called "Lucky Dog." On Sunday, Michael, fortunate to be alive, started the Samsung 500 in the 40th position and finished 33rd.

Michael's nicknames may be "McFlippin" and "Lucky Dog," but he knows who ultimately kept him alive on that Friday. When a close friend asked him later what the accident did for his faith, Michael replied that it gave him a new platform from which to share about his belief in God. The crash gave him a stage, and God asked him to do something on that stage for Him. While his relationship with God was strong going into turn 4, it was even stronger after his accident.

FAMOUS FOR WRECKING

During the week following his crash, Michael made the rounds on the media circuit. He appeared on shows like *Good Morning America, The Today Show, Ellen,* and *Geraldo.* The marketing side of NASCAR says that drivers drive the sales of their own brand and of the brands that deck out the cars they race. So Michael, after walking away from a wreck of such magnitude, was "marketable."

People have looked through NASCAR history to find a wreck comparable to Michael's. His wreck was compared to the wreck his car owner, Michael Waltrip, had in 1990.

On race day in Bristol, Waltrip lost control and took on a concrete barrier where a steel gate was latched. His car blew the gate open, T-boned the barrier, and sat on the track like a dropped egg.

In 2008, car owner and car driver had something more in common: wreckage that the hand of God pulled them from. Maybe this solidarity kept Michael employed with Waltrip's racing team for 18 more races in 2008. Many young drivers who have a bad crash don't get another chance, but Michael was kept in the driver's seat, at least for the time.

Later in the season, however, Michael was replaced in the #00. He did not qualify at Kansas Speedway late in September '08, and that was his last attempt in the Aaron's Dream Machine. But that would not be the end of his stock car career.

In 2009, Michael ran 34 Nationwide Series races, spread out between three different teams. He had five Top-10 finishes. He also ran in eight Sprint Cup races for Tommy Baldwin Jr. In all eight races, Michael started but purposely left after a small number of laps. He would park the car back in the garage, where a problem would be identified and reported to NASCAR officials, and that would end his race day. It's called "start and park," and it is how many small, underfunded NASCAR teams try to stay relevant in racing.

For Michael, this "start and park" approach to racing has become his way of being persistent. He's resolved to stay relevant in the sport he loves. He has the heart and the desire, but he doesn't have much funding.

To cut down on costs further, Michael drove to each race stop with his wife and children. Like many families across America heading out on vacation, the McDowells simply load up the motor home and go.

Michael believes God has called him to racing, but he isn't seeking fame and fortune on the track. Like any race car driver, he would love to be a champion, but he says that's "a distant third or fourth" on his list of what he wants to be known for. Michael's top desires are to be a loving husband and father and to honor God above all. He wants to be where God wants him to be, and if that means grinding out races from the garage when he'd rather be on the track, he'll take it.

Michael has spent each Sprint Cup season since 2008 primarily as a "start and parker." Of his 114 career Sprint Cup races, he has 87 DNFs. Said another way, he has finished just 27 races he started.

VISITING ORPHANS, JOE GIBBS, AND DAYTONA

One has to wonder if Michael has, at some point, ever wanted to hang up his fireproof suit and helmet, call it a career, and look for something else to do.

After the 2010 season, Michael felt like his career was stuck in neutral. Most people would probably have agreed with him. He started 24 races and finished only one, and he drove to the track for another eight but then didn't qualify. That's a rough stretch of road.

The welcome off-season arrived, and Michael, Jami, and some friends went on a missions trip to Mexico. On the trip, Michael pondered that itching question about quitting. Answers came to Michael. He told Lee Warren of *The Christian Post* this story:

> We fed the kids and the community, and as I was walking around handing out food and talking to people, I was praying at the same time, saying, "God, where do you want me to be? What do you want me to do? Do you want me in racing? Do you want me on the mission field?"
>
> I felt like the doors [on my racing career] were being closed a little bit. I didn't hear a trumpet or a microphone or a speaker, but what I heard, I know I heard and what I heard was, I just needed to do what I was doing and God would take care of the rest.

After the trip, the phone rang. It was the call that closed the door with the team Michael had been racing for in 2010. It looked like Michael had his answer.

But then the phone rang a second time that day. Joe Gibbs Racing (JGR) was giving him a shot to drive part-time in its Nationwide Series car in 2011. So Michael had another answer. And his response: "As exciting as that was, it was an extremely emotional and humble experience for me because, while driving the #18 car would be a dream come true, it's not about that. It's about God saying He'd take care of the rest."

In 2011, Michael did the Sprint Cup "start and park" thing again. But he also drove in five races for JGR. He recorded four Top-10 finishes, but maybe more importantly he finished 835 of a total 835 laps. JGR offered Michael five races again in 2012, and he got them the same kind of results.

As the 2013 season arrived, Michael and the team worked diligently to secure sponsorship. They have come sporadically. His finishes have also been irregular. Until a primary sponsor comes around and stays, he will be a "start and park" driver—like he is for Phil Parsons Racing in a Mike Curb–owned car.

That's the same Mike Curb of Curb Records, who wrote the lyrics to Billboard-charted songs such as "Hot Wheels," "Hell Rider," "Last Ride," "Midnight Rider," and "Time to Ride."

Curb's a racing fanatic. Remember Richard Petty's 200th win at Daytona in 1984? Curb owned Petty's car in that race, meaning his NASCAR days go back to before Michael's birth. Michael gets pretty excited at the prospects of having the likes of Curb involved with the team. And his team owner, Phil Parsons, is a committed Christian who serves on the board of directors for Motor Racing Outreach.

Picture Michael standing in an interview at the Daytona International Raceway, also known as the "World Center of Racing." The 2013 Daytona 500 has just been run, and he is all decked out in smiles because he has just completed a career-best day, finishing ninth.

"I wanna thank Jesus, first and foremost," Michael tells interviewers. "It's very cool, just very thankful to have this opportunity, feel very blessed. To walk away from a Daytona 500 with a Top 10 is unbelievable."

Some dreams seem unbelievable, even after they have been accomplished. Hard work, sweat, and sometimes tears have gone into your efforts. Trials have harassed you, but you find a way to press on in spite of them.

That's Michael's story, too. It's an ongoing saga. It's the human experience. Michael had been in the Daytona 500 before. But he'd also failed to make the qualifying cut before. But now he was standing in the birthplace of NASCAR, thanking his team owner, his car owner, his sponsor—"positive, encouraging" K-LOVE radio—and Jesus, last but not least.

4

DAVID REUTIMANN:
A BUILDER RELYING ON FAITH

You know that feeling when you're running an event and suddenly realize you're one important man short?

That's how NASCAR All-Pro racing banquet event organizer Les Westerfield must have felt the night the scheduled preacher didn't show up to say the blessing before the meal. Westerfield scanned the crowded room full of hungry racers, WAGs (wives and girlfriends), and industry personnel. He didn't want to pass the job to just anyone. The man he picked needed to be known as having a credible faith, as a man who could stand in front of a room full of his colleagues and pray out loud without anyone batting an eye.

That's when Westerfield's eye fell on David Reutimann—the driver known for having a cross painted next to his name on his car.

David later called it a "nerve-wracking" moment. But the way he walked to the mic, bowed his head, and led the room in prayer showed he was ready to spiritually lead the evening.

David's dad, racing legend Emil "Buzzie" Reutimann, later said it was one of his proudest moments ever.

LIKE FATHER, LIKE SON

The fact that Buzzie Reutimann was as proud of David's spiritual accomplishments as he was of his son's racing prowess says a lot about the Reutimann family.

David was born on March 2, 1970, to Buzzie and his wife, Linda. Buzzie was a second-generation racer, making David the third generation of Reutimanns to race cars around a track. The family home is in Zephyrhills, Florida, a town of 13,000 located 30 miles northwest of Tampa. Zephyrhills is where their family's race shop is located and where the Reutimann family racing tradition started.

Emil Reutimann—Buzzie's father and David's grandfather—immigrated to Tampa from Switzerland in 1920. Five years later, he moved to Zephyrhills and opened the Zephyrhills Auto Shop, which later morphed into the town's first Chevrolet dealership. From there, Emil got into racing, and his son Buzzie soon followed in his footsteps.

As a boy, and later as a young man, Buzzie traveled to race tracks up and down the Eastern Seaboard and throughout Florida, eventually becoming a legendary racer. He grew up tinkering with cars, rummaging for parts in the junkyard behind his dad's dealership, and building race cars from the chassis up. And then he listened to his father's advice on how to drive them fast.

Buzzie took what he learned from his father and passed on all he knew to his son, David. Of course, the joke is that David's mother wanted him to be a doctor or a lawyer—professions he wouldn't get banged up doing. But that wasn't David's bent. Instead, he carried the family banner into racing's ultimate series, NASCAR Sprint Cup.

David learned a lot more than how to turn left on a banked curve. Like his father, he was a whiz with mechanic's tools in his hands. But a love of driving enticed David more than any other career path. Plus, there were uncles and cousins racing all kinds of cars at various levels. Darrell Waltrip, who eventually gave David his first full-time NASCAR ride, said his "racing bloodlines" were one reason he liked David so much.

David's close-knit relationship with his father is the stuff country songs are made of. He really wanted to walk in his father's shoes, and he really wanted to make his way through life like his father did. There was never a time when he didn't want to be like his dad.

Young David watched his father much the same way a child stares out a car window daydreaming of his future. He watched his father slide around the short oval dirt tracks and stick to his line. He watched his father overtake other cars to win on the last lap. And he saw how gracious his father was to the cheering fans, giving preferential treatment to some and paying tribute to others. In David's mind, Richard Petty, Dale Earnhardt, and other NASCAR greats didn't measure up to his father.

Yes, David wanted to be just like Buzzie Reutimann. But to reach that goal, he'd have to travel a long, challenging road.

RACING TO MAKE A BUCK

David began his racing career on dirt tracks on weekends, always hoping his hard work would lead to bigger and better opportunities. He married his girlfriend, Lisa, and during the early years of their marriage, the two lived, for the most part, paycheck to paycheck, race to race. Lisa worked at a local realty office to help support the couple, but she and David spent their weekends at race tracks, where David struggled to earn purse money.

That's another of the similarities between David and his father. As a young man, Buzzie drove a bumpy path of his own. At times, there was barely enough money for food *and* racing. But David, like Buzzie, kept his dream.

Year after year passed with David's big break failing to materialize. In 2000, when he turned 30, he began to wonder if he'd been passed over. Maybe he was too old to begin a career in elite-level racing. Sure, he'd had some success along the way—but it was all relative. He could always compare himself to someone else and see he wasn't where he wanted to be. Three years earlier, he had earned Rookie of the Year honors in NASCAR's regional Southeast Series. That same year, though, a driver named Jeff Gordon was already a six-year veteran of NASCAR's top series and making millions of dollars. And Jeff was a year younger than David.

In 1991, Bill Davis, a team owner at the top two levels of NASCAR—Sprint Cup and Nationwide—had taken a chance on the young up-and-comer Jeff Gordon. His gamble paid off and inadvertently turned the tables on the old way of thinking around NASCAR—that young guns were too aggressive to put behind the wheel. The conventional wisdom was that it would be better if teams stuck to hiring seasoned drivers.

David still followed the old paradigm of thinking. He stayed busy putting in time getting seasoned, and while he was busy following the old rules, NASCAR changed right under his nose. Young drivers were getting hired right and left—while he was getting left behind in the dust.

MOTORING ON

Never one to quit—and one with the survivalist instincts of his immigrant grandfather and famous father—David pressed on. He continued racing the Southeast Series, all the while praying for a better opportunity. His well-mannered demeanor, along with his good humor, didn't go entirely unnoticed, and his solid character helped earn him the Most Popular Driver award in 2000. And his sheer racing ability (as Buzzie described it, the ability "to get an extra ounce of speed out of his car") made him the Bud Pole Award champion two years later.

During that 2002 season, David finally caught a break. At 32, he landed a deal that put him in a stock car for a few Nationwide Series races, which at the time was still called the Busch Series. That opportunity came thanks to Joe Nemechek, a fellow Floridian who owned Nemco Motorsports and evidently knew that speed, not age, was the main winning factor in the Reutimann family. David came to Nemechek with a résumé that was metaphorically covered with dirt and oil, badges of honor from thousands of laps on smaller circuits. He was infused with excitement at the opportunity to break into NASCAR.

David and Lisa were thankful for the big break for another reason. Their daughter Emelia had been born just a few months prior, in January.

David's debut race with Nemco Motorsports took place in Richmond, Virginia, at the Hardee's 250. He didn't make a big impression on anyone during the qualifying heats. His #87 car, sponsored by Geico Direct, started back in Row 17, in the 34th position. The lead announcer in the broadcast booth went through the starting lineups without even mumbling David's name.

But all that changed when the starting flag dropped. David ran fast and worked his way up from the back of the pack to gain 18 positions over the course of the 187.5-mile race. When the checkered flag dropped, he was the last car on the lead lap—meaning none of the leaders had lapped him—a commendable finish for his first big race. David went on to run in three more races for Nemco in 2002.

David's next season proved almost identical to 2002. In 2003, he ran a limited number of races for Nemco and spent the rest of his time working in Nemco's garage to help earn his keep. On the track, he recorded three Top-10 finishes, two of which were fifth place. Again, a respectable season.

In a NASCAR team shop, just like in any work environment, people often play practical jokes, particularly on the new guys. David was no exception. The guys around the shop all knew that David longed to race full-time, so a familiar joke over the intercom went like this: "Paging David Reutimann . . . Roger Penske is on line 1." Howls of laughter would ensue. A little later, someone would take the intercom and say: "Paging David Reutimann, Richard Petty is on line 2." And so on. David was always a good sport.

Then came the moment when what appeared to be another practical joke was actually a big break for David.

One night, David had just gotten up from the dinner table when his home phone rang. He answered, and the voice on the other end said, "Hi, David. This is Darrell Waltrip."

David, certain that someone at the shop was playing another practical joke on him, thought about hanging up. But then his eyes flashed to his caller ID.

The name said *Darrell Waltrip.*

By this time, Waltrip sensed David was fumbling around. "Should I call back at a more convenient time?" he asked.

"No way," David said. "It's great to hear from you."

Waltrip explained that he was starting a NASCAR truck series team for the 2004 season and was looking for a driver with speed. He was calling to gauge David's level of interest. The two talked for half an hour. Waltrip had known Buzzie, but he'd never talked to David. Darrell soon realized the apple hadn't fallen far from the tree and that David, just like his father, was a great guy. He was a strong Christian and a good family man—exactly the type Waltrip could build his team around. At the end of the conversation, Waltrip asked David to join his truck team.

The offer reinforced one thing in David's mind: God was taking care of him and his young family. David had just landed a full-time ride in one of the top three levels of NASCAR, and he was sure to learn a lot from Waltrip, a NASCAR legend and strong Christian man himself. With Waltrip, David would have a chance to help build a formidable racing program.

Waltrip's venture also introduced Toyota to NASCAR. Automobile manufacturers such as Chevy and Ford had been involved with NASCAR for decades, but Toyota was still relatively new to the premier ranks. Waltrip knew the truck series (NASCAR's Camping World Truck Series, as it is currently known, feeds into Nationwide Series and top-tier Sprint Cup Series) was the best place to start something new. And David understood that the truck series was a great place to start out as a new NASCAR driver.

When the 2004 season arrived the following February, the #17 Toyota headed to Daytona for its much-anticipated unveiling. David had his first full-time ride in one of NASCAR's top touring series, and he was determined to make the most of it. In his first truck race, David led for seven laps and finished inside the Top 10 at the ninth position. A great beginning for the team.

In his second career start, David won his first career pole and went on to finish third. Waltrip believed he'd found the most underrated talent in any garage.

David raced with Waltrip through their first season together and garnered four Top-5 finishes, 10 Top-10 finishes, and two poles. David finished the season 14th in point standings and was named Rookie of the Year.

For the first time in his career, David had found some financial security for his family. He and Lisa were able to put a down payment on a house outside of Charlotte, where many other racers live. Lisa was also able to quit her job to take care of Emilia full-time. Their next big-ticket purchase: a motor coach so they could travel as a family.

While the road to racing success had seemed incredibly long, David made sure to point out the purpose the Lord had for him. Cliché or not, God was at the wheel. In David's own words: "God had a plan, and waiting, buying time, was just part of it."

David ran with Waltrip again in 2005, competing in another 25 of 25 truck races. The most memorable of those races was the 16th of the season, at the Nashville Superspeedway, where David won his first NASCAR race. He battled Mike Skinner—back and forth they went for the lead. David finally won by seven-eighths of a second—less than a truck length. With that win, David began to make NASCAR history. He would become the first-ever driver to win a race in each of the top-three touring series.

Toward the end of the season, in mid-November, David doubled up when he raced the boss's Nationwide car following the truck race. That year (2005), David also ran his first Cup Series race for Michael Waltrip. It was the fall race in Charlotte, and David finished 22nd after starting 26th. For David, the ever-burgeoning process toward full-time Cup racing continued.

The winter off-season passed, another February arrived, and David climbed back into the race truck. He also slipped into the seat of a stock car for 15 Nationwide races. For 12 of them, he was teamed up with Michael Waltrip, Darrell's younger brother. It was the start of a great friendship . . . and a working relationship.

AN OLD ROOKIE

In a 2007 ceremony in which David was presented the key to Zephyrhills, Michael Waltrip announced that the city's favorite son would be the franchise driver for his new NASCAR Sprint Cup team. Once again, David was helping to build something from the ground up.

It was another first for Toyota. What Michael's older brother did in the truck series, Michael set out to achieve in the Cup Series. The common denominator was David Reutimann—now a 37-year-old Sprint Cup rookie.

David's rookie season as a NASCAR stock car driver arrived in hurried fashion. He was one busy driver. There are, on average, 10 more stock car races each season than there are truck car races. But this would become a moot point once the 2007 season started.

David raced more than 12,000 laps his rookie year for a total of 17,369 miles. That's a lot of laps and miles. Comparatively, the number of laps in a normal season averages 10,500 for around 14,000 miles—and that's if you're racing full-time in a Cup car. Here's some perspective on David's rookie year: if you were to pack up your car, drive coast-to-coast across the continental United States six times, you would have driven as many miles as David did that year.

David covered that much pavement because he would climb into the cockpit of Michael Waltrip Racing's Nationwide car one day, then board the team's Sprint Cup car the next. In total, David ran in 35 Nationwide races and 26 Sprint Cup races as a rookie. And, incredibly, David reached these totals while failing to qualify the #00 Toyota for nine of the season's Sprint Cup races. There was one race that almost made David's Did Not Qualify (DNQ) number a nice round 10. Only due to unforeseen circumstances did he stay in the race at Daytona—his first Daytona 500.

Because his entrance fate was out of his hands after failing to qualify on speed, David stood beside Buzzie on top of his hauler and did the only thing he knew to do. He gripped the hauler's railing tightly and prayed out loud with his father that a last-second spot on the starting grid would open up. The prayer worked. David made it into the Daytona 500.

While that's a nice story of faith, David freely admits to falling short of the ideal Christian example. He talks openly about the challenge of living a life that represents Christ and following the teachings of the Bible. On his testimony card, which Motor Racing Outreach handed out, David says, "I'm no expert on scripture, and I'm probably as big a mess-up as anyone. Just go to Jesus—it doesn't matter whether you are at church or you are sitting in your car."

David knows the Bible is the place to go when he falls short. He likens God's Word to the NASCAR rulebook—except "there's no gray area, and it's been around longer."

When David talks about just "going to Jesus," he is sharing from his own experience. And he is also saying it's simple to talk to God.

David grew up in a Christian home, but he wandered away from God as a teen. The road back went through a schoolyard bully who threatened to beat him up if he showed up for school the next day. At the time, David hadn't prayed in years. But God answered a simple prayer for safety when the bully was absent that day. David gives the Lord the credit for getting him out of that situation and called the incident a simple reminder of how easy it was to go to the Lord with anything.

Back on top of the hauler in 2007, David and Buzzie hugged and cried when they learned that David would be in the 2007 Daytona 500. It was at the expense of another driver, who had fallen just a few feet behind, but in NASCAR's arcane qualifying rules, feet, inches, seconds, and tenths of seconds all come into play. It would be a few feet that would get David into the race and onto the starting grid on Sunday's showdown.

That year, the Daytona 500 was held on February 18, 2007. That was the first race of David's Sprint Cup rookie season.

David's #00 car ran fast for 173 laps. But with 27 laps to go—and with just a few cars behind the 2006 winner Jimmie Johnson—David got caught between the wall and the apron in a pack of cars that spun out of control in Turn 2. Johnson's car broke loose, hit the wall, and bounced off the barrier and into the pack. He had nowhere to go but straight into David. They both barreled into the wall and spun off the track and onto the apron.

Other cars in the crash (those driven by Denny Hamlin, Jeff Gordon, and Tony Raines) sustained damage, but not enough to keep them from finishing the race. But Jimmy Johnson was out, and so was David Reutimann. His Toyota, with a Domino's Pizza decal across the hood, looked like a delivery box that had been dropped from the sky and landed on its corner.

David didn't fare much better in his second Sprint Cup start. Once again, late in the race with only eight laps to go, David pushed his car hard into turn 4 with Greg Biffle right behind him. Biffle bumped David and sent him into a spin. The car banged into the wall. Parts and pieces went everywhere, and David's engine caught fire. The impact destroyed the Domino's Pizza #00 and knocked the wind out of David. NASCAR later reported that the g-force impact during the crash was one of the highest ever recorded, although NASCAR didn't disclose the exact figures.

Even with the wrecks and the DNQs, David had a respectable rookie year.

The Nationwide Series went a lot better for David. He finished second in point standings after nailing his first Nationwide win in late October and earning his first Nationwide pole the following week. For the season, he had twelve Top-10 and five Top-5 finishes in the Nationwide Series.

After David's successful 2007 season, Michael Waltrip signed him up for another year. In 2008, David again raced full-time in both the Sprint Cup and the Nationwide Series, logging 16,694 laps and more than 22,000 miles.

In the final race of the year, at Homestead-Miami Speedway, the MWR team qualified for its first Sprint Cup race pole. David took the 1.5-mile oval in 31.462 seconds at 171.636 miles per hour to gain the starting line advantage. This made David the first driver in history to earn the pole position in all three of NASCAR's top divisions.

LET IT RAIN, LET IT POUR

Professional sports stadiums that play host to Major League Baseball or NFL football games are sometimes built with retractable roofs that can open and close due to weather. But all NASCAR speedways are open to the sky. If it rains, it rains, and if it pours, it pours—but just a little rain can have a huge effect on racing conditions.

On Memorial Day weekend in 2009, the Charlotte Motor Speedway hosted the 50th running of the Coca-Cola 600. The 600 is nicknamed the "Ironman" due to the endurance driver and teams need just to finish the race. With 600 miles facing them, drivers race longer, engines get pounded harder, and pit crews must be ready for more stops.

The Coca-Cola 600 race is regularly scheduled for Sunday evening under the lights and is considered the capstone for the "Month of Speed"—May for NASCAR. Drivers and their teams come to Charlotte, the hub of NASCAR Nation, and spend three weeks in the region. Since Charlotte is the epicenter of the sport, many teams keep their shops in the area, and many drivers and team members live in the small towns around the city.

Since Charlotte is also home to the NASCAR Hall of Fame, the city veritably beats as the heart of the fan experience during three racing weekends in May. Folks everywhere have racing on their minds, as evidenced by the appearance of colorful banners and signs on every downtown street corner. Hotels, motels, and campgrounds fill up early. After a long winter and spring thaw, NASCAR fans see summer approaching, which means it's time to renew summer rituals like barbecuing.

But before the real heat of summer strikes, the spring rains often fall. And in May 2009, the springtime showers poured on the Charlotte Motor Speedway. NASCAR officials tried to get the track dry enough for the Sunday race, but they wound up postponing the Coca-Cola 600 a day until Monday, Memorial Day.

David was slated to start in 21st position on the grid of his third Coca-Cola 600. Rain was still in the forecast for Monday, and his crew chief and team were looking at track conditions, making adjustments, and preparing to "chase the race track," a phrase that gives the track a "will" or a life of its own. When the track's conditions change, the teams must make the proper adjustments due to weather, temperature, moisture on the pavement, how rubber reacts on the surface, and several other factors.

The green flag finally dropped at noon. As the race progressed, there would be six cautions—three of them for rain. David's crew chief, Rodney Childers, had created scenarios for running the best they could under that day's conditions.

On lap 164, NASCAR race officials waved the fifth caution of the day. But this yellow flag wasn't for rain or a crash or any track-related incident. The driver slowdown was about carrying out the White House Commission on Remembrance's and President George Bush's request that Americans everywhere pause their day's activities at 3 p.m. for a moment of silence noting the ultimate sacrifices millions throughout U.S. history had made in the cause of freedom.

Silence at a NASCAR race?

Well, NASCAR has a history of pulling off the seemingly impossible. Besides, NASCAR is as patriotic a sport as there is. NASCAR's community of racers, fans, and industry personnel strongly supports military servicemen and servicewomen and often begins races by paying tribute to all branches of the military and to the men and women who have died in action.

As 3 p.m. approached, NASCAR officials brought out the caution flag. A pace car slowed the field and then brought 42 thundering race cars to a halt. Along the front straightaway, drivers lined up their cars and shut off their engines. Crews lined up along pit road. Each driver got out of his car, then took his helmet in hand and placed it over his heart. Fans took to their feet. Flags around the speedway flew at half-staff.

"A moment of silence please" came the directive over the public address system. The crowd hushed. The roar of NASCAR—the squealing, screeching, popping, and backfiring of engines had stopped.

After a long minute of absolute quiet, a huge uproar of applause and cheers streamed from the bleachers.

The drivers got back in their cars and fired up their engines once again. They followed the pace car for several laps as rain threatened from the southern horizon. David was in 14th place when racing resumed. He soon climbed to 12th, then fell again to 14th. He was in that position on lap 222 when rain began to fall and the caution flag came out again.

By that point in the race, the drivers had completed 333 miles. Each team examined its options. Would the rain stay or pass? The NASCAR rulebook states that if a race is halfway finished or more, then the officials have the option to call it. In this instance, the 600 was more than halfway finished.

The immediate decision confronting the teams was whether or not to pit under the caution flag. Each teams' radar screen showed that the rain was going to stick around awhile, and the sky said the same. But if the race went back to green, the cars that did not pit under the caution flag would almost certainly fall behind later in the race. That's because they would need to pit later to refuel.

The top 13 teams pitted. David, in 14th place, consulted his crew chief by radio. The chief, sensing that the race would never restart again, opted not to pit. It was a risky move, but it put David in first place.

Five laps later, still under caution, NASCAR called the race. Since David was cruising behind the pace car at the time, sitting in the rocking chair, he picked up a rain-shortened victory. The gamble had worked.

David had made NASCAR history, becoming the first driver to earn a victory in all three of NASCAR's top series.

Some people put an asterisk next to David's first Sprint Cup win, believing he just gambled and got lucky. Though David admits that taking a victory in a race shortened almost by half wasn't his first choice for how to win, he still considers the Coca-Cola 600 a huge victory. He and his crew had, after all, put him in a position to win.

That day in the finish circle, tears and hugs abounded. Lisa and Emilia were there, and so was Buzzie. David swept up Lisa and Emelia in his arms and gave both a strong embrace. This was David the family man on display. Michael Waltrip punched the air and then gave David a hug and some friendly, playful punches. The rain may have dampened the track but not the spirits of the winners.

David's win was a trifecta of firsts: David, Michael Waltrip (as owner), and crew chief Rodney Childers had all captured their first Sprint Cup win.

For the 2009 season, David had ten Top-10 and five Top-5 finishes and finished a solid 16th in the point standings.

ERASING THE ASTERISK

Forty-two races had passed since David's Memorial Day win, and he was ready to leverage his Toyota's horsepower at Chicagoland Speedway. It was time for the 2010 Lifelock.com 400, the frenetic race that kicks off the second half of the season.

David had raced a good first half of the 2010 season, taking three fifth-place finishes, the first of which came at the Daytona 500. Before coming to Chicagoland, David finished one spot outside the Top 10 in the Fourth of July weekend race in Daytona. With Independence Day celebrations lingering around the Windy City, David was poised for another big race.

Chicagoland Speedway, which sits 50 miles southwest of Chicago in Joliet, Illinois, opened in 2001 and quickly became a driver favorite. The public address announcer set the stage for the nighttime race when he called out the most famous words in racing: "Gentlemen, start your engines!" David reached for his starter switch, and the 358-cubic inch, 900-horsepower engine rumbled to life. The other cars joined the wildness.

David started the race in seventh place and kept pace with the race leaders. Lap after lap went by as David inched closer and closer to the front of the pack. He steadily moved into sixth place, then fifth, then fourth, then third, and then second.

Going into the last lap, David and his Tums-sponsored Toyota were out in front of everyone. He had a two-second lead—about 500 feet—on Carl Edwards, who drove a Ford. When David came around the final turn, he blazed wide open and took the checkered flag. David had earned his second career Sprint Cup win.

With tears in his eyes, David tried to please the cheering crowd by making a few tire-smoking donuts. His burnout needed work. Then, when someone tried to hand him the checkered flag, he fumbled around until he successfully held it in his grasp. Once he had the checkered flag flying out the window, he sped off to Victory Lane, where he was met with more cheering, tears, hugs, and smiles. Buzzie was present, and David was overcome by the moment. Other than a quick comment thanking his sponsor and car owner, David was at a loss for words.

Two weeks earlier, David had signed a contract extension with MWR, giving him his first multi year deal. For the first time in his career, he enjoyed a bit of job security. Maybe the security of the new contract gave David the boost in Chicagoland. More likely, however, David's key to victory was a combination of years of experience, expert wrenching in the garage, and mental and physical toughness behind the wheel.

The final 17 races of the season gave MWR more excitement. David was comfortably wheeling in the #00. He finished every race he ran and placed in the Top 10 five more times. At Bristol, the late-August night race, David finished second. When the final driver point standings were tallied in November, David was in 18th place.

After all the success of the 2009 and 2010 seasons, David and Michael Waltrip Racing eyed 2011 with hopes set high. Since David joined MWR Sprint Cup team in 2007, they had collected 23 Top-10 finishes and two wins. They approached the new season confidently.

Unfortunately for David, his team's hopes for continued improvement did not materialize in 2011. His average starting position dropped five places. He did earn the pole position at Richmond in September, but it was his only one for the year. He earned only three Top-10 finishes and only one Top 5. To make matters worse, he dropped ten places in the final driver point standings. Three-fourths of the way through the season, the team was already calling the year what it was—a scratch—and talking about changing things around in 2012.

RACING TOWARD AN UNCERTAIN FUTURE

The 2011 season was an obvious disappointment for David, but what happened next would test his faith beyond anything he'd ever known. The MWR team released him from his contract, meaning that, after 171 races in the #00 Sprint Cup car, David was looking for a new ride in 2012.

The Bible includes several good definitions of faith, and one of the clearest is found in Hebrews 11:1 (NIV): "Now faith is being sure of what we hope for and certain of what we do not see."

After learning that he was a driver without a car, David told *Bleacher Report*, "Nine times out of ten, faith was really the only thing that was constant that you had to fall back on. You never were really 100 percent sure that you were going to have a ride the next week. It's kind of the nature of our business, unfortunately, so the faith side of things was the only thing that was constant."

As a seasoned racer who also happens to be a Christian, David had a lot of experience trusting God for his future. He knew he could talk to God through prayer at any time or in any place.

When the New Year rang in, David's faith was rewarded when he found a ride with Tommy Baldwin Racing. Baldwin acted as owner and crew chief and worked on his own cars to keep them racing. David, who is cut from the same cloth, made for a good fit. He raced in 21 Sprint Cup events for TBR in 2012. He also ran in four other races as a freelancer; two of those rides were for a new team, BK Racing.

One of David's races for BK Racing was the 2012 Daytona 500, where BK hadn't tested a car or done much of anything except get its NASCAR licensing together. Even though BK was a newbie to NASCAR, a well-seasoned "D-Reu" was there. He took the helm of the team's #93 car, but, unfortunately, he got caught up in a wreck with only a couple laps to go.

David had a good year in 2012, which opened the door to racing full-time with BK Racing in a Toyota car. He was content in his role as a driver *and* a builder.

He once said, "I think that there's nothing more fulfilling than starting with just a rack of 22-foot length, inch-and-three-quarter .095 tubing or something and building a car, hanging the body and doing everything to it—running the brake lines and wiring—and then going out and racing it and winning with it, knowing that it was your creation."

David was a builder with his father in the family garage as he was growing up in Zephyrhills.

David was a builder when he worked as a fabricator with Joe Nemechek.

David was a builder when he drove for Darrell Waltrip's NASCAR truck series team.

David was a builder with Michael Waltrip in the Nationwide Series and the Sprint Cup Series.

And David was a builder with the BK Racing program.

There's an important lesson here. Sometimes before you can become a driver and gain all the acclaim that comes with performing well, you have to get your hands dirty.

David Reutimann has never been afraid to roll up his sleeves and do the grunt work needed before he can send his machine onto a NASCAR race track.

It's all about building for the future—and for whatever the Lord has in store for him.

5

TREVOR BAYNE:
REACHING HIS BIG DREAM

The smooth-faced kid entered the media room and sat down quietly next to his crew chief, Donnie Wingo, and team owners Eddie and Len Wood. The eyes of the young race car driver were hooded by a decal-emblazoned hat, and he nervously adjusted the microphone in front of him.

Fortunately for him, the first question was directed at team owner Eddie Wood, who was asked what he thought of Trevor Bayne, now that the Daytona 500 was over.

Wood shifted in his seat and flashed a grin. "The kid just might be the next big deal," he enthusiastically told the assembly.

"What is it that made you so bullish on the kid's ability?" another reporter followed up.

This time, Donnie Wingo handled the question. "He knew how to go fast *and* control the car," he answered.

Trevor Bayne sat politely with his hands in his lap, like he had just returned from a Sunday afternoon drive with his family. He took a moment to look around the room and realized *why* he was there. The revelation caused him to put his arm around Wingo's shoulders. He shook the teddy-bearish man for a few seconds, then blazed a huge smile.

Thanks to the kid's driving, the Wood Brothers team had just won the Daytona 500. The name of the celebrated track, "Daytona International Speedway," was printed on the backdrop behind them. A NASCAR Sprint Cup linen covered the table where the four of them sat.

In the world of NASCAR auto racing, they had "arrived."

On the starting grid five hours earlier, sitting buckled in the Wood Brothers' #21 Ford, the kid had prayed, "God, thank You for this opportunity to be here and drive these race cars. Lord, thank You for the platform You've given to all of us. I just pray we will glorify You with everything we do, because You're the reason we're here."

Now the kid was living his dreams. Though the full impact of his life-changing victory would take weeks to sink in, the barely-out-of-the-teenage-years driver hoped he'd be on center stage for a long while to come.

KIDDING AROUND AND GETTING AROUND

Like his car owner said, Trevor Bayne was about to be the next big deal. From New York to Los Angeles, bookers for daytime and late-night talk shows wanted him—and the sooner the better. The public craved a fresh face and a refreshing story. So did the media.

Back in the media room, on the night of the race, there were a few hoops and hollers when Trevor took the checkered flag. Even though the racing journalists followed the time-honored dictum of "No cheering in the press box," these writers and reporters knew they had a great story—and a lot of entry points to choose from when writing it:

- Trevor turned 20 years old one day before the race
- It was the kid's first Daytona 500
- It was only his second Sprint Cup Series race
- He was the youngest driver ever to win the Daytona 500
- The kid broke Jeff Gordon's record for being the youngest driver to win Daytona
- The Wood Brothers were the oldest team in NASCAR

While sitting at the table facing the journalists, another explosion took place, this time of unrestrained laughter. It was during Eddie Wood's answer to a question by ESPN's Marty Smith. A little banter broke out about the brothers "now having this kid racing for them; this kid who wasn't even hardly born" in 2001, when Wood Brothers Racing was last victorious. (Actually, Trevor was born in 1991.) Trevor stepped into the mix, pointed at Smith, and quipped, "I bet 1991 even makes you feel a little bit old, don't it?"

Laughter erupted around the room. The press was delighted to overhear the good-natured exchange between the new sheriff in town and a media heavyweight like Marty Smith.

One journalist said he had been watching social media's reaction to Trevor's win, and in the last hour, Trevor's Twitter numbers had climbed by 8,000 followers. *What did Trevor think of that?* he was asked. Trevor smiled ear-to-ear, laughed, and said he'd been working at Twitter a long time, which everyone in the room knew was total smoke. What Trevor did was reveal himself to be one of the most fun-loving drivers in NASCAR.

In the coming months, Trevor would prove that only a small part of his positive demeanor hinged on his racing performance. A larger reason for it was his natural enjoyment for life, and a still larger part was his Christian faith, which his parents and several key friends had helped cultivate along the way.

Trevor's parents, Rocky and Stephanie Bayne, raised him, as well as his younger sister Sarah and his younger brother Tray, in a Christian home near Knoxville, Tennessee. God first started working on his heart when he was in middle school. By this time, Trevor was already heavily into racing and had been for years.

As a two-year-old, Trevor rumbled around in a battery-powered jeep that he "raced" in the backyard. That led to him getting a dirt bike when he was three. Rocky left the training wheels on the bike until his son was four. And then, at five, Trevor graduated to racing on four wheels when he jumped into go-karts.

Actually, the Bayne family's racing roots extend deeper than Trevor's father. Both of his parents have racing blood in their veins. One of Trevor's grandfathers raced boats and the other raced stock cars. His grandfather, William Bayne, enjoyed success around the local stock car tracks of South Carolina. Rocky grew up around the sport and helped his father with projects in the garage. He too knew racing, cars, and engines intimately.

For Trevor, God's plan was apparently to cross these speed genes with the Christian walk. During Trevor's freshman year of high school, he became serious about his relationship with Christ. He went with a friend to a youth meeting and heard a message that really struck him. At home later that evening, Trevor talked with his mom about the message of the Cross and then knelt beside the couch to invite Christ into his life.

A few months later, when Trevor was 15, he moved to North Carolina for the next step in his racing career. With his parents' support, he left his family behind in Tennessee and made the move on his own. His new commitment to Christ and his fierce competitive spirit would help keep him on track and out of trouble.

To back up a step, the success Trevor had seen in his eight years of go-karting—three world championships and more than 300 wins—had led directly to the Allison Legacy Race Series (ALRS) when he was 13. The ALRS is considered a stepping stone series for drivers looking to further their racing careers. Trevor spent his 13th and 14th birthdays in Allison Legacy cars, which are three-fourths the size of a Sprint Cup Series car. Added good fortune came when Donnie Allison spotted Trevor's natural talent and became his mentor. In Trevor's first year in the ALRS, he became the youngest top rookie in the series. He followed that up by winning the 2005 series championship. In 41 starts, he earned 14 wins and 30 Top-5 finishes. Trevor's success at the lower levels of racing set up his big move.

Coinciding with his move to North Carolina was his move up in racing to the X-1R Pro Cup Series, which is also considered a proving ground. This series tests young racers against veteran short-track stars who have made a career of racing outside of NASCAR and has propelled several young drivers into NASCAR's ranks. Trevor hoped for the same. He was apparently on the right path for a NASCAR career.

THE NEXT BIG THING

Like other major sports leagues, NASCAR has its scouts. They travel out to the lower levels of racing to tracks with names like Ace, Motor Mile, and Lonesome Pine, looking for the next fresh face who can run fast and win. If the scout spots a diamond in the rough, he'll sign the young driver to the team's developmental program. If the young driver shows talent, he'll get to race and not just practice.

The developmental driver is someone a team wants to groom to become the next big thing. The grooming process is solely up to the team management. After a team signs a developmental driver, one of two things happens: either that driver tests for the team by practicing a car at different tracks, or he races right away in one of the lower-tier series.

In 2006, Trevor was that fresh face and became a developmental driver for Dale Earnhardt Inc. (DEI). He was 15 years old when he signed the contract with DEI. It had been more than four years since Earnhardt died when his black #3 Chevy hit the wall at Daytona. Trevor had watched that year's Daytona 500 with his family over at his grandparent's house. He saw the wreck, but he didn't hear the news of Earnhardt's death until he was back home. There, when he tuned in to the post-race coverage, he heard the horrible news. The 10-year-old boy stood in his living room and cried. Now, years later, he was racing in the shadow of that man's greatness.

"T-Bayne, the developmental driver" has a little different ring to it than "Ironhead," "The Intimidator," and the "Man in Black"—all nicknames for the legendary Dale Earnhardt. If Trevor needed a daily reminder that he had a ways to go in racing, then being part of Earnhardt's legacy was that prompt. But Trevor embraced the challenge. During the X-1R Pro Cup Series racing seasons of '06 and '07, he competed in 31 races and capitalized on the experience by winning two times, finishing in the Top 5 nine times, and placing two more times in the Top 10.

At Greenville-Pickens Speedway in April 2008, DEI had Trevor start racing the #1 car in the K&N Pro Series East. Trevor made 13 starts in the series, and he won the pole position in his sixth start. To get the pole, he blazed around the track at 110 miles per hour, and later won the race by averaging 70 miles per hour. The race was held at the historic Thompson Speedway in the northeast corner of Connecticut. The farm-turned-speedway, which opened in 1940, was the nation's first asphalt race track.

Trevor performed excellently for DEI in 2008. Being under a long-term contract, he believed the news when others told him he was the next big thing. But when 2009 arrived, the Great Recession was in full swing and took its toll on NASCAR. Trevor would be one of the drivers the scaling back of corporate sponsorship would affect.

Trevor was out at DEI, a casualty of the weak economy. It didn't matter whether or not people thought he was the next big thing. Each driver needed a few million bucks backing, and, unfortunately, the bucks stopped before they reached Trevor.

GOD WILL DIRECT YOUR PATH

Being laid off hit Trevor hard. He slipped away from regular prayer and Bible reading. He had fallen into the trap of thinking that he was a good enough race car driver to make it on his own, but now, through no fault of his own, he was sidelined.

Trevor would stay sidelined for several months, and God would use the time to redirect his thinking and strengthen his devotion. Today, Trevor says that being let go at DEI was the best thing God could have done for him. During that difficult season, God brought people into Trevor's life who helped lead him back to a right relationship with Christ.

His "comeback" began with a simple prayer before a meal. Trevor had fallen out of the habit of thanking the Lord for the food he was about to eat, but a business manager took him out to lunch one day to help him go over his options. At the start of the meal, the manager offered to pray. Trevor found the offer "refreshing." It had been awhile since he'd heard someone speak with reverence for God like that.

Still, months passed and no offers to race came. Trevor continued to wonder about his life's direction. Then one day, he was out wakeboarding and realized he was trying to do too much on his own. He went back to shore to pray about his career. He asked himself these questions:

• Am I supposed to be in racing?
• Should I be trying to put a ride together?
• If so, will the Lord open doors or create opportunities for me?

And in words that resemble Proverbs 3:5–6, Trevor asked God to direct his path.

God answered the prayer. Trevor was soon introduced to Gary Bechtel, who'd been a NASCAR car owner for much of the '90s. Bechtel was interested in getting back into racing and wondered if Trevor would join him. In March 2009, Trevor climbed back behind the wheel. It was a promotion of sorts from his last driving gig. Michael Waltrip Racing had a Nationwide Series car. They just needed a driver and money. Trevor was the driver, and Gary Bechtel had the money. So Trevor found himself with MWR's Nationwide team for a limited schedule, beginning at Bristol Motor Speedway in Tennessee.

Bristol felt like a home court advantage. "Thunder Valley," as the half-mile track at Bristol is called, was only a two-hour trip down the interstate for the Bayne family. They'd made the trip annually since Trevor was nine.

As a boy, Trevor would get to explore the pits to find his favorite drivers—none so favorite as Jeff Gordon. Then he would climb the steps of the aluminum grandstands to find his place among the 160,000 seats that tower up and around the tiny concrete oval. From there, he'd soak up the experience as though his senses were one giant sponge. He'd never forget those road trips, or seeing his hero Gordon, or the rattle of his seat, or the smell of burning fuel waft up into the coliseum's seats. Season after season found him cheering his favorite drivers to victory. The experience fueled his dream.

On that chilly spring day in Tennessee, no longer was Trevor the kid doing the watching and hollering. Now he was the guy being watched. He had raced Bristol three times before, when he was part of the X-1R Pro Cup Series, but the Nationwide race would be his debut in a NASCAR-sanctioned event. That all translated to big numbers of spectators in the stands, numbers Trevor had never seen from the driver's side. More than 100,000 fans showed up to watch the spectacle.

Trevor finished 23rd in Bristol that day—an okay result. He drove 14 more races that season, finishing seventh twice. The team officials agreed that two Top-10 finishes was a pretty good result for a young driver on a limited schedule.

Twelve months later, another season of racing began. Gary Bechtel and Trevor, still working with MWR, unveiled a sponsorship that would give them virtually a full 2010 Nationwide season. This time around, Bechtel had 28 of the 35 races covered.

Trevor had run well in '09, and he was hoping to follow it up with a great 2010. He did just that. He started races 19, 20, and 21 from the pole. It's virtually unheard of for a driver in his first full season—or any driver, for that matter—to pole for three races in a row. He also claimed several Top-10 finishes.

Then God directed Trevor's path again—this time toward racing legend Jack Roush. The transition didn't happen as smoothly as it could have. During the 2010 season, Trevor had again gone back to thinking he could race well without total dependence on God. He ran well, and his spiritual slippage wasn't deliberate. It just happened over the course of a busy schedule. He says he journeyed away from consistently reading the Bible.

Trevor brings his testimony back to the relevance of scripture and the role it has in his life. "It is still relevant for today," he says. "When you get into it, and are reading it, it's not just something that was written 2,000 years ago, but it is living and active. So if you're not staying in it, your impact on this world will fade away."

Trevor needed to be reminded that God would direct his path, a path that would take him over some rough spots.

YOUNGEST DRIVER JOINS OLDEST TEAM

Careers can change fast in NASCAR. What car you're driving, if you're driving, or for whom you're driving—any of these can change suddenly . . . and without explanation. With seven races to go in the 2010 Nationwide season, an offer and contract with Jack Roush and Roush Fenway Racing were suddenly on the table.

Trevor said yes in a heartbeat, and then debuted for his new team on October 2 at Kansas Speedway. Then, with three races to go on the Sprint Cup schedule, Roush farmed out Trevor to the oldest team in

NASCAR, Wood Brothers Racing, to race in one Sprint Cup event. Both are Ford teams, and in NASCAR that connection is vitally important when drivers need to get seat time on a substitute basis.

The team managers were toying with the idea of Trevor racing in the following season's Daytona 500, but to get Trevor approved from NASCAR to race at the 500, the managers needed to insert him into at least one of the last races of the 2010 season. So the first race the Wood Brothers put Trevor into was the 2010 AAA Texas 500, held on November 7.

"You will love this kid," Roush told Eddie Wood. Sure enough, Trevor lived up to Roush's hype. He brought the #21 car across the line in 17th place—much better than an "okay" result.

Trevor passed 140 times during the race and was passed only 104 times, and that stat stood out to Eddie Wood. Trevor's Texas racing was acclaimed as the best of any Sprint Cup debut in NASCAR history. Rookie stripes or not, the Wood Brothers and Wingo decided right then to stick Trevor in the Daytona 500 in the spring. The stage was set.

THE DAYTONA 500: GOING BACKSTAGE

With the Texas race for the Wood Brothers behind him, Trevor had just two more Nationwide events for his new Roush Fenway team before his season would be over. That final race, in late November at Homestead-Miami Speedway, ended with a fifth-place finish. Finishing in front of him were three Sprint Cup drivers who were pulling double duty that weekend, including Trevor's close friend Ricky Stenhouse Jr.

The off-season kicked into gear. Trevor, 19 years old by then, had initially made plans for a trip to Jackson Hole, Wyoming, for some snowboarding and snowmobiling. But his good friend and fellow racer, Michael McDowell, invited him to instead join him in a weeklong mission trip to Mexico to work alongside Back2Back Ministries.

By the time of his post–Daytona 500 press conference, Trevor knew firsthand about Back2Back Ministries, so when a reporter asked him if he planned to splurge with a little of the $1.5 million prize money, he replied that he knew where some of the winnings would go. "There are a lot of foundations and ministries that need support, Motor Racing Outreach being one of them, and Back2Back Ministries in Mexico with Lonnie Clouse is another one," he said. "There are a lot of good organizations that need some help, and we will help them out as much as we can."

Motor Racing Outreach (MRO) is a ministry that provides drivers and teams with access to traveling chaplains, Bible studies, and chapel services on race weekends. Through MRO, Trevor met Lonnie Clouse, chaplain for the Nationwide Series. Trevor took part in the Bible studies, attended chapel, and sometimes took an active role in the service by reading scripture or praying. Lonnie was available down on the track to pray with Trevor before the drivers got in their cars. At the time of the Daytona 500, Lonnie was on staff with Back2Back Mexico, a ministry that serves ten orphanages and three impoverished communities in Monterrey, Mexico.

The snowboarding trip could wait. When the 2010 season ended, Trevor was on his way to Monterrey.

While in Mexico with Lonnie and Back2Back, Trevor fell in love with the ministry and with the orphans. He worked and played tirelessly. He didn't care about getting dirty working on a construction project, nor did he care about getting sweaty playing soccer with the neighborhood kids. He was serving the orphans around him out of the joy of the Lord that was within him. When the children ran up to him, he'd swoop one up and then another—sometimes he'd have a child in each arm. They would cling to his neck, wrap their skinny legs and arms around him, or ride on his back. All the while, Trevor would smile and laugh right along with them.

In the impoverished communities, Trevor took advantage of opportunities to meet people's needs. At an orphanage in one village, the team found the pantry empty, so Trevor and Michael drove down to the local grocery store with the caregiver, and Trevor purchased an abundance of food for the kids.

The children made quite an impression on Trevor and Michael. Many of them went without essentials such as clothing and shoes, but they still smiled and laughed. And the guys made quite an impression on the children as well, telling stories about being race car drivers and how fast they went.

One day, Trevor and Michael held a barbecue for the orphans. They went out and bought a bunch of burgers, but they didn't have proper grates or a grill, so they improvised with a wheelbarrow and wire. They looked a lot like a misfit race car team that showed up at the track without a car or tools. It was rough going; they were singeing the hair right off their arms. But they just kept on grilling.

At one point, Lonnie, seeing that the guys were searing themselves, hollered over to them, "Aren't you guys hot?" Trevor replied, "Nah, this is nothing compared to being in a race car."

Before leaving Monterrey and the orphan ministry to head home, Trevor asked Lonnie when he could return to serve the orphans again. Lonnie told him he had an open invitation and was welcome anytime.

Serving with Back2Back Ministries had a tremendous impact on Trevor, so much so that defending the cause of the orphans was on his mind when he won the Daytona 500. For Lonnie to hear Trevor's public statement in support of orphan ministry was a proud moment.

During the lull in racing before the start of the 2011 season, Trevor grew stronger in his relationship with Christ than ever before. He became intentional in his spiritual walk—in prayer and Bible reading. He was still thinking a lot about Back2Back Ministries and Lonnie when the 2011 NASCAR season rolled around.

Two days before the start of the season, Trevor sent his chaplain friend a text, asking for prayer that he would be able to handle the highs and lows of the sport. Ahead was a full Nationwide schedule for Roush Fenway Racing and 17 Sprint Cup races for Wood Brothers Racing. Of course, Trevor didn't know he would go on to win the most difficult race of the year.

DANCING THE TWO-STEP AT DAYTONA
NASCAR Speedweeks is the name given to the annual series of events held in Daytona, Florida, each February. The events lead up to and

include the Daytona 500. For the 53rd annual Speedweeks, in 2011, Daytona International Speedway boasted a new-and-improved $20 million surface.

The new surface smoothed the bumps and introduced a new style of racing. Two-by-two was the new way to speed around Daytona. If you found yourself single for a lap, you'd better start looking for someone quickly, or you could count yourself out of the running. With two-by-twos, drivers team up for maximum speed and efficiency. They hunt for a partner on the track, ride their partner's bumper, seeking to confuse the wind and create a draft, then try to stick with that partner to fly by cars—those that may be out of step for a moment—in tandem. Not having a partner to hook up with, or not being trusted as a pusher or puller, spells defeat at Daytona.

Going into Speedweeks in 2011, the odds were against Wood Brothers Racing. Some teams have two, three, even four cars on the track in each race. But Wood Brothers had only one—Trevor. That was going to make it harder for him to find a partner. To make matters worse, Trevor's car had bright yellow stripes on the back. *Rookie stripes*—a clear warning for other drivers to be cautious.

Despite the challenges, Trevor embraced the new style of racing. He watched others and then went out and practiced the technique himself. He took advice from Donnie Wingo and from his favorite driver, Jeff Gordon. Jeff proved an incredible ally. He soon came to trust Trevor's driving, which he saw firsthand during the earlier Gatorade Duel race. Trevor looked for someone he could get in step with, and that someone happened to be Gordon. Trevor proved to be an awesome pusher.

On the evening of February 19, Trevor's twentieth birthday and the night before the Daytona 500, he and some friends hung around the hauler parking lot. They were relaxed, and they raced wheelbarrows, just like kids like to do. He confided in his friends how he had grown a little tired of just reading and studying all the time; he wanted to experience the power of God firsthand. They promised to pray for him.

February 20—the big day drivers, teams, and fans had waited for all winter—had finally arrived. Country artist Martina McBride performed the national anthem, and the U.S. Air Force Thunderbirds flew through the "Petty blue" skies. The racers readied themselves mentally for what legendary driver-turned-TV-analyst Darrell Waltrip called "the toughest 500 ever to win."

In 2011, more than 35 million people tuned in to watch the Daytona 500 on TV—many times more than the 182,000 fans who packed the stands. Fox Sports, which telecast the race, featured Trevor as he walked along pit road. Being the good-humored kid he is, he talked about how he had arrived to drive for the Wood Brothers.

Trevor was decked in the Wood Brothers classic colors: the white car with red hood and red top and a gold #21 on its doors. Like every NASCAR color scheme, this one was intentional. Longtime racing fans would recognize the tribute. It honored David Pearson's 2011 induction into the NASCAR Hall of Fame. Pearson drove for the Wood Brothers from 1972 through 1978 and won the last Daytona 500 for them in 1976. That meant Trevor was following up a legend in a legendary car for the oldest continuously operating NASCAR Sprint Cup team, the famous Wood Brothers.

Trevor started in row 16 on the outside of Bobby Labonte. (The rookie and the veteran Labonte, who was racing in his 19th Daytona 500, would bump into each other four hours later, though both kept going.) Toward the back was not a bad place to start for a rookie, and Trevor knew a lot of aggressive driving would take place in front of him. If he could see his way through the smoke, he'd be fine. That is, if he could find a partner for the biggest dance of his young career.

The cars started and the green flag fell. The race was on. The trust Gordon showed in Trevor during the Duel convinced other veteran drivers that they could also trust the kid. Throughout the race, Trevor had no problems hooking up. And he always did it in the right way, never causing a wreck because he bumped unevenly or too roughly into his partner.

Waltrip said during the race, "Many of NASCAR's most dramatic scenes have happened in a Dayton 500." Indeed, it's where records are set and then broken. One of the records set in the 2011 race was the number of caution flags—16. Twelve of them were for accidents, which only makes sense since a staggering 32 of 43 cars that started were caught up in some sort of accident during the race.

But Trevor's car was not among them. He kept his car *clean*. That's an owners' dream, and it didn't go unnoticed. During the last caution of the race, Waltrip wondered aloud what many others must have been thinking: "Can Trevor Bayne win this race?" Trevor was up with the leaders late in the race. He was dancing with David Ragan. Waltrip answered his own question: "He's been awfully good during *Speedweeks*. And there's not a scratch on the car." (Yes, the bumper on the #21 was torn up, but Waltrip was referencing how Trevor had stayed out of the wreckage.)

With the 500th mile coming up, more cars got turned and wrecked. The pace car once again came out to lead the race, and the field got in line. The 500th mile came under caution, but NASCAR rules state that a race can go with a "green-white-checkered" flag sequence to avoid finishing a race under caution. That means essentially two laps to the finish at that point.

This 500 would take two attempts at the green-white-checkered before it finished.

In the first attempt, Trevor was in the lead and on the inside. David Ragan was on the outside of him. When the green flag fell, David dove down in front of Trevor, almost as if they had planned things that way. But they didn't even make it back to the white flag before more cars got turned around and a caution came out again.

In the second attempt, Trevor would need to hook up with someone other than Ragan because he had been black-flagged for a violation on the first restart.

When the green flag came out again, Bobby Labonte gave Trevor a great push. All Trevor could do from there was to try to keep Bobby in tow and hug the inside of the track. Several veterans, hungry for their own first 500 win, were nipping at Trevor's heels as they came around the track. When the white flag came out, Trevor was in the lead. All he needed to do was hang on.

Races almost always create some suspenseful moments before their climactic finish. The green-white-checkered provided the suspense in 2011.

In the 60s and 70s, NASCAR fans came to the realization that if an event contained a "Cinderella" story or historical ending, the #21 car was probably involved. The #21 car owned by the Wood Brothers had been around nearly as long as NASCAR, and the list of drivers who had driven the legendary #21 car included Cale Yarborough, A.J. Foyt, Dale Jarrett, and David Pearson, who won 43 times with #21 painted on his side panels.

Trevor was 2011's Cinderella. He was in the right car with the right lead for a historical ending. As he rounded the fourth corner, Carl Edwards slid up on the inside in the #99 car. David Gilliland, in the #34 car, came up on the inside of Labonte, and Labonte gave Edwards room. Edwards bumped Trevor. It was the last bump of the race. As most NASCAR fans know, the bump pushed Trevor home, and he went all the way to the checkered flag.

During the race, Trevor had talked with Wingo on the radio using "Sir" and "Thank you." But now he was hollering at him, "Are you kidding me? Are you kidding me? Am I dreaming?"

Then he needed to ask directions to Victory Lane.

When Trevor stopped the car, he was surrounded by well-wishers, including two who wanted to shake his hand: 85-year-old Glen Wood and 76-year-old Leonard Wood. It was their seventh decade as a team and their 98th win. For Ford, it was the 600th win.

Records had been broken or tied. Previously, Jeff Gordon was the youngest driver to win the 500, but Trevor broke that record by five years and sixth months. Trevor also joined Jamie McMurray as the only other driver to win a race in his second start. And Trevor also became the seventh driver to get his first Sprint Cup win in a Daytona 500.

The year before, Trevor was just a kid watching the race in blue jeans. This year, he was setting new records. Four hours earlier, he was on the starting grid thanking God for the platform he was given. Now he was on the platform in Victory Circle, with a whirlwind of media appearances coming in the coming week.

Trevor's first stop was Daytona International Speedway's media center. He entered looking completely composed as he sat down at the table with Eddie and Len Wood and Donnie Wingo. After several routine, how-does-it-feel-to-win questions, he got the loaded one: "What is the biggest thing that has happened in your life before today?"

Before Trevor answered, he choked up for the first time. Speaking through the brief falter in his voice, he answered, "Finding Christ. He is the reason I'm here. He is the whole platform. If it weren't for Him, I wouldn't be sitting here. These wins are great, but they go away with time."

PERSPECTIVE WHEN FACING TRIALS

Two months after the media was reporting on Trevor's remarkable Daytona 500 win, they were writing tons of articles speculating about Trevor's mystery illnesses. You can't drive a race car if you are experiencing double vision, fatigue, and nausea—and Trevor had suffered some of those very symptoms.

A series of hospital visits began after the April 9 Sprint Cup race. Trevor had finished 17th but climbed out of the car so fatigued that he had to go straight to the ER. But whatever Trevor's problem was, it wasn't diagnosed or solved that day As it turns out, he would need several more hospital visits before that happened. In the meantime, he kept racing.

The following weekend, at the Saturday race at Talladega, Trevor boarded his Roush Nationwide car and ran to a sixth-place finish. The following day, he raced for the Wood Brothers in a Sprint Cup race but wrecked after 89 laps.

The next Saturday would be Trevor's last race for several weeks. It was for Roush's team and, like the previous week, he finished in sixth place.

With symptoms still hampering Trevor's daily routine, he checked himself in for a weeklong stay at the Mayo Clinic, where the world's best doctors could examine him. At the time, Trevor believed that there was a possibility that his condition may never be diagnosed and that his racing career could be over. Every day, he asked the doctors how long it would take to get back in the race car.

The Mayo Clinic doctors eventually diagnosed and treated Trevor for Lyme disease, an illness carried by a pinhead-sized tick. The disease wouldn't end his career, but it would keep him out of the car until June. He returned, fully recovered, to Nationwide in early June and the Sprint Cup later that month.

Many people watched Trevor to see how he would respond to this new trial. Would he still praise God now that his platform—at least temporarily—was a hospital bed?

Trevor admits to being scared throughout the ordeal. But he didn't waste his time in self-pity or complaining. That's because he realized that God had already blessed him in his career as a race car driver. Through his faith in God, he found peace in his heart about the unknown. He had the inner assurance that the whole trial would be for God's glory.

When Trevor returned to strength and to the track, he ran well. He ran nine more solid races for the Wood Brothers and recorded nine more Top-10 finishes—giving him 14 for the year—for his Nationwide team.

The next season brought new trials for young Mr. Bayne. He had hoped that his success at Daytona would translate into sponsorship, but it didn't happen. Everybody involved with Trevor's racing career was banking on some momentum from 2011 to create a more stable future—possibly even a full-time Sprint Cup ride. But that was far from what took place.

After a six-day, six-city media tour to promote the 2012 Daytona 500, Trevor settled into a wholly unsatisfying part-time schedule. Roush Fenway Racing's sponsorship contracts expired at the end of 2011, and even with Trevor's youthfulness and charm, the economic climate did not afford him more than a handful of Nationwide races. His relationship with both Roush and the Wood Brothers allowed him to race in 16 Sprint Cup events. But in total, he scored only five Top-10 finishes in 22 NASCAR starts during 2012.

PERSEVERANCE

When the 2013 Daytona 500 arrived, Trevor was once again in the seat of the Wood Brothers #21. It was his third 500 in the storied car—a story he has contributed to with his win in 2011. After having a hard time finding a sponsorship in 2012, Trevor was back to running a full-time Nationwide schedule with Roush and a part-time schedule with the Wood Brothers. But Trevor didn't race as well as he hoped in the Daytona 500, starting 33rd and finished 27th.

On the Nationwide side of his schedule, Trevor was back to finishing well. He was back to having a full-time ride, and he consistently excelled in that ride. Ten races into the season, he had earned four Top-10 finishes.

Trevor's highlight in the Wood Brothers car in 2013 came at the Coca-Cola 600 in Charlotte in May. It marked the 1,400th start for Wood Brothers Racing and Trevor's 39th start with the team. He finished 16th in the milestone race.

Trevor had a milestone of his own planned, and it didn't have anything to do with racing, other than it included several of his racing friends. Between the Dover and Iowa races on his Nationwide schedule, Trevor married his longtime girlfriend, Ashton. The honeymoon would need to wait until later because they had squeezed their wedding between two racing weekends.

Trevor finished fourth at Dover International Speedway, which moved him into the Top 10 in driver standings. Since he was in a full-time ride during the 2013 season, he had a shot at winning the Nationwide Series points championship. Reaching the Top 10 was a significant step for Trevor. Throughout the season, Trevor had a solid hold on the middle of the Top 10 standings, but he received some disturbing news when Mayo Clinic doctors told him that he did not have Lyme disease but a more serious affliction—multiple sclerosis. However, he was cleared by his doctors to continue to compete in NASCAR. His wedding was two days after the Dover race, and five days later he and Ashton were off to the Iowa Speedway for the DuPont Pioneer 250.

Trevor and Ashton received a wedding gift of sorts in Iowa: a giant gas pump, the race's unique trophy. Trevor capped an emotional but sensational week by winning the 200-mile race. In his post-race comments, he spoke tearfully of his special wedding week. Then, in his characteristically good-humored way, he added, "I should have gotten married a long time ago."

After Trevor won the Daytona 500, he made a call from the media center to his chaplain friend in Mexico. During the call, Trevor cried, and as Lonnie said later, "With him in tears, he recognized that his win was not about himself but all about Jesus Christ."

What Lonnie wrote in February 2011 is still true of Trevor today: "On the biggest stage of his life, with millions of people watching, Trevor summed up God's two greatest commands: love God and love others."

Trevor is actively fulfilling those commands still today. He is not all about himself, but about Jesus Christ and about sharing His love with others.

6

JUSTIN ALLGAIER:
THE TRIUMPH OF THE "LITTLE GATOR"

When Justin Allgaier was a youth, his midget car sported a message on the back that read, "Follow Jesus, Not Me."

The outspoken teen aimed to promote Christ's message of salvation to any tailgaters on the race track as well as to fans sitting in the grandstands. His inspiration for sharing his faith came from hearing evangelist Billy Graham saying, "One person's voice can make a real difference." That's why he aimed to keep speaking out for Jesus everywhere and in any way he could.

Today, no matter whether he wins or loses a race, Justin—one of the dominant drivers in NASCAR's Nationwide Series—is often heard thanking God publically for both the thrilling wins on the race track and for the lessons he learns from hard defeats.

Justin is sure God has a purpose for his racing, and he wouldn't want that to change. But if there was one thing this driver, who was 27 at the time of his writing, could change, it would be his height. He barely stands 5 feet, 5 inches, and that's in his racing shoes.

Justin sometimes gets a little tired of being teased about looking like some old grandpa hunched behind the wheel, trying to find his way around an oval track with four turns. All he knows is that his right foot can reach the gas pedal, and that helps him to be one of the most competitive drivers in NASCAR.

"LITTLE GATOR" KEEPS WINNING AND WINNING
Justin "Little Gator" Allgaier was born on June 6, 1986, in Riverton,

Illinois, to Mike and Dorothy Allgaier. His dad gave him the nickname "Gator," and Justin later added the "Little" to preface it. Make no mistake, though, his moniker had nothing to do with his short stature or with his being an aggressive racer. Those associations came later.

Here's how the story goes regarding Justin's nickname: when his father was born, the nurse at the hospital mangled Justin's grandfather's name and called him "Mr. Alligator." Mike's father was amused at the error, so he played along and started calling his son "Gator." When Justin arrived on the scene years later, it was "tag, you're it." Now it was Justin's turn to be known around the house as "Gator"—or actually "Little Gator," to differentiate father and son.

The nickname stuck for good after Mike started talking frequently about his "Lil' Gator" while doing business at race tracks. One day, when young Justin was hanging out with his dad, a business associate looked down at Justin, then back at his dad, and said, "This has to be 'Lil' Gator' you always talk about."

"And that was it, it stuck," Justin said about the nickname.

Mike and Dorothy raised Little Gator in Riverton, a small farming community along the banks of the Sangamon River. Riverton's claim to fame was that in 1831, according to American writer Carl Sandburg, a 22-year-old Abraham Lincoln "floated a canoe down the Sangamon River, going to a new home, laughter and youth in his bones, and in his heart a few pennies of dreams."

Justin, too, had a few pennies of dreams. One evening when his dad was away on business, Justin called him from a payphone. There was a definite agenda to the call. Earlier that day, his mother, looking for something to occupy her son, had taken Justin down to the Quarter Midget track by the Route 66 drive-in. There, they'd watched one of Justin's friends race, and that's all it took for Justin to be hooked on racing.

Years later, Justin explained the instant connection: "We watched him race, and I fell in love with it." When the race was over, Justin's friend's parents offered to let Justin borrow their car and try a practice run. But Justin's mom wanted to check with his father first. Thus, the call from a nearby payphone.

"No way," said his dad. "Too dangerous."

It took a child's art of persuasion—the notorious squeal of "but Mom said . . ." in the background—to get Mike Allgaier to agree to let his young son get behind a wheel and compete against other kids.

Mike was cautious about giving his son the green light because he knew plenty about the sport. He and Dorothy had friends who drove race cars, and they owned Hoosier Tire Midwest, a distributor of racing tires, so they had been around the track a few times. But there was still the big problem in Mike's mind—Justin was only five years old.

Mike had one big stipulation: if they did this racing gig, then they needed to do it right. No ingredient would be left out. Pedal to the metal.

So the family jumped into the sport as a team, and Justin's love for racing soon translated into wins. By the time he was 12, he had racked up more than 100 victories, taking five Quarter Midget National Championships in the process. Moreover, Justin became a huge NASCAR fan during the 1990s—a time when the sport saw exponential growth in popularity. From an early age, Justin followed NASCAR, rooted for his favorite drivers, and charted his dream to destiny.

One of Justin's favorite drivers was a family friend named Ken Schrader, whose NASCAR racing career went back nearly three decades. Schrader soon became Justin's mentor and a lifelong hero. Another of Justin's favorite drivers was Richard Petty, the indomitable, hypercompetitive King of NASCAR. Justin's favorite TV show growing up was the weekly 30 minutes of *Inside Winston Cup Racing*, which "looked at the men and machines that make up the world's most popular motorsport." And his favorite color became purple because purple was the trademark color for Hoosier Tire Corporation.

While a big part of Justin's youth was racing, an even bigger part was the Christian faith. Riverton Christian Church was Justin's home church when he was a youngster—and a church he still attends when he's back in Illinois as a grown-up. Though it was often impossible to attend Sunday morning church services on out-of-town race weekends, Justin saw from an early age the importance of church and "the benefit of the Lord's Word," as he described it on the Motor Racing Outreach website.

Those benefits have kept him grounded to this day. His longtime friends say his fame hasn't changed him. He doesn't worry about himself, doesn't put on airs, and does his best to place everyone else ahead of himself.

TURNING LEFT FOR A LIVING

By age 15, Justin was already hearing whispers of greatness directed toward him. He was out of Quarter Midgets by then and into racing Midget, Micro Sprint, and Late Model cars. He was winning, too. The size of track didn't matter, nor did the surface, nor whether or not the car had fenders. He could win a race in anything he drove.

In 2001, Justin set the record as the youngest driver ever to advance to the A-main at the famed Chili Bowl Midget Nationals in Tulsa, Oklahoma. The annual event began in 1987 and had seen hundreds of participants by Justin's day, but no one as young as him had ever reached the main event.

That same year, Justin's Late Model team ran in 51 dirt track races, earning two wins and 24 Top-10 finishes.

Around that time, Justin met Ashley Hanson, a cute girl his age, when he was at a local hockey game. A friend of Ashley's had an older brother who worked on Justin's Late Model car, so she knew who Justin was, thought he was really cute, and even predicted to her mom she would marry him. Justin still says that right after he met Ashley, he also knew he would marry her. That would turn out to be true in time, but there was some growing up to do . . . as well as a lot of racing.

Justin moved steadily up the ranks toward a stock car career. In 2002, when he was 16, Ken Schrader turned over an ARCA (Automobile Racing Club of America) car he owned to Justin for three races. Justin's first ARCA race was held at the Illinois State Fairgrounds in Springfield, and he finished 17th. In his next race, he finished 11th. And in his third race he finished 17th again. Pretty good results for a teen, observers said.

A rule in ARCA racing holds that a driver must be at least 19 years old before he can race on a track more than a mile long. That rule limited the number of races Justin could participate in—at least until his birthday in 2005. When the big day arrived, Justin was ready to race full-time.

When Justin moved into ARCA racing full-time, Ashley stayed by his side. The couple married in 2006, when they were both 20 years old. She became involved in the race day experience as much as any other team member, always cheering Justin to the finish and always doing whatever it took to help out the team. Ashley arranged travel, paid the bills, and worked as the team office manager. Each race day, she made sure the whole team had sandwiches and their radios in hand. During each race, she sat on top of the pit box, recorded lap times, and performed other crew tasks.

Justin raced in the ARCA Series until he was 22. The team ran on a shoestring budget, and Justin's dad owned the car. Justin came away with eight victories between 2002 and 2008. Two of those victories came after he got married: one in 2006 and one in 2007.

Results would be different in 2008. Justin approached the new year with vigor, and the entire team saw the season as another great opportunity from the Lord. In Justin's first three races, he finished second, first, and second, respectively. The season progressed just as well. Justin ran in all the ARCA races and wowed fans by grabbing 16 Top-10 finishes. But the most spectacular part of the season was the way it ended. Justin won his last three races, which turned the heads of NASCAR scouts, one of whom happened to work for Penske Racing.

Justin first shook hands with Roger Penske in September 2008, when he was at home in Illinois for the Chicagoland ARCA 200. In October, representatives from Penske Racing called, and within days Justin and his dad were on a flight to Detroit to meet with team management. This was the big break Justin had been waiting for.

Justin signed a contract to drive for Penske's Nationwide Series team the following year in 2009. But first, he needed to wrap up the 2008 season. He had four more ARCA races and an additional four races for

Penske's Nationwide team to close out the year.

In Charlotte that October, Justin climbed into his first Nationwide car, but he soon got caught up in a wreck. He knew he'd need to learn a few things about his new machine in order to thrive. Just two days later, riding the wave of back-to-back ARCA victories and of the thrill of signing his new contract, Justin traveled to Toledo and ran the Allgaier #16 Chevrolet car to its final ARCA victory. He finished the ARCA segment of his career on top. Not only did he capture the checkered flag in his last race, he also earned the '08 ARCA Series Champion.

To finish off the season, Justin ran the final three Nationwide races—in Fort Worth, Phoenix, and Homestead—behind the wheel of Penske's Dodge Charger. In Phoenix, he posted his best result, an 11th-place finish, good enough for Tim Cindric, Penske's President of Racing, to say, "We'd had our eye on Justin for some time, [and] we're now fortunate to be in a position to bring him on board."

ROOKIE STRIPES WITH VETERAN RESULTS

Justin was on board. He was a team driver for Roger Penske. More importantly, he was an ambassador for Jesus Christ. His new car number was #12. His new sponsor was Verizon Wireless. Justin embraced all of these roles admirably.

Justin's 2009 Nationwide Series rookie season came around fast, and so did his lap times. In 35 races, he finished in the Top 10 twelve times and in the Top 5 three times—a remarkable feat for a rookie. He placed sixth in driver standings and also won the Raybestos Brakes Rookie of the Year award. With the award came a lot of praise from veteran drivers:

"Great competitor."

"Aggressive."

"He knows no limits."

"He just pushes it as hard as he can every lap."

"Fearless."

"Very talented."

After a brilliant rookie year, there was no locking up the brakes. In

2010, Justin almost doubled his Top-10 finishes and tripled his Top-5 finishes. It was another remarkable year, and he boasted in the Lord's blessing as much as he thanked his sponsor, team ownership, crew, and family. Justin exemplified the apostle Paul's appeal to give thanks in all circumstances (1 Thessalonians 5:16–18).

On March 20, 2010, two months into the season, the #12 team was at Bristol Motor Speedway, the short track in Tennessee. With a colossal crowd of 85,000 fans in attendance, Justin found a groove and drove like a champion, cutting through rows of strong competitors to take the lead on lap 274 of 300, snatching it away from veteran driver Brad Keselowski. Seasoned drivers Kyle Busch, Carl Edwards, Kevin Harvick, and Greg Biffle stayed on Justin's heels. Justin raced them all hard to the finish, but he managed to keep them in his rear view mirror to capture his first-ever NASCAR checkered flag.

After thanking Penske, his crew, and sponsor, Justin said, "Thanks goes to God. He gives me a lot of good doors to walk through." Then he turned to his wife, Ashley, and gave her a big hug, a quick kiss, and a warm smile.

Bristol holds special meaning for Justin and Ashley. Back in 2004, when they were both 18 years old, they made their first trip to the storied track with Ashley's parents. They took in the whole atmosphere: they camped out, shopped the vendor stands, and sat down near the track. They walked away from Bristol covered in those tiny rubber marbles from tires the track had torn up—and with the hidden hope of winning there someday. That hope was fulfilled in 2010.

Justin's season with Penske closed in a bittersweet way. The sweet part was that he finished fourth in the driver standings, behind three Sprint Cup drivers—Keselowski, Edwards, and Busch. As the top Nationwide-only driver, Justin would have captured the championship if Cup drivers' points hadn't counted.

But then the storm clouds appeared on the horizon. Justin was hearing rumors that his sponsor, Verizon Wireless, was pulling back from NASCAR. If a new sponsor couldn't be found, then he wouldn't have a ride with Penske in 2011.

As in any workplace, some rumors around the garage are just that—rumors, and unfounded ones at that. Sadly for Justin, the rumors proved true. Verizon drove off into the sunset, leaving everyone else behind. Penske gave Justin the news and freed him to go looking for work.

Good news soon arrived for Justin when Turner Motorsports announced the formation of a NASCAR Nationwide team. With the 2010 season winding down, Turner made its announcement in Fort Worth just as Justin was getting ready to race in his third-to-last race for Penske. The two sides met in negotiations, and Justin signed a new two-year contract.

More exciting news came Justin's way when Brandt, a leading agricultural retailer and manufacturer, agreed to become his new sponsor. Brandt is located in Springfield, Illinois, and Justin was raised just a few miles away in Riverton, so the union proved an excellent fit. The Brandt sponsorship gave American farm families a chance to root for a NASCAR team with a Midwest kid behind the wheel.

FUEL: FILL IT UP!

Racing fans sometimes overlook the significance of what is called fuel strategy. But for crews and drivers, fuel strategy is of utmost importance. During the 2011 season, Justin and his new crew showed just how important fuel strategy can be.

Most modern family sedans get around 20 miles per gallon and need to be filled about every 300 miles. But race cars need to be topped off much more frequently. Running flat out on an oval track, a NASCAR vehicle burns through fuel at the rate of about five miles per gallon. Most race cars have an 18-gallon fuel cell (the NASCAR name for a gas tank), meaning the car can only go about 90 miles before the tank is empty and the car stalls out.

Teams take many precautions to avoid empty fuel cells. Racing conditions are always changing, and much depends on driver skill. But teams also depend on engineers who crunch mileage numbers and then inform crew chiefs how many laps a car can go on the fuel left in the fuel cell.

One of the best scenarios for filling a fuel cell during a race is when a caution flag comes out. This gives teams the opportunity to bring their cars into the pits to be refueled. But the unscheduled pit stop changes the mapped-out strategy for the race, which can cause problems down the road. Other complicating factors include differences in tracks, differences in drivers, and changing race-day conditions. These factors mean that fuel strategy often changes during the course of a race. Frequently heard during a racing broadcast will be the phrase: "So much for that strategy."

At the start of 2011, things looked bright for Justin. He had a new team and a new sponsor. He also had a new fuel in his fuel cell. NASCAR made Sunoco's "Green E15," a highly oxygenated unleaded racing fuel, its official fuel. The change to Green E15 demonstrated NASCAR's commitment to improving race competition as well as to doing what was best for the environment.

Many drivers have been one-time winners, and Justin didn't want to be one of them. After his win at Bristol with Penske in 2010, Justin was eager to earn another Victory Circle appearance. With the fresh start with Turner, and with his new sponsor supporting his efforts, his heart was set on continuing his success. He approached the starting grid of each race with this winning mind-set. As he raced through the beginning of the season, Justin finished inside the Top 10 seven times and just outside the Top 10 another six times.

Race 14 arrived on the schedule. It was early June, and Justin was in his home state of Illinois, at Chicagoland, hoping for an early birthday present in the form of a "W." That day, on the mile-and-a-half speedway, Carl Edwards and Justin entertained the fans with a thrilling two-car battle that went down to the wire. Edwards had dominated most of the day, leading a total of 144 of the 200 laps. But on lap 198 of 200, Justin closed in on Edwards.

Crew chiefs for both teams were playing the fuel mileage game, and everyone knew that fuel would play a role as the final few laps passed. Behind the leaders, a couple drivers were already coasting on the apron, signaling that they were out of fuel. Meanwhile, the battle between

Edwards and Justin came down to the white flag—one lap left—with Edwards slightly ahead.

Driving hard on the backstretch, Justin inched closer with every second and watched his front bumper draw up on Edwards' rear bumper. With only a few feet between the two cars, Edwards' car sputtered and ran out of fuel. Justin swerved to avoid plowing into him from behind and continued hard into turn three.

The finish line was in sight, and Justin could almost taste victory. Then his car sputtered and ran out of gas, too. All he could was coast toward the finish line and hope that the drivers behind him wouldn't pass him before he took the checkered flag.

When you're going 150 miles per hour, it takes a long time to slow down to nothing. Fortunately for Justin, his car had enough momentum to carry him across the finish line for the victory. Edwards coasted in to claim second, with Trevor Bayne right behind him.

Justin got a big win, and fans got the thrill of a close finish. He quickly forgot the angst running out of fuel had caused him as he thanked God for being with him during the race and talked about how blessed he was to be in a winning situation.

Think about it: Justin led the race for just three-eighths of a mile, and most of that was without fuel in his car. But in NASCAR, at least that day, that unlikely scenario was enough to win.

MORE FUEL STRATEGIES

Justin enjoyed mostly excellent finishes—up until the road course race at Road America in Elkhart Lake, Wisconsin, in late June. At that race, fuel mileage would also play a role. Road America that day was hosting only the 29th road course race—a race where the track isn't shaped like an oval—in NASCAR history. At Road America, the trophy—a brand-new Harley Davidson—waits in the winner's circle for the victor. (Wisconsin is, after all, where it all began for the legendary motorcycle brand.) Starting 14th, Justin hoped to run well enough to find out what he might do with a new Harley.

From a bird's eye view, and looking north toward Elkhart Lake, the track at Road America looks like a bizarre twist of a large upside-down fishhook, except with frequent bends and kinks around the hook. The course sprawls out over the 640-acre facility and measures 4.048 miles around. What sets Road America apart is 14 turns ranging in radius from 100 feet to 550 feet and hundreds of feet in elevation changes.

Veteran NASCAR racer Mark Martin gives two definitions of a NASCAR road course. The technical definition says that they are "race tracks with complex configurations of left and right turns at varying angles. The track may have elevation changes as well." This less-technical definition states it in ways the average race fan can understand: a road course, like Road America, more or less resembles a winding country highway with a number of sharp, difficult turns—some hairpin, others sweeping. There are peaks and valleys, dips and slopes. It is like driving through a great, big, hilly field, or racing through a maze.

Some teams employ what NASCAR calls a road-racing ace, or a "ringer," for the road course races each year. For instance, Michael McDowell is considered a road course ace due to his extensive experience in open-wheel racing.

USA Today reporter Jeff Gluck, an expert on all things NASCAR, noted that on intermediate tracks, aerodynamics is everything: on short tracks, the lightweight car with a low center of gravity is the secret, but at road courses, the skilled driver is still more important than the car. A driver can manhandle a car on a road course and stand a good chance of winning.

Justin thought he was prepared for the wildness of the course, but the unbelievable sometimes happens and hampers preparedness. One hundred times Justin could practice downshifting quickly to enter a hairpin turn at a crawl so as not to skid into a gravel pit and plug his car's radiator with dirt. He could practice turning right, right again, then left, and left again, then right again, all at 70 miles per hour hundreds of times and still not be prepared for happenstance.

With five laps to go, and with road course ringer Michael McDowell in the lead, Justin was running strong in seventh place. On lap 46 of the scheduled 50 laps, a car ran out of control and skidded into the grass beside corner eleven. The crash took out a sign and scattered debris over the track, drawing a caution flag. Because it took some time for officials to clean up the mess, the 50-lap mark passed under caution. NASCAR decided to apply the green-white-checkered rule to the end of the race. That meant two additional laps of racing. The first lap is called the green lap. When the field comes back around again, they see the white flag (meaning one lap to go), then it's a race to the finish line. At Road America, those two laps mean eight more miles than originally planned.

For the Road America race running in overtime, new fuel strategies came into play. Crew chiefs scrambled to adjust their fueling strategies. Jimmy Elledge, Justin's crew chief, told Justin they were undoubtedly good until lap 56—or six extra laps.

Justin was still in seventh place after the track was cleared of the debris. The pace car led the leaders back toward the green flag to restart. McDowell and Ron Fellows were in the first row, and Justin wasn't far behind.

The restart didn't get off well. Barreling down "Road America Straight" (RA's front stretch) and into turns one and two, several drivers behind the leaders engaged in reckless attempts at passing. Multiple cars wrecked, and the caution immediately came out again. That meant a second attempt at a restart and more fuel management questions.

When the second attempt came, McDowell raced ahead with a fast start. Justin moved up directly behind him. They came down a hill called Moraine Sweep and into turn five, the sharpest turn on the track. McDowell overshot the corner and went wide, while Justin braked hard and slid perfectly into the corner. Justin took advantage of the pressure, cut tight on the inside of the corner, and squealed ahead into the lead.

In corner six, McDowell lost control again, and soon his car, along with several others, lay scattered around the grassy edges of the track. Justin pressed on into corners seven, eight, nine, and ten. The caution flag came out again. There would be a third and final attempt at the green-white-checkered, and Justin would now be the lead car when the racers went to green.

With all the driving under caution and the two restarts of the race, Justin was getting very low on fuel. Yet at least two more laps remained. The hope in Justin's camp was that he'd take the lead into turn 1 and a bunch of cars would crash behind him, allowing him to coast into Victory Lane under gas-sipping caution flag conditions.

Justin got a good jump on the restart and raced ahead. As his crew hoped would happen, a car spun out into the gravel pit in turn six, but officials let racing continue. Justin remained out in front with one lap to go. Only four miles to victory.

There were more spinouts behind Justin, prompting officials to bring out another caution flag. Things were looking good for Justin. The field of drivers lined up behind him, and the procession to the finish line started. There were no more chances for restarts. The finish line was only a few turns away. Justin's crew chief came on the radio and shouted, "Shut it off and coast! Shut it off and coast! Shut it off and coast!"

Animated, Justin shouted back, "We just won this race! You guys are freaking awesome!" He raced under Sargento Bridge and down the hill of Moraine Sweep into turn 5 for the last time, and passed under Corvette Bridge. Going into turn 6, his Chevy slowed and the engine sputtered. Justin couldn't believe his ears. Then his car coughed and sputtered as it slowed to a crawl. One car passed.

And then another.

And then another, and another, and another. He didn't have enough fuel to finish a race that went an extra 28 miles.

In all, 18 cars eased by Justin's car that day as he limped and sputtered his way to the finish line. In a matter of minutes, he went from first place to 19th. The only bright spot for Justin was that one of his teammates, Reed Sorenson, won the race for Turner.

Justin mustered the strength after the race to congratulate Reed and thank his sponsor and Turner. He told an ESPN interviewer, "Unbelievable. I thought we won it."

Justin paused and took a long breath before adding this thought: "What a disheartening way to lose a race; it would have been great to win. I don't know. No words I could really say." And then, echoing what he said in the winner's circle during his Chicagoland victory speech, Justin denied himself a pity party in front of ESPN's viewing audience and said, "God definitely blessed me to be here and be up there where we could be capable of winning the race. It just wasn't the right time."

Justin put into practice the apostle Paul's meaning of "do not lose heart" (2 Corinthians 4:16). It's not that he wasn't disheartened; he admitted that he was. Even so, he didn't let the bad break get the best of him. Instead, he gave glory to God.

Following the fuel shortage debacle, Justin offered an amazing example of the Spirit-filled life. When Jeff Gluck asked him to define himself without NASCAR, or any racing at all, Justin replied, "Number one, I'm first and foremost, a Christian." That summed up Justin's Road America reaction, but it is what you'd expect for someone whose father once said he could raise the best race car driver in the world, but if that son wasn't a good person, he lost.

Over the remainder of the season, Justin pulled in nine more Top-10 finishes. That landed him squarely in third place in the driver standings.

ROAD COURSE REDEMPTION AND MINISTRY

When Justin's 2012 season came around, he received an opportunity to redeem himself on a road course. The race was set for mid-August, in Montreal, Quebec, at Circuit Gilles Villeneuve, which was named after a famous Formula One driver.

Justin ran strong the whole race. With moments to go, Penske driver and hometown favorite Jacques Villeneuve—and the nephew of Gilles Villeneuve—had the lead on Justin under the green-white-checkered rule.

Sound familiar?

Going around a corner, the little fuel remaining in Villeneuve's tank sloshed around. His engine, unable to slurp up the needed fuel, momentarily stalled, finishing Villeneuve. Justin raced by him to claim the lead and the victory. Over the radio Justin shouted, "Awesome, awesome, awesome! God's great, man! God's great!"

For the season, Justin finished in the Top 5 six times and in the Top

Bobby Labonte, one of NASCAR's most popular drivers of the last twenty years, followed the tracks laid out by his older brother "Texas Terry." Together, they are the only brothers to each win NASCAR's premier series championship. Bobby's consecutive career start streak ended in 2013 with 704 races. (AP Photo/Autostock, Russell LaBounty)

Mark Martin climbed into his first stock car in 1973; forty years and 40 Cup wins later, he is legendary. Even if he never takes the wheel of another race car, NASCAR fans know he'll be around a track somewhere because this future Hall of Famer won't be found in a rocking chair. (AP Photo/Autostock, Nigel Kinrade)

Michael McDowell, known as the lucky dog who survived one of NASCAR's most horrific crashes, is as determined as the next young racer to overcome challenges to be a champion. He invests his winnings back into the sport, drives his own RV to the track, and produces his own media clips in a persistent drive for racing relevance. His constant smile and positive attitude are another story—one that wins him fans all across America. (AP Photo/Nigel Kinrade)

David Reutimann, the consummate family man, is building his racing career on a family tradition that dates back to his immigrant grandfather's small garage in Florida. Watching his father become a famous racer, David discovered exactly what he wanted to do and set his sights on the highest level of racing—NASCAR. (AP Photo/Wade Payne)

In 2011, 20-year-old Trevor Bayne won the Daytona 500, becoming the youngest driver to win the "Great American Race." Since then, he has continued to make a name for himself as one of the most exciting young racers in NASCAR. Though every season presents new challenges, Trevor faces his share triumphantly. (AP Photo/Terry Renna)

Justin Allgaier, who hails from the "Land of Lincoln," made his Sprint Cup race debut at Chicagoland Speedway in 2013. He has been strictly a Nationwide Series driver for the last six years, but his 84 Top 10 finishes may move him to full-time Cup racing ahead of other young drivers. Whatever the future holds for the young star, his laser-like eyes see what it takes to succeed. (AP Photo/Nam Y. Huh)

Jeff Gordon came of age as Richard Petty retired. Though NASCAR wasn't necessarily looking for a new star to carry the banner, Jeff proved more than capable of the weighty responsibility. Today, as a four-time Cup champ himself and the early mentor for six-time Cup champion Jimmy Johnson, Jeff is the stalwart that the veteran Petty was; he is recognized internationally as a compassionate man and sports superstar. (AP Photo/Autostock, Russell LaBounty)

Michael Waltrip, co-owner of and part-time driver for Michael Waltrip Racing, is a two-time Daytona 500 winner. He grew up as the little brother of NASCAR great Darrell Waltrip to become a racing statesman in his own right. Through big wins and tough losses, on and off the track, he remains a fan favorite. (AP Photo/John Raoux)

David Ragan's win at the Talladega Superspeedway last season was the first trophy for Front Row Motorsports and the second trophy for David as a wheelman in the Sprint Cup series. But he has been a winner since committing to racing as a young man. He has risen to slay some metaphorical giants over his career, and is genuinely gracious and compassionate. (AP Photo/Rainier Ehrhardt)

After retiring from driving, Hall of Famer Ned Jarrett discovered that he was good at broadcasting races, both from the pit and in the booth. He was sometimes partial, as proud dads often are, when he called events his son Dale raced in. If there's a Hall of Fame for dads, Ned's in it. (AP Photo/Ric Feld)

Morgan Shepherd is the oldest driver in NASCAR history to start a Cup race; but at 71 he's not racing to make history. He hauls his "Racing for Jesus" car to the track every weekend to encourage and evangelize his fellow drivers and racing fans of all ages. (AP Photo/Jim Cole)

10 nineteen times. He came in sixth in the overall driver standings.

For Justin and Ashley, the off-season meant spending time with family back in Illinois, as well as serving on a Motor Racing Outreach–sponsored missions trip to Monterrey, Mexico. While south of the border, Justin and Ashley were able to have a special visit with Magali, a young girl they had sponsored. Justin also did off-season promotional work on behalf of his sponsor, Brandt, and enjoyed being home with family for Thanksgiving and Christmas.

The New Year brought Justin a return to Midget racing. He hadn't been in an open-wheel car since he was 21. But the 2013 Chili Bowl Midget Nationals, held during the first couple weeks of January in Tulsa, Oklahoma, was on his schedule. While he didn't reach his goal of returning to the A-main, like he'd done as a teen, he still had a great run.

Before the Allgaiers knew it, the 2013 season was upon them. They made plans to head to Daytona, where every NASCAR season begins. But first, they had one more trip to make—this one a cruise sponsored by K-LOVE Christian Radio. One of their ports of call was Cozumel, a Caribbean island off the coast of Mexico's Yucatan Peninsula. But instead of spending all their time lying on the beach, Justin and Ashley dedicated much of their time to working in an orphanage.

The off-season recharged Justin's batteries, and his wife's encouragement spurred him on. "There have been times when I was ready to give up, ready to quit, but she has been the one behind me, pushing me," he said.

Justin's other big motivation was serving others, like he has on missions trips, so he can bring a little happiness to others who are less fortunate than he is.

Back in Daytona, Justin and Ashley sat in the Steak and Shake restaurant just outside of Daytona Beach. They were with family and friends after a race and planned to use the time to announce that a new "Baby Gator" would be arriving in August. This announcement took place at the same Steak and Shake where Dorothy announced to Mike that she was expecting Justin. Apparently, some treasured moments in the Allgaier family are worth repeating. In early August, Justin and

Ashley welcomed their new baby girl, Harper Grace, into their family—and dare we say, into the NASCAR family?

Repeating or re-signing—both can be good. For 2013, Justin re-signed with Turner, which is now called Turner Scott Motorsports. He also proudly re-signed with Brandt, which celebrated 60 years in business in 2013. Being the local kid who teamed up with an established Midwest business had made racing possible for Justin. He hoped that having everything in place would allow him to run for the NASCAR Nationwide Series Championship in 2013.

Justin had a good go, finishing in a tie for fourth place, in the Nationwide series driver standings. Earlier in the year, after 14 races, he had a firm grip on second place, just 28 points behind leader Regan Smith.

A second-place finish at Road America in Elkhart, Wisconsin, kept him high in the driver's standings and was a bit of a payback. Justin raced his #31 Chevrolet to a second-place finish at the road course where two years earlier he had stalled due to an empty fuel tank.

In one sense, Justin was thrilled to finish second. Justin was part of the I Am Second video ministry, which inspires people to live for God and for others. His message was simple, and a message he lives. With a black backdrop and stark lighting illuminating his face, Justin looked into the camera and spoke from his heart:

> *Growing up, I've faced quite a bit of intimidation. Being younger, being a rookie, the fact that I'm not so big of a person, I'm only 5 feet, 5 inches, I've faced a lot of intimidation. I'm not the type that's going to go out there and be an enforcer. Other people look at that as a weakness. But I'm able to overlook that.*
>
> *When I'm in the race car, those differences all go away. My race car is just as big. It weighs just as much as anyone else's. I have the same rights that they have to be out there. There is no one that's better than another, whether it be size or race or color or anything.*
>
> *I love racing. Hopefully I'll be a race car driver for the rest*

of my life and be successful at it. But I trust God's plan for me. I want to succeed. But I want to succeed on His terms, not mine. I'm having a great time being a race car driver, and I'll continue to do that as long as He provides the success to do that.

But at the same time, if God wants to use what He has given me to help another person, or if there's another direction that He's calling me, I'm going to follow His lead and do just that. I'm doing the things that He has given me to do.

I am Justin Allgaier, and I am second.

No, Justin, you've got it wrong.

Because you've chosen to follow Christ and stay in His slipstream around the track, you'll finish second, but in an eternal sense, you're going to finish first.

7

JEFF GORDON:
THE GREATEST DRIVER OF THIS ERA

In 1986, John and Carol Bickford sold their house and John's bustling auto parts business in Vallejo, California, and moved 2,222 miles east to Pittsboro, Indiana. Why?

Because that same year, their 14-year-old son, Jeff Gordon—Jeff kept his father's last name after his mother remarried—was an open-wheel racing prodigy who sped past his youthful competitors like they were stuck in third gear. A move to Indiana, the mecca of sprint cars, would give him the opportunity to test his skills against better drivers. The Hoosier State was right where Jeff needed to be.

The Bickfords carefully researched and planned their move, which was also a reaction to a California rule that blocked their path like a phalanx of stock cars in turn 4. More about that in a bit.

Regardless of their reasons, the move set the stage for Jeff's future in stock cars, although, strangely enough, stock car racing wasn't on Jeff's radar—Indy car racing was.

Did the big move pay off?

Sure, it did. Then again, Babe Ruth didn't regret being sold to the Yankees, and LeBron's glad he moved from Cleveland to Miami.

Today, Jeff Gordon is none other than a living legend. But his path to greatness contains more twists and turns than you might think, which is partly why his ascension to the top of the NASCAR totem pole is so interesting.

Most diehard NASCAR fans know the main contours of Jeff's life and his remarkable career, beginning with how, from the age of five, he progressively climbed the racing ranks until he arrived as a NASCAR driver at the early age of 19. But what many may not know about Jeff is how God has been in the pole position throughout his life and has graced him with faith, bestowed on him the gifts of showing mercy and healing through his charitable work, and along the way helped him achieve four NASCAR Cup Series championships to date. (Not to mention three Daytona 500 wins!)

You might also not realize the full impact Jeff has had on NASCAR racing.

Oh sure, you've seen him talk about NASCAR on the nation's biggest talk shows—*Late Night with David Letterman, The Tonight Show with Jay Leno, Jimmy Kimmel Live, The Late Late Show with Craig Ferguson, Late Night with Jimmy Fallon, Good Morning America, 60 Minutes,* and more.

You've seen his persona grow so big that he's been an easy target of parody on *King of the Hill, The Simpsons,* and *South Park.* You've seen him as the cover driver of the video games such as *Jeff Gordon XS Racing, NASCAR Thunder 2002,* and *NASCAR 09,* plus his appearance in *Gran Turismo 5* as himself. You've seen him guest-host *Live! With Regis and Kelly* ten times and play on the Sports Superstars edition of *Who Wants to Be a Millionaire.*

But you might not know about the battles he faced early in his career. You might not know that when the economy tanked in the late '00s, Jeff took a pay cut to secure jobs for members of his team and to help NASCAR, too. Last but not least, you might not know that, despite some mistakes along the way, Jeff is essentially a caring family man who deeply loves his wife, Ingrid, and their two young children, Ella and Leo.

So, even if you don't wear a Jeff Gordon T-shirt or ball cap, even if you haven't purchased a Jeff Gordon lunch box for your kids or trinkets like a key ring or a #24 flag to hang in your front window on race day, you'll still enjoy learning about his far-reaching impact on NASCAR Nation. That's simply because his story is novel—and sweetly refreshing, too.

If you're tackling monstrous decisions, then you can take away from

Jeff's story the confidence that comes from having absolute assurance in the God who has ordered Jeff's life. His story is an example of why there is never chance or mischance in God's appointed way.

LIVING WITH FAME AND FAITH

Critics have claimed that Jeff's ride to the top was too easy, that he didn't pay his proper dues along the way. But these critics are ignoring the hidden hand of Providence. It was no accident that Jeff was a racing demon before he was out of middle school. It was no accident that John Bickford—a patient man who was mechanically gifted, who knew carburetors and filters and hoses and gaskets and plugs and timing, and who was capable of crafting superb racing parts—became his stepfather.

Ironically, some occasionally slight Jeff for keeping his faith in God to himself—at least in comparison to his outspokenness earlier in his career. When Jeff first became a Christian, he'd go out of his way to thank God in Victory Lane. He doesn't do that these days—not that he has to. Keeping his faith more under wraps has been a conscious decision.

Then there's the celebrity side of fame that comes with ruling the NASCAR roost, which made him fair game for the tabloids. He didn't help his quest for privacy by choosing to live in New York City, the center of the media universe, during the prime of his career. (The Gordons have made Charlotte, North Carolina, their main residence since 2010.) Being based in Manhattan certainly raised his national profile and gave him endorsement opportunities that wouldn't have been available if he had chosen to live in Huntersville, North Carolina, or Delray Beach, Florida—other places he's made his home. But living in the Big Apple was a two-edged sword.

While he makes more than $10 million annually in endorsements, he was and continues to be a sitting target for the poisonous pens of tabloid writers and snarky reports of entertainment reporters. Why is the media so interested in Jeff Gordon? Why is the public—love him or hate him—so fascinated with him?

The answers lie in how he became a rock star stock car racer, and how's he handled the fame of being one of the brightest stars in the NASCAR firmament.

RACING AGAINST MOM

Jeff Gordon was born August 4, 1971, and spent his first 14 years growing up in Vallejo, California, across the bay from downtown San Francisco. If the freeway traffic is moving well, Vallejo is only a 30-minute drive to Oakland and a 40-minute drive to Fisherman's Wharf and Union Square.

As a boy, Jeff was more drawn to the San Francisco side of the bay. He chose the 49ers as his favorite pro football team, which made perfect sense considering they won more often than the Oakland Raiders and had Joe Montana engineering comeback wins week after week. By the time Montana was a superstar, Jeff was also winning week after week in his Quarter Midget car.

How did Jeff get behind the wheel of a race car, even one as diminutive as a Quarter Midget? He originally wanted to race BMX dirt bikes, but his mom felt he was too young and considered BMX racing too dangerous. Her decision was prudent; after all, Jeff was only four at the time.

Right around that same time, John Bickford brought home a Quarter Midget car and quickly showed his young stepson how to drive. The car was six feet long and black, with steel bumpers and a roll cage. At the Vallejo fairgrounds, John created a makeshift track for Jeff. As the boy began to learn the art of controlling the machine, he embraced racing with a natural talent and true humility born out of understanding the danger in racing. At first, five-year-old Jeff didn't place well, but he'd caught the competitive bug. A year later, the first-grader won 35 main events and set five track records.

Quarter Midget tracks stretch all across the United States, and Jeff and his stepfather charted out a schedule where they could race all 52 weekends a year. In addition, Jeff practiced up to three times a week and even raced against his mom, though nobody is saying whether she ate his dust.

All that time sitting behind a wheel paid off. By age eight, Jeff had won his first National Quarter Midget championship. Two years later, he won again. Amazingly, he was beating kids twice his age. There was a strategy to "racing up." Jeff was playing by a little-known life rule— actually it was more his stepfather's rule than his—that went like this: "When you're a kid, you need to be a learner. If you're better than the people you're racing against, you're a teacher." More often than not, Jeff was the teacher on the track. So he continually needed to find tougher competition so he could become a learner again.

Jeff's parents also thought he was ready to learn to drive a new car—a sprint car. When Jeff was in sixth grade, he and his father John built a sprint car, complete with the standard 650-horsepower engine. (By comparison, an average full-size family sedan has a 200-horsepower engine.) The effort didn't come cheap; out the door, the new sprint car set them back $25,000.

When they were ready to race, John and Jeff had a real battle on their hands. You see, state licensing, track rules, and insurance companies say you can't race sprint cars until you're 18—there's just too much horsepower under the hood. But Jeff and his family appealed to the insurance companies, and their persistence paid off when 13-year-old Jeff was allowed to run in the All Star Florida Speedweeks.

Being allowed to run in a race and being an actual racer were different things, however. Before Jeff's entry could be accepted, there was still one final roadblock to clear. Because Jeff and his family lived in California, they fell under legal restrictions barring kids under 18 years old from racing full-sized sprint cars. The family tried various angles to get the ruling flexed, but officials wouldn't budge.

Then the family found a way to insert Jeff into the starting line. They learned that Indiana's law allowed 14-year-olds to race full-sized sprint cars. Thus, the family's decision to pack up and leave California was a no-brainer. In 1986, John and Carol Bickford moved their family—Jeff had an older sister named Kim—across the country to Pittsboro, Indiana, a small town of 3,000 located 20 miles northwest of Indianapolis.

"THIS IS WHAT I WANT TO DO"

The family found that settling into the racing lifestyle in the heart of sprint car country wasn't too difficult. Jeff immediately showed a strong talent for racing the larger, faster machines. Actually, he had explosive success, soon capturing several track championships. Very quickly, he became the most talked-about young talent on the American racing scene.

Jeff also began receiving national attention via ESPN, which produced a show called "Thursday Night Thunder," featuring racing from the United States Auto Club (USAC). Jeff was a member of the USAC and he raced sometimes seven nights a week during the summer. It wasn't long before the hotshot teenager was hogging TV coverage because of his young age.

Larry Nuber, a racing analyst for ESPN, was the first racing insider to ask Jeff if he'd ever thought about racing stock cars.

Jeff immediately said no. His dream was to head for Indianapolis to race open-wheel cars—as in the Indy 500 on Memorial Day Weekend. Larry insisted that Jeff really needed to drive stock cars instead. Jeff, never shy, asked how that was possible. Larry told him about the Buck Baker Driving School at the Rockingham Speedway in North Carolina. Before you could drop a green flag, Jeff and his mom rented a car and headed to Rockingham. At 19, Jeff was about to meet NASCAR Hall of Famer Buck Baker, the man who would help change the direction of Jeff's life for good.

Baker retired from racing in 1976, but he wanted to stay involved in the sport, so he opened a racing school at Rockingham Speedway. There, he quickly developed a penchant for training future NASCAR drivers, including Jeff Burton, Ward Burton, Ryan Newman, Joe Nemechek, and Tony Stewart. But Baker's most famous pupil turned out to be a young open-wheeled racer named Jeff Gordon.

John Bickford had worked out a deal with ESPN and the school to tape a feature of Jeff learning how to drive a stock car for the *Thursday Night Thunder* broadcast. Baker, who'd seen Jeff on TV, was curious about what the boy could do in a heavy stock car. Once on the track, Jeff didn't disappoint. He drove the school's car faster than it had ever been driven. When Jeff completed his first timed laps, he climbed out of the car acting like he'd just won the Daytona 500. He exclaimed to his mom, "This is it! This is what I want to do for the rest of my life!" The next thing he did was call his stepdad to say, "Sell the sprint cars! I've found my calling in stock cars."

Through Buck Baker's school, Jeff met restaurateur Hugh Connerty, who arranged limited funding through Outback Steakhouse for Jeff to race in one Busch Series event (known as Nationwide Series today) at Rockingham toward the end of the 1990 season. Jeff's NASCAR debut wasn't memorable, however; he drove only 33 laps before crashing.

In 1991, Bill Davis asked Jeff to be the driver of Davis' #1 Carolina Ford Dealers car for the full season. By season's end, Jeff won Rookie of the Year honors, prompting Davis to quickly secure Jeff for the 1992 season. Davis also hired Ray Evernham, a former driver and race car designer, to join the team as crew chief.

The #1 team started from the pole position 11 times, three of those translating into victories in 1992. For the next eight years, Jeff and Ray prospered, but '92 was the only one with Bill Davis as owner. There was another man looking on: retired race car driver and business entrepreneur Rick Hendrick. He met Hendrick, and a bond formed between them.

ON STAGE WITH KING RICHARD

Hendrick first saw Jeff race in March 1992, at the spring Busch Series race in Hampton, Georgia. Jeff started from the pole and took the lead, which he maintained for most of the race. Jeff was still leading with a few laps to go. Hendrick was walking toward his skybox when he spotted Jeff's white Baby Ruth–sponsored car smoking through the turns because he was pushing so hard. Hendrick muttered, "That guy's tail is gonna bust loose and wreck." But Jeff didn't spin out and kiss a wall. He went on to win.

At the race shop the following Monday, Hendrick was talking with his guys about what he had seen. It turned out that one of them shared an apartment with Jeff. Hendrick told his general manager to get in touch with Jeff and "get him signed to a Winston Cup contract, whatever it took."

Jeff signed with Hendrick Motor Sports and climbed into a Winston Cup car for the first time—at the 1992 season finale, which took him back to Hampton. Of that day, Jeff said, "I pretty much felt out of place . . . I was looking around, looking at these great drivers and celebrities, wondering what I was doing there." Yet Jeff also knew that nothing was recklessly assembled in God's economy. The Lord had given him superb racing abilities, and now He was putting him on stock car racing's biggest stage for the first time. Though Jeff was a young phenom, his Cup debut wasn't the lead story at Atlanta Motor Speedway on that gorgeous fall Georgia day. Instead, his story just happened to meld beautifully with Richard Petty's.

More than 160,000 fans ringed the track—the largest crowd in Georgia history to gather for a sporting event. The fans had gathered to witness Richard Petty's final ride, which was part of a year-long "Fan Appreciation Tour" recognizing a 35-year racing career that began in 1958. It was also the day NASCAR would crown the 1992 Champion. Due to the mathematical possibilities of the point system, six different drivers had a shot at emerging on top by the end of the race. That made the '92 championship the closest contest to date.

ESPN cranked up the coverage, putting NASCAR greats Ned Jarrett and Benny Parsons in the booth. The speedway was spectacularly bathed in pomp and circumstance, as befitting a king who was giving up his crown. Country supergroup Alabama sang the "Star-Spangled Banner." Fans poured out their thanks to Petty with every lap, and he was trying to do the same for them in return.

The whole scene wasn't lost on Jeff. Before the race, Petty personally handed each of the 42 drivers a commemorative money clip. Jeff's was engraved with his name and his race starting position—21st. The money clip was imprinted with the name of the race and the date: "1992 Hooters 500, November 15, 1992." On the other side, the inscription read, "Thanks for the memories, Richard Petty." With 200 wins in 1,184 career starts, Petty had a lot of memories to be thankful for.

NASCAR fans of a certain age look back on that day with awed reverence. Many of those same fans feel that a mysterious baton was passed that day from the king of NASCAR to the new prince, Jeff Gordon. When you look back at Jeff's 22 years of triumphant racing and how he has acted as NASCAR's ambassador of growth and popularity, in a manner similar to Richard Petty, you have to feel like the sport of stock car racing has been kept in good hands.

Certainly, the departure of Richard Petty created a vacuum in NASCAR racing, but there was another void that needed to be filled— the spiritual hole in Jeff's heart. Whether Hendrick or Petty or anyone else around the sport understood it at the time, Jeff was also on a spiritual journey that would send him into a higher orbit as well.

"I'M JUST A CHRISTIAN"

What does it mean to believe in God?

Sounds like a simple enough question, but in 1992, Jeff wasn't sure he knew the answer, although he says he had some sort of faith. Jeff didn't grow up going to church or subscribing to any kind of religion. At the same time, way back there in his mind was a belief in God.

Not until Jeff began racing in the Busch Series did he start to sort through exactly what he believed about God. He starting sticking around for the short chapel services that followed the mandatory drivers' meetings, and he met some Christian drivers there. This habit carried over to his rookie season in the Winston Cup as well. "I started paying more attention," he said.

As a result, Jeff became friends with fellow driver Bobby Hillin Jr., a 10-year racing veteran. In 1992, early in his NASCAR career, Bobby became a Christian after driver Lake Speed invited him to a Bible study that met in the hotel room next to his. Bobby accepted Christ that night, and everything about him changed. Even the guys around the garage noticed the difference in him.

Jeff also got to know Darrell Waltrip, who was a very unpopular driver before he became a Christian in 1988. Waltrip got together with Lake Speed and Max Helton to found the Motor Racing Outreach ministry.

Years later, when Jeff sat down with sportswriter Dave Caldwell to talk about his faith, he also mentioned Max Helton as being important. "He was a big influence on me. I admired him . . . he never really was pushing people. He just very subtly would talk to me about God," Jeff said.

Then Jeff met Brooke Sealy, who became his wife in 1994. Having a relationship with Christ and attending church were important to her, and she wanted that to be important to the man she married. Jeff said he could ask her questions that he couldn't ask anyone else, and from there, his faith grew and grew until he committed his life to Christ. Shortly before he married Brooke, Jeff was baptized in the same church as his fiancée.

Jeff has never expected all of NASCAR's fans, or the world, to comprehend his faith or how he lives it out. He succinctly says, "I'm just a Christian." He understands if some fans don't get it. He still remembers his reaction when his sister Kim told him she had become a born-again Christian. This was six or seven years before his own conversion, and he laughed at her when she announced her newfound faith. "I told her she was crazy," he said in an interview with *Stock Car Racing* magazine. "I really thought she was nuts."

Jeff's testimony, which is posted at jeffgordon.com, includes a section of him sharing about the significant role God and prayer play in his life:

> I welcomed God into my life a few years ago, and I regret that I did not do it sooner. Embracing this faith has made a tremendous difference in my life and my overall well-being.
>
> I know that through the good times and bad times, He is always there for me. Racing is a very tough and dangerous sport, and I rely on Him to keep me safe and overcome adversity.
>
> I think life is more than just about winning and losing,

and God helps to remind me of what is important in setting priorities for my life. I am very fortunate to have had such an amazing life, and I am very blessed to be able to share it with my wonderful wife and precious daughter [and son].

We all have to experience our own spiritual journey. But if you embrace God's power, I believe you will live your life with a renewed joy and a heightened sense of fulfillment.

WITH PURPOSE ON THE TRACK

On the track, Jeff is known as a winner and a champion. After winning the Winston Cup Rookie of the Year award in 1993, Jeff and the #24 team, with primary sponsor Dupont, started winning plenty of individual races. By the end of the 2001 season, at the age of 30, Jeff had collected 55 wins. Only Richard Petty had more wins by that age, with 60 to his credit.

In 2007, at Phoenix International Raceway, Jeff recorded his 76th win, tying him with Dale Earnhardt Sr. The next week, he surpassed Earnhardt by winning for the 77th time. Jeff won two more times the next year. He currently holds third place in the all-times wins list, but it's highly unlikely that he'll even get within a sniff of Richard Petty's 200 trips to Victory Lane or catch David Pearson with 105 wins. Earlier in Jeff's career, some commentators thought he was on pace to pass Petty's mark, but that one appears out of reach.

But Jeff Gordon is the greatest driver still racing today. His NASCAR winning began in 1994 when he started from the pole for the Coca-Cola 600 in Charlotte and went on to win the marathon-type race handily. Two months later, Jeff and the team won for the second time.

On August 4, 1994, Jeff turned 23 years old and was at home in Indiana. But he wasn't home just to celebrate a birthday; he was also home for the inaugural running of the Brickyard 400 at Indianapolis Motor Speedway on August 6. Jeff started in third position and battled all day, mostly from the lead. The "Rainbow Warriors," as his crew was famously branded, had the #24 multicolored Chevrolet transformed into a wild horse that would not be tamed. Jeff led in 93 of the 160 race laps, including the white-flag final lap that took him to the checkered flag for the victory. The Indiana boy heard the fans in his home state speedway erupt for him.

On that day, Jeff made history as the winner of the first stock car race run at the famed Indy car track, home to the Indy 500. Since then, he's won at Indy three more times—in 1998, 2001, and 2004.

Heading into the 1995 season, Jeff, Rick Hendrick, and crew chief Ray Evernham found themselves answering a lot of questions about young guns paying their dues. Those questions about Jeff's youth and inexperience surfaced time and time again as the season progressed. Even as the team kept winning, the media skepticism kept coming.

It wasn't like they were cheating. They were just dominant. They logged 23 Top-10 and 17 Top-5 finishes, with seven victories—in Rockingham, Atlanta, Bristol, Daytona, Loudon, Darlington, and Dover. In the spring race at Bristol in 1995, they began what turned out to be a four-year winning streak. The same pattern emerged in the fall race at Darlington. From 1995 through 1998, #24 never lost in those two places.

THE "BOO BIRDS" ARE OUT

When you're winning often in NASCAR—or finishing in the back of the pack, for that matter—chances are someone will slap a nickname on you. Most nicknames describe a personality quirk or some intrinsic ability. Thanks to Dale Earnhardt, Jeff became known as "Wonder Boy."

Jeff has also been given a number of unflattering nicknames that can't be reprinted here. Those nicknames came from a number of NASCAR diehards known as the "Boo-Birds."

Their motivation was simple—they couldn't stand Jeff winning race after race. They were fans of other drivers, and with Jeff in the starting grid, their favorite drivers didn't stand as good a chance at winning. So they made a sport out of hating Jeff. The "Boo-Birds" showed up at tracks holding signs saying things like "Anything but Jeff," and they would boo Jeff lap after lap. Other times, he would pass the grandstands and receive one-finger salutes. They weren't hailing him as No. 1.

When the 1995 season finale, the NAPA 500 in Atlanta, rolled around, Jeff was in a position where all he needed to do to win the season championship was to lead for one lap—or to have one driver drop out of the race. Both happened. After three hours of racing, Dale Earnhardt burned rubber into Victory Lane, while Jeff was taking his victory lap for winning the championship.

For the rest of the decade, the winning ways continued for Jeff and his #24 team. In 1996, they missed winning the championship by 37 points but amassed 24 Top-10 and 21 Top-5 finishes, along with 10 wins. That included a three-race win streak in September.

During the next two seasons, Jeff and his team won back-to-back titles. The 1997 season began with Jeff winning his first Daytona 500. At season's end, the championship was in reach for Dale Jarrett, Mark Martin, and Jeff, who needed to finish the final race better than 18th to win the title. He qualified slow and got involved in a fender bender during practice, resulting in a 37th-place starting spot. With his main car wrecked, he needed to drive his backup car on race day.

But Jeff didn't dwell on the setbacks; instead, he ran hard. Around and around he went, elbowing his way through the pack. He was 30th, then 25th, and then 20th as the race neared the end. With one final spurt of great driving, Jeff passed three more cars and finished in 17th place to clinch the championship.

Spring at Bristol and fall at Darlington were pretty much counted on as wins for '98. But did anyone think Jeff and his team would win another eleven races that year to tie Richard Petty's record of 13 wins in a season? That's what the Rainbow Warriors and Wonder Boy accomplished. Along the way, they won four in a row and finished in the Top 10 in 28 of the 33 total races. They won the season championship in '98 by more than 350 points. Before heading into the winter off-season, Jeff won the final two races of the season. That success spilled over into 1999, when he won the Daytona 500 for the second time.

Changes came to the #24 team in 1999. Crew chief Ray Evernham planned to leave the team at season's end. To fill the vacancy, the team hired Robbie Loomis, the former crew chief of Richard Petty. The team sputtered through an adjustment period, but they soon meshed like a synchronized gear box.

By 2001, Jeff and the rest of the team were contenders for the Winston Cup crown. With back-to-back second-place finishes in early spring, then back-to-back first-place finishes in June, Jeff took over the top spot in the standings from Dale Jarrett.

Like any good champion, Jarrett hung around, and the two stars were tied with 2,515 points midway through the season. They stayed tied for another week when they finished one-two in Loudon, New Hampshire. But then Jeff put together another set of back-to-back wins, at Indianapolis and Watkins Glen, which gave him sole possession of the top spot in the points standings as the drivers headed into the last race—the Napa 500 in Atlanta. Still at stake was the 2001 NASCAR season championship.

On Sunday, November 18, 2001, after attending chapel with Robbie Loomis and several other drivers, Jeff returned to his transporter and changed into his race suit. With driver introductions just 30 minutes away, he stretched and grabbed some lunch. Before the introductions, Jeff gathered the team together to go over any last-minute issues. Then he led the group in a short prayer and a chant.

A chant?

That's what Jeff calls the cheer the team has memorized. It's usually a word or a short phrase "that represents something we've worked at or a goal we're striving to accomplish at a particular track." For the 2001 NAPA 500, the chant was, "Finish the job!"

Once he was strapped into his custom-fit seat by a six-point harness, Jeff went through a series of routine steps that he has down to a science. He locked his steering wheel onto the steering column, then checked a series of switches. About 15 seconds before the public address announcer called out, "And now for the greatest words in all of sports . . ." he hit the battery switch to get the electrical system up and running.

Then Jeff flipped four more switches: tachometer switch, voltmeter switch, crank switch, and then when he heard the announcer's directive—"Gentlemen, start your engines!"—he flipped the final switch, which started the car's motor.

It's cliché to say it, but it's also accurate: when 43 drivers fire their engines at the same time, it sounds like thunder. "I think it is the sweetest sound in the world," Jeff says.

Jeff ran the race hard but soon realized he probably didn't have a winning car that day. He thought he had a Top-10 car, but not a winner. So he practiced what he learned from Dale Earnhardt Sr., who said, "Bring it to the house."

Bound up in that short phrase is the idea that there is no sense pushing a car too hard if it isn't capable of winning the race; it would be better to just finish and get the points. If you don't follow this simple advice, you could find yourself in a wreck, or damage your car and be towed into the pits, thereby losing a lot of points. By driving conservatively, Jeff finished sixth that day and wrapped up his fourth championship.

FAME SETTLES IN

In 2005, when NBC News producer Alice Rhee was researching an article about the faith seen in NASCAR drivers, she happened to witness Robbie Loomis and Jeff sitting in the front row of a chapel service. She approached Robbie and inquired about the practice, and he told her, "It doesn't matter what level of talent you have, you're not going to get success without God blessing you to get it."

A few months earlier, Jeff had won his third Daytona 500, which quieted the "Boo Birds." Or maybe they were just outnumbered—Jeff and the #24 team had a considerably larger fan base by then. Probably the largest contributing factor to this growth was Jeff's consistency. He wasn't just posting great results race after race, but he was also an ambassador for the sport. He was everywhere, doing everything—taking interviews, signing autographs, shaking hands, and gathering fans to NASCAR.

Analysts credit Jeff's influence for attracting an inestimable number of fans to NASCAR. His impact on the sport has broadened the appeal of NASCAR racing far beyond the Deep South. He wasn't just filling the trophy case at Hendrick Motor Sports headquarters, but he was filling the seats at dirt tracks and speedways across the country. There were little kids who wanted to be like Jeff Gordon, and there were women who watched just because Jeff was young, attractive, and well spoken. And there were diehard fans who encouraged their friends to watch him race—simply because seeing Jeff win time and time again was a hoot.

In 2006, Jeff married again, this time to Ingrid Vandebosch, whom he had met four years earlier. Jeff kept his relationship with Ingrid quieter and more private than he had his relationship with his first wife—a lesson learned out of experience. (He and Brooke had an acrimonious divorce that finalized in 2003.)

Jeff's dominance continued in 2007. He finished in the Top 10 in 30 out of 36 races—unheard of in NASCAR. He also raced to Top-10 finishes in 10 straight races. Sure, he'd accomplished or bettered that feat two times earlier in his career, but that was before NASCAR had more than 75 million fans coast to coast.

Something else happened for NASCAR while Jeff was dominating the sport: he paved the way for other young drivers to get good rides. He changed the demographics of NASCAR; the prototypical driver could now be younger than 30 years old. And it was even cool if they wanted to display their faith as proudly as they did their corporate logos.

WITH PURPOSE AWAY FROM THE TRACK

Jeff wasn't the first race car driver to share his faith from a NASCAR stage and won't be the last, but he certainly has had a lot of fans closely watching him over the years.

Knowing this, he made this statement early in his career:

Racing is important to me. It is an important part of my career, but I really don't know what I would do without the Lord in my life . . . It really has made a big difference, not only on the race track but off the race track. I mean, it's a dangerous sport that we're in out there, and it's not really whether you win or lose on the race track, it's whether you win or lose with the Lord. I've come to realize there is a far greater place; there are so many bigger goals for me to set out there than just whether or not I win this race or that race or win a championship.

That coveted fifth NASCAR season championship still eludes Jeff, but he has reached some of his "many bigger goals." Even though his best seasons are likely in the past, it still seems like Jeff is bigger than ever and everywhere in the media. Newspaper and magazine writers still write often about him and his family, and he keeps himself busy doing television commercials for his sponsors and the companies he endorses. He must be one busy guy, because it's estimated that 75 percent of his earnings come off the track.

As mentioned before, Jeff frequently makes the rounds of the late-night and daytime talk shows. He's even "gone Hollywood"—he appeared in the 2005 Disney movie *Herbie: Fully Loaded,* and in 2011 he got behind the mic for a cameo role in *Cars 2.*

But what really turns Jeff's starting crank these days is his charitable foundation, named the Jeff Gordon Children's Foundation, which supports children battling cancer and funds programs for medical research.

Early in his career, Jeff got behind organizations such as Make-a-Wish and March of Dimes, but his inspiration to start his own foundation came in 1992, when Ray Evernham's 11-month-old son was diagnosed with leukemia. Jeff established his foundation in hopes of helping children facing critical illness to realize their dreams. The foundation has raised more than $11 million to date.

Jeff is also a spokesman for the Jeff Gordon Children's Hospital in Concord, North Carolina. For his efforts, the Boy Scouts of America named him the 2009 Silver Buffalo Award winner for distinguished service to youth.

Jeff reaches out to help children on one end of the social spectrum and seniors on the other. In 2011, he teamed with the AARP Foundation's "Drive to End Hunger" campaign among elder Americans. The AARP also became his car's primary sponsor that year.

In 2013, Jeff's #24 teamed with Alan Gustafson as crew chief and raced in the all-new Generation-6 Chevy SS in search of that coveted fifth championship.

Although the results were not similar to his glory years, millions of eyes were still watching Jeff Gordon racing hard around the track.

8

MICHAEL WALTRIP:
TIMING IS EVERYTHING

"God's season is the best season," wrote John Bunyan, the 17th-century preacher and writer. "God has set aside a time for every purpose."

Bunyan's words echo those of Ecclesiastes 3:1 (NASB): "There is an appointed time for everything. And there is a time for every event under heaven." As the men featured in this book would likely tell you, this verse would include every NASCAR race, every win and every loss, every wreck, and every near miss for every driver, every time.

Michael Waltrip, a two-time Daytona 500 winner and owner and part-time driver of his own racing team, can attest to that. After winning the season-opening truck race at Daytona in 2011, he proclaimed, "I believe in God. I believe in Jesus. I believe everything happens for a reason." Michael has said similar words after other races, many times. *God has His reasons, His timing.*

The 2014 season marked Michael's 30th year in NASCAR, and from year to year and race to race, Michael has seen God's plan for his life unfold in ways he could never have predicted.

In addition to doing his job as a race car driver well, Michael's ultimate purpose is to let people know what it means to be a Christian. "As I grew up, I learned more about the Bible," Michael said, "and I learned more about a personal relationship with Jesus Christ. I prayed, asking Him to come into my heart and forgive me of my sins, and now we walk this field together."

Whether Michael is lining up in the field of 43 cars, or whether he is managing Michael Waltrip Racing from his desk, he's convinced that he's right where God wants him. But God's plan and purpose haven't always been easy for Michael to discern or embrace. On a number of occasions, Michael has questioned God as to why certain things have happened in his life.

In a few key areas, Michael has failed big-time. He's been embroiled in controversy, and he's had other drivers angry at him. Yet no matter how rough the road has been, he has held fast to his faith.

Those who hold to what Bunyan, the author of Ecclesiastes, and Michael believe—that everything happens in the life of a believer for a reason—know that however gut-wrenching, tear-jerking, and faith-testing life's circumstances may be, God has His hand on the wheel.

With that in mind, Michael's life story can be an encouragement to us all.

CREATING OPPORTUNITIES

Margaret and Leroy Waltrip were living in Owensboro, Kentucky, when Margaret discovered she was pregnant with the couple's "little surprise"—a fifth child. At the time, Leroy worked 10 or more hours a day at the Pepsi bottling plant, while Margaret worked as a part-time clerk at a local grocery store. Their baby, Michael, was born on April 30, 1963.

Sixteen years separated Michael from his oldest brother, Darrell—quite a gap for a pair of siblings. To this day, Michael still remembers having to stay home with his mom while Darrell—an up-and-coming driver—and his dad went to the races. "Man, that killed me," Michael said. "I wanted to be at the races, too."

Once in a while, Michael got to tag along with Dad and big brother, and what he saw and heard at the track "made me fall in love with NASCAR." When Michael was nine years old, his older brother began to race in NASCAR's Winston Cup Series, and soon after, Michael decided he wanted to be a race car driver, too.

Michael was a huge fan of *Stock Car Racing* magazine. He read and reread the feature stories on the drivers a dozen times over and studied the glossy color pictures until he became familiar with every driver's number and car color scheme. "Every month," Michael remembers, "there was a fold-out poster of a driver and his car in the center of the magazine." Those colorful posters covered his bedroom walls, including one of his brother—and his hero—Darrell.

Occasionally on Sundays, Michael's mom would drive the younger kids an hour out of town where they could pick up the radio station that carried the NASCAR races. Once they could get the static-filled station tuned in clearly, they'd pull over on the side of the road and listen. Those were the days before cable TV and iPhone apps, so that's what they had to do to keep up with Darrell's racing career—at least when they couldn't see the races in person.

The radio broadcasts, magazine articles, and sporadic TV highlights on the local news fueled Michael's imagination about someday following in his brother's footsteps and becoming a racer himself.

First, though, Michael needed to figure out an actual plan to make his dream a reality. His parents had already been through the whole racing venture once with Darrell, and they weren't interested, or financially able, to go through the gauntlet again. So Michael called on his big-time racing brother for advice and support. But instead of immediately telling Michael he'd do anything to help him fulfill his dream, Darrell looked at his younger brother and said, "You're wasting your time, Mikey."

That was a huge blow for a youngster still in elementary school. All Mikey, as his family sometimes affectionately called him, was looking to do was drive a go-kart. But everywhere he turned, doors slammed in his face.

This turned out to be a teachable moment for Michael, a time when he would learn about God's support through bad times.

If Dad and Mom couldn't help out, and if his big brother told him he was wasting his time, then he would have to find someone else to help him race. Michael eventually asked his other brother Bobby about letting him race in his go-kart. Bobby, the middle Waltrip boy, was set on pursuing a racing career in go-karting.

"Sure, I'll help you," Bobby replied.

Michael's first race in Bobby's kart was at the old Smyrna Speedway in Smyrna, Tennessee. Michael was nervous about the race and didn't sleep well the night before, but when the race went green, the 11-year-old was ready. So was his brother's kart—it proved faster than the rest of the field. But after watching Darrell, and after being a NASCAR fan his whole life, Michael knew that fast wheels were only half the game. The other half of the winning equation was up to the driver. Michael proved he had the Waltrip genes for driving when he won his first go-kart race convincingly, taking home a trophy to Owensboro.

Michael raced karts for several more years. Then, in 1981, when Michael was 18, he moved into stock cars, at first racing Mini-Modifieds. He got into this area of racing independently with a friend named Kerry.

Then Michael's dad—taking advantage of some connections at work—hooked up Michael and Kerry with Pepsi as a sponsor. The boys took the opportunity to paint their car to look a lot like his famous brother Darrell's #11 Mountain Dew car. For Michael's first race with Pepsi, he and Kerry hauled their Mercury Capri to Kentucky Motor Speedway and got it ready for a 25-lap main event.

The cars started, and Michael surged to an early lead. He was racing mostly against veteran drivers, and with only a few laps to go another driver passed him. Michael reacted quickly, swerved past the lead car, and tore off down the track toward the checkered flag. "My first big win on my first night out," Michael recalled. "And I had to conquer a giant to do it."

Michael's persistence and dedication paid off that season. At Kentucky Motor Speedway later that year, he became the Mini-Modified division track champion.

EVERYTHING FOR A PURPOSE: WINNING AND LOSING

Soon after Michael graduated from high school, he began renting an apartment with a friend. He hoped to simply keep on winning and earn a ride in the Dash Series, the smaller division of NASCAR. Race after race, Michael piled up win after win. And winning fit perfectly with his plan to move up one more rung on the NASCAR ladder.

The Dash Series, which has since evolved into the International Sport Compact Auto Racing Series (ISCARS), is considered the "entry level" to NASCAR, much like minor league baseball is to the big leagues. The Dash Series was (and still is) a viable way for a driver to work his way toward a full-time NASCAR career.

In 1983, 20-year-old Michael won the NASCAR Dash Series championship. The future looked bright. He'd won championships at every level of racing he tried and believed he'd be joining his brother in the upper echelon of NASCAR within a short time. All he needed to do was stick to his plan: move up to the Busch Series (the Nationwide Series today) and use that as a stepping stone to the big time—the Winston Cup (the Sprint Cup today).

But the next year, Michael's plan didn't progress as he had hoped. "I really didn't have any opportunities to race much," he said about the 1984 season. With time on his hands, Michael moved to North Carolina and got a job working on race cars. While in the shop, he made a connection that would eventually put him back on track . . . with none other than the King himself—Richard Petty. Michael had gone to work for Petty Enterprises, and Richard and his wife, Lynda, took a liking to him. In the fall of '84, they offered to rent him a room.

This was Michael's big break. The advice and guidance this First Couple of NASCAR gave Michael while he sat in their living room was instrumental in preparing him for a future in racing.

One day, sitting in his comfy recliner, Richard asked Michael what he hoped would come next for him. Michael talked about the success he'd enjoyed the past couple of years . . . as well as the difficulty he'd had finding a ride for the NASCAR Busch Series.

Richard's advice was surprising. He told Michael to skip the next logical step in his well-thought-out plan and not mess with the Busch Series. Instead, the King suggested that Michael shoot for the top. "If you want to be a Winston Cup driver," Petty said, "go get yourself a Winston Cup car. If that's where you're going to wind up, you don't need to waste all your time racing in cars that aren't your ultimate goal. Go find a ride and see if you can make something happen."

Michael listened to Richard that fall day and changed course. With Richard's help, Michael made some key connections over the next few months. By the start of the summer of 1985, Michael had himself a Winston Cup ride.

On Memorial Day, Michael found himself in his debut race. He would be driving in Charlotte's Coca-Cola World 600, behind the wheel of a car owned by Dick Bahre. Dick operated on a small-scale budget that he managed with a heart of gold.

Not only was Michael in the major leagues, but he would also be racing against his big brother. It might sound strange, but Darrell and Michael didn't know each other that well at the time, mostly because of the many years between them. But they were still brothers as they lined up on the starting grid.

Darrell started in the second row, on the outside of Geoffrey Bodine and behind pole leader Bill Elliott and Harry Gant. Michael was much farther back, in the twelfth row, starting 24th.

Bill Elliott and his sleek Thunderbird were a considerable force in '85, winning the Daytona 500 and the Winston 500 at Talladega leading up to the Coca-Cola 600. (Indeed, when Bill won the Southern 500 later that season, he collected a $1 million bonus check for winning three of the four major races. Fellow drivers called him "Million Dollar Bill" after that.)

Harry Gant took the lead from Darrell on lap 278. Darrell had already led for 76 laps, and he went on to reclaim the lead and win the race after battling Gant, Bobby Allison, and Dale Earnhardt. Michael, on the other hand, left the race after lap 278 with a busted transmission.

Michael basically won gas money in his Winston Cup debut—$2,050 for his 28th-place finish. For taking the checkered flag, Darrell took home $90,733. In fact, what Darrell earned at the Coca-Cola 600 was almost 10 times what Michael would earn for the five races he would run in Dick Bahre's car during the '85 season.

What Michael didn't know after his debut race was that winning a race at the Winston Cup level would be a long, long time coming. He was about to watch 16 Februarys pass by and burn through 16 hot summers of racing without making the turn into Victory Lane.

THE "O-FER" TAG

Michael had no problem putting his 1985 season behind him—it was only five races. That year, Darrell won the million-dollar payout for winning the NASCAR series championship.

In 1986, Michael was deemed a NASCAR rookie and ran a full-time schedule with a new car owner, Chuck Rider. His results were nothing to write home about, although his two 11th-place finishes placed him second for the Rookie of the Year award. As the 1987 Daytona 500 rolled around, Michael hoped to build on his rookie season, but not much happened for him during his sophomore year.

In 1988, Michael tasted the high life momentarily by breaking into the Top Five at Pocono International Raceway in Long Pond, Pennsylvania. His second-place finish was his highest to date—and it would be his highest finish for the next 13 years.

Darrell owned a Busch Series car in 1988, and that year he suggested to his little brother that he race in NASCAR's lower series races—the series Richard Petty had advised him to drive past five years earlier. This time around, Michael's comfort level at taking advice was higher because of his brother's involvement, plus he knew he needed more race day experience near the front of the field.

"A plan is important," Michael says, "but you have to be ready, willing, and able to see opportunity when it comes along. Don't skip it just because it isn't on your checklist. It might be what is necessary for you to continue on down the road."

Michael won in his fourth start at Dover, and 11 of his 16 career NASCAR wins would come in Busch or Nationwide races. Some of his most violent wrecks would come at the second-tier level as well.

The wreck that stands out in most people's memories occurred at Bristol in 1990. Michael was driving high on the track right before getting ushered into a concrete barrier head on. His Pontiac was virtually sawed in half on impact, and it looked like Michael had bought the farm. Fans and pit crews alike feared that no one could have survived such a violent wreck.

Darrell—who wasn't racing until the next day—immediately sprang from the pits and sprinted to the car. He and several first responders yanked off the shredded shell and dug through the wreckage to find his brother. There were some long, anxious moments, but Michael was all right. Darrell's first words after seeing that Michael had survived were, "Praise God, he's alive!"

When a visibly distraught Darrell was interviewed on TV 10 minutes later, he said, "I walked up there, and the car was gone and everything. The roll cage was all bowed up. I looked at him, and he looked at me and winked, so Mom, Dad, he's a Waltrip. He's got a pretty hard head."

Most commentators agreed that Michael should never have survived such a horrific wreck. That Michael stayed safely tucked inside his roll cage meant that NASCAR engineers had done their job right. The wreck brought the Waltrip brothers closer. From that day forward, they viewed each other in a different light. Life, and their relationship, was more precious to the both of them.

Somewhere between the Winston Cup losses and the Busch Series wrecks, Michael had time to meet and court Elizabeth "Buffy" Franks. In 1993, Michael stood in Victory Circle at Bristol for a Busch win, and Buffy stood beside him. On that day, Michael let the viewing public know that Buffy was his girlfriend and that he intended to marry her someday. Moments later, after an interviewer inquired whether that would happen any time soon, Michael turned to Buffy and got down on one knee to propose. The couple married on November 27, 1993.

CHUGGING ALONG

With the possible exception of a racer like Jeff Gordon, most drivers will change owners sometime during their career. Michael's stint driving for Chuck Rider lasted through the 1995 season. In 1996, he went to work driving the famous #21 Wood Brothers car. Michael struggled to find an identity as a Nextel Cup driver (the series' name from 2003–07), but folks in the know were talking about him and watching him tough things out. Michael had some shining moments during that era, and in familiar Michael Waltrip fashion, he shared them with the fans.

For NASCAR aficionados, one of the shining moments of every season is the All-Star weekend in Charlotte every May. Packed with racing and street fair excitement, the All-Star weekend flows right into Coca-Cola 600, held a week later on Memorial Weekend on the same track in Charlotte. With two consecutive weekends of racing to enjoy, many NASCAR fans take advantage of the holiday and stick around the entire week.

In 1996, the annual All-Star race was called the Winston Select, which was the main event of the weekend and paid the winner over $200,000. "Select" meant that not all drivers were eligible to race. Historically, only race winners ran in the All-Star race and got a shot at the big money.

On some occasions, however, NASCAR has made exceptions by changing the rules. For example, the rules in 2013 held that drivers were eligible for the All-Star race if they had won a race since the previous year's All-Star race, were a past NASCAR Cup Champion, had placed first or second in the qualifying race earlier in the day (known as the Sprint Showdown), or won a fan vote. After Ricky Stenhouse Jr. finished second in the Showdown and Danica Patrick captured the fan vote, both joined the field of race winners.

Changes in NASCAR rules happen more often than you might think. Sometimes a rule stays the same from one year to the next, but other rules—like NASCAR safety developments—change regularly to enhance the sport. Rules for All-Star eligibility vary year to year—sometimes insignificantly, sometimes much more noticeably—because NASCAR wants to keep the race fresh and exciting. Some fans like the changes, but some don't.

Even with this history for NASCAR, the rules for 1996 stand as an anomaly in All-Star race history. Why? Because the 50-lap qualifying race called the Winston Open had a field of 36 that year. Win that race, and you automatically joined the main event, the Winston Select.

In the Winston Open, Michael started sixth in the Wood Brothers car. He didn't lead a single lap, so of course he didn't win (he finished fifth). But the anomaly was this: for 1996, NASCAR rules stated that the

Top-5 finishers in the Winston Open qualified for the Winston Select. The rules change meant the last possible entry spot for the main event belonged to Michael.

The 70-lap Winston Select ran under the lights of the Charlotte Motor Speedway. Most drivers love running under bright lights because they can see so well. And since Michael's debut race had been at the superspeedway, he had it marked as his favorite. Michael, however, started dead last, making him the underdog of underdogs. Although he hadn't won a race in 309 starts, he didn't mind lining up with guys who had won plenty.

Lined up in front of him were NASCAR's biggest winners. If he could have seen the front of the line, he would have recognized Jeff Gordon's rainbow-colored Chevrolet. He could have counted off drivers like Dale Earnhardt Sr., Rusty Wallace, Mark Martin, the Labonte brothers (Terry and Bobby), the Burton Brothers (Ward and Jeff), and his brother Darrell, who was up in ninth.

The race began, and Michael drove as hard as he could. With 10 laps to go, he had worked his way up to an astonishing fourth place behind Earnhardt, Wallace, and Terry Labonte. Then Michael found a groove and passed Wallace on the outside. He took dead aim at Earnhardt and hugged the Intimidator's bumper until his rival got a little loose going into the turn. When Earnhardt floated up the bank, Michael reacted by hitting the boosters to zip by #3 on the inside line and take over the lead.

The lead!

Of the All-Stars race!

For the next several laps, Michael fought off Earnhardt and Wallace. Michael's car ran so well that he forged a 20-car gap going into the last lap. Just a mile and a half to go . . . and plenty of gas in the tank.

Michael circled again, and then the checkered flag was his. In Victory Lane, Darrell gave his little brother a big hug. Then a TNN Motor Sports pit reporter, Glenn Jarrett, thrust a microphone in front of Michael's chin and asked him what this moment was like after years of never winning. After saying how excited he was and thanking the fans, Michael blurted, "I'm building my Mom and Daddy a house!"

Michael had wanted his parents to move to his hometown of Sherrills Ford, North Carolina, and the winner's check of $211,200 would more than cover the cost of building them a house next to his. The interview closed with Jarrett commenting on the magnitude of the win for the Wood Brothers, whose last win at Charlotte came in 1987, and reminding viewers that Michael was the first driver from a qualifying race to win the Winston Select.

After Jarrett's last comments, in an ever-so-slight but soberly poignant moment, Michael looked away from the reporter, then straight back to his eyes and said: "But I still ain't won a race, have I?"

Michael smiled, gave a halfhearted chuckle about his own condition, and turned away from the interview into more congratulatory embraces. Jarrett tried to add a redeeming quality to the sting in Michael's words by saying that the Winston Select victory was the first of what would surely be many wins in the Winston Cup Series.

Michael had stated the technical truth. Even though winning the All-Star was an incredibly difficult thing to do, the race had never counted toward a Cup Series championship. Michael may have earned his first career win in dramatic fashion, going from underdog to top dog, but the Winston Select was the shortest race of the season and not a regular season race. Michael was still in the never-having-won-a-major-series-race doghouse.

LOSS AFTER LOSS

If you think Michael used his Winston Select victory on All-Star weekend as a springboard to Victory Lane, think again. A string of losses followed, as did some other nasty Busch Series wrecks—notably, back-to-back season-opening wrecks at Daytona.

Michael wrecked horribly at Daytona in 1999. His Band-Aid–sponsored car hit the wall square on. A split-second later, another car sandwiched him. Though battered, Michael walked away, needing just a few Band-Aids for the scrapes.

Later that year, at Bristol, with his dad watching from a track suite, Michael finished second. That second-place finish looked good on paper but actually crushed his spirit.

Remember the house Michael said he was going to build for his mom and dad with his All-Star winnings? He followed through on his word, and the new home was constructed. But before his parents could move from Owensboro to Sherrills Ford, Michael got word that his dad had lung cancer.

For Michael, his father's life-threatening disease was all the more reason to bring his parents to the Tar Heel State. Beyond the family support, a move to North Carolina meant his dad could see more of his races while undergoing treatment.

The father-son bond had grown stronger over the years. Michael had felt that he didn't have a very close relationship with his dad, who had been vitally involved with Darrell's racing career. But when Michael was around 11, he and Leroy started spending more time together, and their relationship grew closer. That enduring bond was extremely important to Michael, which was one reason why he had been thinking about building a house for his parents.

At Bristol in August '99, Michael finished second for what seemed like the umpteenth time. His dad was in the grandstands that afternoon. The mounting frustration caused him to direct questions to the heavens: *Why? Why, God? Why couldn't You let me win this one for Dad?*

There was urgency in Michael's conversation with the Lord. Leroy Waltrip was getting weaker. His 30-month battle against the cancerous cells swirling in his body was taking its toll, and he was losing weight and strength. Michael knew his father was wasting away. Some days were better than others, and Michael was hoping the race in Bristol would be a big breakthrough. That's why he wanted so badly to win the race.

For his dad—just once.

It was God's grace, working through his dad's reaction to his second-place finish, that rescued Michael. His dad told him he did an "amazing job" and that his day would come.

Michael's transparency and honesty before God should be an encouragement to believers today. Afterward, Michael wrote words that could have come from the book of Job: "I hate when I question God's grace and mercy. I don't have any answers. Who do I think I am?"

A couple weeks later, at another Busch Series race, Michael got what he wanted most. That day in Charlotte, he started his Band-Aid car in the back, but by race's end he was in the lead. He drove skillfully, and his cause was helped when several other drivers ran out of fuel. For the first time in a long, long while, the checkered flag was his. Michael was able to say, "Thank you, God, for allowing my dad to enjoy this win."

At the 2000 season-opener at Daytona, Michael wrecked badly on lap 101 of the 120-lap race when another driver tapped—*tapped* at 200 mph—the right bumper of his Band-Aid car. Michael skidded into a slide that ended abruptly when the back of his car took off like a helicopter before coming back to earth and bouncing into a barrel roll. After five high bounces, Michael and the car were ready for their final landing. First, the front bumper bashed down, then the back bumper smashed down. A fulcrum of air kept the middle of the car suspended. Like a teeter-totter, the car went back and forth two times—bash, smash, bash, smash—and then stopped in a heap of dust and smoke on four flat tires. Michael's day was over. Incredibly, he again walked away from a frightening crash unscathed.

The barrel rolls happened on Saturday during the Busch Series race. The following day, a Sunday, was the granddaddy of motor racing—the much-anticipated 42nd running of the Daytona 500. The previous year, Michael had finished a strong fifth in the race, but he never cracked the Top 10 for the rest of the season. He hoped the 2000 Daytona 500 would be his breakout race and give the family a ray of hope.

You see, Leroy Waltrip wasn't present that day. This would be the first time in 22 years that the senior Waltrip missed a Daytona 500. The 76-year-old World War II veteran's three-year battle with cancer ended a month before the race on January 10, 2000, when he passed away in Michael's arms. Michael resolved to one day win a Winston Cup race and thereby honor the memory of his father.

Michael rolled off the starting grid in the 10th position for the '00 Daytona 500. Darrell, in his final 500—he had announced that he would be retiring at the end of the season after 29 years of racing—was feeling the weight of his father's death as well as his poor start position in last place. With 10 of the 200 laps to go, Michael was running 17th. On lap 192, several cars spun out of control in turn 4 with Michael dead center of the melee. His recorded finish was 39th.

Another day, another wreck, and another loss brought his total Winston Cup losing streak to 429.

WHY WINNING ISN'T EVERYTHING

During the two worst years of his career, 1999 and 2000, Michael's faith held him together like nothing else could. He said in one interview, "I want to win, but my life doesn't hinge on whether I do or not. Through my faith, I have an inner peace. I have a lot of things in my life figured out because of my faith. I'm thankful to God for putting me where I am today."

Michael could certainly have found something else to do in the NASCAR race world. He was a Waltrip, after all, and his last name held connections. But his faith kept him in the center of the sport he loved. Like Abraham, the patriarch of old, Michael believed God had a purpose for him. In Michael's case, that purpose was racing—not managing a car or running a pit crew.

Even though he hadn't won on the biggest stages, Michael never lost confidence in his abilities. It helped that he had strong support from Dale Earnhardt Sr., who had befriended him over the years. After the 2000 season ended, Earnhardt put together a proposal for a car and sponsorship package that included Michael. His hopes ran high as the negotiating process ran its course. Never had this kind of opportunity come his way. If it all worked out, Earnhardt's team would be the biggest and best-funded team he would ever race for.

Toward the end of the deal making, there was a three-day wait. Michael prayed and hoped everything would work out. The package came together, and Michael signed with Dale Earnhardt, Inc. (DEI). Earnhardt's decision turned the talking heads of NASCAR; after all, Michael was winless in well over 400 starts. Skeptics will always be skeptical, but Michael believed what the Man in Black told him: that he would become a winner in a DEI car.

When the 2001 Daytona 500 arrived, Michael was confident he could win, but as fate would have it, that race would turn out to be the most horrible day of his life.

Most of the racing world knows what happened on February 18, 2001. Doing what he loved best, racing hard and constantly charging, Dale Earnhardt Sr. was running third late in the race. His son, Dale Jr., and his friend Michael Waltrip were the only two in front of him, with Michael in the lead.

On the last lap, Dale Sr.'s car was hit slightly. In the blink of an eye, #3 careened into a concrete wall. Up ahead, Michael saw the checkered flag in front of him and Junior safely in his mirror. In a matter of nine seconds, Michael crossed the finish line as victor.

If you've seen the YouTube video, you've heard Darrell Waltrip in his first race as a television color commentator cheer Michael to victory: "Come on man! That a boy! You got 'em Mikey! You got it!"

This is the sort of stuff you can't make up—a legendary driver in the booth for the first time, calling a race in which his younger brother takes the checkered flag for the very first time in his 16 years of racing. After Michael's victory was secure, Darrell, overcome with joy and in tears, said, "My Daddy would be so happy!" The whole scene was punctuated with love—love from one brother to another, and love for a father who had passed away a year earlier but who was never really gone.

In Victory Circle, family, friends, crew, sponsors, media personnel, and Michael's wife, Buffy, surrounded him. "Thank God. Thank my Daddy. I love him so much," Michael exclaimed. He continued by thanking Dale Jr. as a great teammate, and Dale Sr. for believing in him. His final comments wrapped up the joy from Victory Lane:

> *Momma, I love you. Momma, I wish you were here. Golly, if my daddy were here, it would be complete. This is the day the Lord has made. And I'm proud, and I never gave up. You know, you can't win if you give up. I didn't care how many O-fers I*

had. I showed up every Sunday and did my job. And today I
finally won one of these things.

Michael picked a pretty good time to win his first Winston Cup race—
the Daytona 500. The thrill of the victor coursed through his veins.

But then disconcerting news swept through the crowd: Dale
Earnhardt had been rushed to the Halifax Medical Center by ambulance
and was in grave condition. His crash didn't look especially bad, at least
by NASCAR standards—just another collision that crumpled the front
end of his car. He usually walked away from smash-ups like this with an
appreciative wave to the crowd.

What Michael didn't know as he rolled into Victory Lane was that
his close friend and fellow warrior had been killed instantly when his
car hit the wall at approximately 160 miles per hour. Around an hour
after the race, the rumors and whispers circling pit row were confirmed:
the Intimidator was dead.

The human spirit never feels quite right when incredible highs are
followed by the lowest of lows. What happened next is impossible for
anyone but Michael to talk about. In his autobiography, he took his
readers on an extensive journey through his grief following Dale's death.
There was guilt, confusion, darkness, questions, and unfathomable
angst. "Human beings aren't designed to go through the range of
emotions I went through," Waltrip said later.

There is perhaps no better modern writer on the subject of grief
than Christian apologist C.S. Lewis, who lived in Belfast, Ireland,
more than 50 years ago. His book, *A Grief Observed,* is arguably his
best on the subject. His stepson Douglas Gresham said, "This book is
about a man emotionally naked in his own Gethsemane." The same
could be said of the fourth part of Michael's book, *In the Blink of an
Eye,* in which he recounted a time when he found himself emotionally
naked in his own Gethsemane.

Michael's wife, Buffy, was the one who broke the unexpected news
to him. "Dale is dead," she said through her sobbing.

"I reached over and grabbed her," Michael wrote, "and I didn't want to let go. Then she said, 'I'm so sorry, honey. You don't deserve this. Nobody does.' "

Questions always lurk in dark times. Michael stayed up that night asking God his share of questions. But Michael also experienced the Lord's mercy in the aftermath of the grim news. The next morning, he decided that his perspective as a driver for Dale Earnhardt, Inc., a former Daytona 500 winner, and a close friend of Dale's, could help a grieving NASCAR Nation. Michael knew everything happened for a reason. He believed that he could be, and would be, an example of relying on Christ through this time of grief, so as to honor Dale and to bring honor to God.

With Buffy's help, Michael began his mission with a letter addressed to the community of racing fans. In the letter, he shared from the book of Joshua: "Have I not commanded you? Be strong and courageous. Do not be terrified; do not be discouraged, for the Lord your God will be with you wherever you go."

Throughout the racing community, mourning took the form of displayed memorabilia in tribute of the racing legend. Candles and flowers lined roads and race tracks everywhere. Vigils were held. Darrell Waltrip revealed to the press the Bible verse that his wife, Stevie, had stuck on Dale's dashboard for Sunday's race, something she did each week. The scripture was from Proverbs 18:10 (NIV): "The name of the LORD is a fortified tower; the righteous run to it and are safe."

The week after Dale's death, Michael used his platform during a press conference in Rockingham, North Carolina, to play off the verse from 1 Corinthians 15:52 that would later become part of the title of his 2011 book: "In the twinkling of an eye, you are in the presence of the Lord when you die, if you believe," Michael said to the media.

Michael had visible strength about him while in public, but when he was alone, a deep, raw grief haunted him. At home, ghosts of "guilt, self-pity, and anger" scaled his castle wall, raided his family harmony, and robbed him of sleep. What he was sharing with others didn't seem to help him.

What Michael wanted more than anything was to help—and go

back in time when he'd get a friendly slug from Earnhardt or a fatherly hug from his dad. His inability to let go of the past would change his life and eventually factor into Buffy and him separating.

It turned out that Dale Earnhardt's crash caused lots of collateral damage.

LIFE CONTINUES

The NASCAR show must go on. Despite the profound sense of grief he felt over the loss of his friend and boss, Michael kept racing with DEI. Five months later, he was back in Daytona for the Pepsi 400. This time, Dale Jr. finished first and Michael took second, a nice symmetry for fans and the drivers. Michael finished second one more time in 2001—in Homestead, Florida, late in the season. But other than these two Top-5 finishes, Michael wrestled to perform well behind the wheel of the cars that his friend had convinced him he'd win in.

Racing in 2002 looked similar to 2001 for Michael—and actually for his DEI teammate Dale Earnhardt Jr. At the Daytona 500, the defending champ took fifth. Two months later at Talladega Superspeedway, Junior took his fourth career win. Behind him once again, for a second-place finish, was Michael. At the Pepsi 400 in July, Michael started in seventh, and his brother Darrell praised him lavishly, telling Fox Sports viewers how proud he was of him as he drove under the checkered flag for his second Winston Cup victory.

The 2003 season marked 30 years since Michael declared he wanted to be a racer. That year started well and got better. Back at the Daytona 500 in mid-February, Michael became a two-time Daytona 500 winner. Talking to the press following his victory, a race that NASCAR officials had red-flagged for rain after 272.5 miles, Michael thanked God for the "nice rain shower."

Never short with words, he confided to the public, "I prayed for it to rain. I prayed for God to forgive me for the dumb things I do, and to make me a better person, and then I asked for what I wanted, and today, I really wanted some rain." The win gave Michael three wins for his career, and all of them had come at Daytona International Speedway.

Michael's fourth and last Cup Series win to date came at Talladega in September 2003. After starting 18th, he ran his NAPA Chevy to the front of the pack six times, the last time with only eight laps to go. Dale Earnhardt Jr. came in second. The DEI teammates had done it again, a regular one-two punch. Their relationship as teammates lasted two more seasons.

After DEI, Michael got busy on what came next. Toyota wanted to join Sprint Cup racing, and they wanted Michael to take ownership of a three-car team. Toyota would be the car manufacturer backing the team.

Michael agreed. Beginning in 2006, he worked to build Michael Waltrip Racing (MWR) into a force that would be ready for the 2007 season. Everything was done on a grand scale, but at a big cost. Michael confesses freely that, "I wanted to have a team like Dale's."

MWR debts piled up. No one was watching the store, and way more money was going out the door than coming in. By April, Michael and MWR were in serious financial distress. The stress took a toll on Michael's fragile marriage, which was hanging by an emotional thread following the death of Dale Earnhardt Sr.

To escape bankruptcy, Michael sought the help of racing investor Rob Kauffman, who became a partner in MWR. From there, Michael found a route to financial stability. But it was too late to save his marriage. Michael and Buffy divorced in 2010.

In a heart-wrenching conversation with ESPN's Ed Hinton, Michael told his interviewer: "I've got a big race shop and a couple of Daytona 500 trophies . . . but I don't have a wife anymore." Michael was well aware of what had happened to him over the years since Dale's death. He had become a different person.

Managing a team kept Michael busy as he dealt with the new realities of his life. Michael was only racing three or four times a year to keep a hand in there, but during the Daytona 500 weekend in 2011—the 10-year anniversary of Dale Earnhardt's death—Michael felt a desire to get back out on the track again in memory of his friend.

Michael decided to add another race to his weekend schedule—the

NASCAR Camping World Truck Series on Friday night. He proved to be as adept at steering a black truck as he was at steering a stock car, but he needed a slingshot pass off Elliot Sadler at the end of a green-white-checkered flag finish to squeak by with a victory.

The truck series win gave Michael a win at each level of NASCAR racing—Sprint Cup, Nationwide, and Camping World Truck—putting him in rare company. But something else made the victory more special—or, in Michael's case, more poignant. His truck series win at Daytona came on February 18, 2011, 10 years to the day after Dale Earnhardt's death. As Michael, holding his daughter Macy close to his chest, stood in Victory Circle beside a truck he painted black in honor of Earnhardt's black car, he thanked God and paid tribute to Dale's life.

Not long after Daytona, Michael decided to write a book about his life. That meant reliving some of his most difficult moments, including February 18, 2001. He sat down in his living room and watched the Daytona 500 race that changed his life forever. He knew what would happen on the final lap. What followed was a wreck of a man sitting alone on his couch—no big brother, no Richard Petty, no Dale, and no Buffy to turn to.

He was alone, sobbing. In those moments, Michael says, he realized that the emotions he felt following the crash that took Dale's life were as raw as ever. He realized he hadn't dealt with anything properly because he hadn't dealt with his grief properly.

The first thing he did was reach out to Buffy and apologize for his actions. He took all the responsibility for their failed marriage. He confessed he didn't know how to talk about his grief.

Writing about the stinging realities of his struggles in his book *In the Blink of an Eye: Dale, Daytona, and the Day that Changed Everything* proved to be a therapeutic moment for Michael.

Today, Michael is one of NASCAR's most recognizable personalities. You could watch an hour of 30-second commercial spots he's done. He and Darrell continue to live out their faith in tangible ways by annually raising hundreds of thousands of dollars for charity through the "Waltrip Brothers' Charity Championship."

Michael knows he must live daily with reminders of what happened in Daytona back in 2001. When those thoughts crowd his mind, he can retreat to a fortified tower, where the righteous are safe in the Lord's arms.

9

DAVID RAGAN:
DRIVEN BY FAITH AND ACTION

Long-term unemployment was a very real possibility.

The prospect of being without a ride wasn't, however, going to shake David Ragan's confidence in the Lord.

Here's what happened: at the end of 2011, David's team, Roush Fenway Racing (RFR), needed to make cutbacks. When RFR made the decision to trim down from four cars to three, it meant four drivers were going to be playing musical chairs for three spots. When the music stopped, David was the driver left standing.

After his release from RFR, David shot out the door to try to hook up with another team. Three teams gave David a look and rejected him, leaving him stranded at year's end.

Things weren't looking good for David. He had never gone this late without a car.

On December 24, 2011, David celebrated his 26th birthday by reflecting on his go-to passage in scripture whenever he was facing a trial: "For I know the plans I have for you," declares the Lord, "plans to prosper you and not to harm you, plans to give you hope and a future. Then you will call on me and come and pray to me, and I will listen to you" (Jeremiah 29:11–12 NIV).

Plans to give me a hope and a future. David clung to that verse like it was a life preserver holding him up as he bobbed up and down in the middle of the chaotic Atlantic Ocean. He wasn't sure what to do or where to go, but as he continued to pray for guidance, he was confident God would answer his prayers in a miraculous way.

SOUTHERN BOY AND SOUTHERN BAPTIST

David's confidence in God had deep roots. He was born in 1985 in Unadilla, a five-square-mile town in southern Georgia, to Ken and Beverly Ragan. David was Ken and Beverly's second child. His brother Adam, older by 18 months, was born with Down syndrome, though it would take David awhile before he understood the differences between them. He remembers strangers staring at Adam and other kids calling him names. Once, when the brothers were still in daycare, another kid wouldn't stop the name-calling, so David stepped in and fought the boy.

David and Adam grew up as best of friends. Like their dad, they shared a passion for sports, and father and sons enjoyed all the bat-and-ball games, fishing, karate, and, of course, racing. Both boys excelled at their highest levels, even though "highest level" became individually defined as they each got older.

Over the years, David has seen Adam win many of his more than 20 Special Olympics medals. Adam has seen David win at least that many races. They walked the stage together at their high school graduation, and when David got married, Adam was his best man. And today, down at the David Ragan Ford dealership in nearby Perry, Georgia, the nameplate on Adam's desk introduces him officially as "Vice President of the General Manager."

When David was asked about the tight brotherly bond, he had three emphatic words to declare: "Family is everything!"

Racing revealed the brothers' special influence on one another. A family friend of the Ragan's, PURE Ministries founder David Glover, explained it this way: "David would not be the man he is today without Adam as his brother." Indeed, David learned authenticity, loyalty, compassion, ability to listen, and confidence in God from Adam. "That's how God has used Adam, as a teacher," Glover added. "In David's life, faith, and career, heartfelt truths have been learned from his brother."

Adam faces challenges every day, "yet he has a great attitude," David said. "So when I'm thrown a curve, I look at the big picture and appreciate what I have in life. Adam taught me this."

Adam also would not be the man he is today without David as his brother. Their father always encouraged David to become an advocate, not only for his brother but also for whatever was right, even if it wasn't the popular thing to do.

As David's racing career began, he became an advocate for the network of Shriners Hospitals for Children. He also joined former NFL star Kurt Warner, Christian music artist Chris Tomlin, and former Alaska governor Sarah Palin at PURE Ministry events in Atlanta and Birmingham. In a tribute to Adam and the more than 400,000 people in America with Down syndrome, David celebrated World Down Syndrome Day—held every March 21—by filming TV spots for Down syndrome awareness. Adam is also an honorary member of David's pit crew, giving him a second full-time job.

The Ragans' bond as brothers is the type that can only be forged in a loving family and a strong community, and with God's grace. These three entities have prevailed in David's life. "We've had family, we've had community, and we've had church," said his mother. "They all were behind us and helped us."

David acknowledges that God ultimately gets all the glory, but he credits the people at Unadilla Baptist Church with instilling in him a blazing confidence in God.

BUILDING A CAREER ON FAITH

David's love of racing sprung from deep family roots. First of all, he's a third-generation racer. His grandfather, Hugh Ragan, raced cars all throughout the Southeast following World War II, even trying his steady hand at Daytona in the early days of NASCAR. Ken Ragan and his brothers (David's uncles) bought a Bobby Allison race car at auction in the early 1980s, and Ken raced for eight years on the NASCAR circuit as an independent driver. David's Uncle Marvin was Ken's crew chief. Marvin and Ken owned a Chevrolet dealership in Unadilla that subsidized the family's racing.

David followed in his father's footsteps. At age 12, the youngster raced Bandolero cars, which look like miniature stock cars and top out at 70 miles per hour. As a 14-year-old, he won the Bandolero national championship, which only made him want to go into racing even more. As David started high school, he progressed to full-sized cars in the Dash series while working in a friend's mechanic shop.

In 2001, just before David turned 16 and could *legally* drive, Ken posed a question during a serious father-son moment: "How committed are you, son, about carrying on the family racing tradition?"

The meaning behind that question was simple: if David wasn't prepared to throw himself into racing all the way, then maybe he needed to find something else to do. But if he really was serious about racing, then the whole family would be totally behind him. That would mean some major decisions would have to follow—starting with whether to move the family to Charlotte, the epicenter of NASCAR racing.

But then Ken took things one step further, upping the stakes as high as he dared. "If you wanna forget this racing deal," David's father said, "then I'll buy you a brand-new Corvette for Christmas."

David didn't hesitate in answering.

"Daddy," he said, "I don't want a Corvette. I wanna race."

LEARNING ABOUT LOGISTICS: NO MORE SOFT AND SLOW

They were all in. David, Dad, Mom—and Adam.

In 2002, the Ragan family pulled up stakes and moved to Charlotte, North Carolina. Since David was too young to race under NASCAR's sanctioning, he worked out a deal with veteran Cup racer Mark Martin to drive a car he owned in the Legends Pro Division. This was the minor leagues, but it was a good low-key place for a 16-year-old to develop his driving skills. That first season, David finished in fourth place, which only increased his budding desire to race. But he had to be patient because he couldn't give NASCAR a whirl until he turned 18.

It wasn't long after that milestone birthday that David signed to race in the NASCAR truck series for Tom Eldredge of Fiddleback Racing in Mooresville, North Carolina. But the season started extremely poorly for David—five-wrecks-in-10-races poorly. His inexperience showed, and he began to wonder if he could hack it in the big leagues.

David sought his father's advice on what to do.

Ken counseled David to stay the course. "Good things come to good people," he said. "But you gotta work hard." Taken together, this meant that faith required action, Ken explained.

David felt like he didn't have to worry because he and the family trusted the Lord's leading for his racing career. He continued to work hard, which included studying the legendary racers and learning what his engine was capable of. He changed his approach on the track and started racing with eyes wide open, always soaking in what the track was teaching him.

David caught a big break in 2005, when he took part in Roush Fenway Racing's (RFR) "Driver X" program. RFR, one of the elite teams of NASCAR, occasionally held competitions to draw in quality up-and-comers. That year, the audition aired on the Discovery Channel as kind of a reality show. Although David didn't win, RFR selected him as co-driver of the #6 Ford F-150 with teammate Mark Martin. David was back in a stock truck and well on his way, but it would be a long rise to the top.

In 2006, David started 19 truck races and finished in the Top 10 a total of ten times—not a bad showing for the 20-year-old. In 2007, he drove for RFR full-time in both the Nationwide Series *and* the Sprint Cup Series, which was a big step up and no doubt a confidence booster. David showed that he was ready for the Sprint Cup level when he finished with three Top 10s and was named runner-up for Rookie of the Year. Down in the Nationwide Series, he excelled as a young gun and won the top rookie award.

In 2008, the 22-year-old second-year wheelman padded his budding racing résumé with another 35 Nationwide events and 36 Cup races. As the regular season wound down, David was in the hunt for the 12th and final berth in the Chase for the Sprint Cup. (The Chase is NASCAR's version of playoff racing.) In the end, David finished one place out of the Chase, but he stood out among the many new drivers that year.

With 10 races to go in the 2008 season, David received the thrilling news that signaled exciting things to come. Roush Fenway Racing and the United Parcel Service announced David as "the next UPS man," meaning the coveted UPS sponsorship would grace David's #6 Ford beginning in 2009.

Teaming up with a potentially career-long primary sponsor like UPS was like winning a gas card for life, but David would have to keep performing well. UPS, a blue-chip company, hand-picked David because he had racing rock star written all over him—but in a good way. David was a good-looking, humble, down-to-earth guy with strong family values. He'd also shown immense talent behind the wheel and would make a great spokesman for the team.

But the next two years proved challenging for David. He recorded a combined five Top-10 finishes during those two seasons. "We were just slow," David said. "We didn't compete as well as we should have."

The word *compete* is a big deal in racing. And *slow*? That meant the car wasn't up to snuff once the green flag dropped. Nonetheless, those were not the results that big-moneyed teams like RFR expected. They had projected their investments in NASCAR to return a little faster.

Everyone's morale shot up in February 2011 when David ran well at the Daytona 500. He had his car's front bumper stuck up in the front, in contention to win late in the race, but then he made a costly mistake.

On a restart out of a caution, Trevor Bayne was running hot on the inside front row while David was on the outside front row. As the cars cruised toward the start-finish line, David spotted an opportunity open and, in anticipation of the race restarting, jumped in front of Trevor.

David made the move successfully, but a split-second too early, a moment before reaching the start-finish line. David's move was ruled illegal, and he was black-flagged and sent to the back of the pack. The cars were lined up for a do-over, and 20-year-old Trevor Bayne went on to win the coveted Daytona 500.

A few weeks later, with his error at Daytona still fresh in his mind, David made another quick move—but it didn't happen on the track. It was a cerebral move inspired by his sponsor's love for logistics.

The background goes like this: UPS engineers had discovered that their truck drivers could save time and fuel—and therefore money— if they eliminated as many left-hand turns as possible. Over the years, delivery routes have been strategically re-charted so that today, whenever UPS trucks come to intersections, they turn right nearly 100 percent of the time.

Following the Daytona 500, David reasoned some things through and announced a change in his racing style—a new "right turn," if you will. He declared that from now on, he would compete as absolutely hard as possible, every single time he came to race.

"Now is the time to fight for every spot," David told the press. "We can't give away any positions. We've got to be really aggressive."

Believe it or not, it wasn't an easy decision to make. Aggression, even competitive aggression, wasn't instilled in David as a boy. He was raised to be "a good guy, a good Christian, a Southern boy," all endearing qualities. But in the paint-swapping, bump-and-pass world of NASCAR, nice guys finish last, as the old saying goes.

David clarified that his new attitude wasn't going to affect who he was as a person. It was only about competing on the race track.

GO FAST, TURN LEFT

And compete David did. From then on, every race became a battle royale. Each campaign was a last-ditch effort. Each event became his personal Battle of the Bulge.

In the forefront of David's mind was the pressure to impress his car owners. He needed to blitz rumors that UPS and RFR were going to make changes for the next season and show him the door. Success in combat would only be counted by quantifiable results—by laps led, by points gained, and by where he stood in the pack when he crossed the finish line.

On April 3, 2011, while driving his UPS-sponsored Ford at Martinsville Speedway in Ridgeway, Virginia, David's new approach to racing paid off. He came in eighth for his first Top-10 finish in his last eight outings and his second Top 10 in a year. While he was grateful for his performance, he wanted to do even better. "We had a shot to finish in the top three or four," David explained. "Still, I wanna thank the Lord for a good day."

David's determination continued to pay off. In his very next race, at Texas Motor Speedway in Fort Worth, David ran a blistering 189.820 miles per hour during qualifying to earn the coveted pole position. It was his first time ever in the front row of a Sprint Cup race. Racing next to David, on the outside, was RFR teammate Carl Edwards. David went on to finish seventh in the race, making it two Top-10 finishes in two starts. David had turned things around.

In July, the racers returned to Daytona for the Coke Zero 400. Since Daytona hosts two major races each year, a lot of highlights from the last race were talked about before the next race. Leading up to race day, the media rehashed his black-flag incident at the Daytona 500.

David once again drove a fast Ford. He qualified well and started the race from fifth place. From the starting grid, he looked out his windshield at the great talent ahead of him—Jeff Gordon, Clint Bowyer, and February's winner, Trevor Bayne, on the outside of Mark Martin on the pole.

But David never uttered a negative word about starting fifth. He had never been a complainer—a trait that comes from his faith and his family. "David, you get up and count your blessings," his father always said. "You can count your race cars, count your points, count your laps and all that later, but you count your blessings every day because racing is an absolute miracle."

The green flag fell, and the engines whined loudly as the drivers jockeyed for position. David quickly jumped from fifth to first. But the pack stayed patient and reined him in. Little by little, David fell to the middle of the pack as cars passed him. Then he remembered his vow to battle hard.

The race was scheduled for 160 laps. By lap 104, David had reclaimed the lead. He led for a couple of laps and then slowly fell back again. Once more, he picked his way back toward the front.

The Coke Zero 400 was deemed a "restrictor plate" race, meaning the speed and power of the cars was purposely limited. Cars tend to bunch up more in packs during restrictor plate races—in order to draft better—and for that reason, multi car wrecks often result. Several crashes occurred along the way that day, but David avoided them all. Then, toward the end of the race, there was another wreck, meaning a green-white-checkered finish would determine the winner.

The first attempt at the finish resulted in more wrecked cars. On the second attempt, David took the green flag with Matt Kenseth pushing behind him. The cars came around and got the last-lap white flag—less than 50 seconds of racing left. The pack breathed down David's neck from behind, each hell-bent-for-leather driver vying for the win. The checkered flag was in sight. David maintained a slim lead. He kept his foot pressed hard against the floorboard and raced across the finish line, claiming his first-ever Sprint Cup win.

"Welcome to Victory Lane, my friend," Marty Snider of TNT said.

"This is fun. What better place to win one than at Daytona," David replied. Then, before he thanked UPS, RFR, and NASCAR for support, he thanked his Lord for looking after him. What was especially fitting was that his older brother Adam and his parents were looking on. Really, this was a win for the whole Ragan family. Dad, Mom, and Adam all raised their index fingers in the air signifying No. 1 while David hoisted the trophy high over his head.

Throughout his career, David has given thanks to God because he had been taught Psalm 92:1 growing up: "It is good to give thanks to the LORD" (NASB).

The 2011 season proved to be a stellar one for David. He had his first pole and his first win in the books, and he went on to sit on the pole again later in the season at the famous Brickyard 400 race at the Indianapolis Motor Speedway. But despite his newfound excellence, and despite his vow to fight for every spot on the track, neither UPS nor RFR stuck with him. Early that December, he was informed that UPS was moving on and that RFR was going to reduce the team. Once again, David was without a ride.

Days turned into weeks as David looked at his options. His options were becoming fewer and fewer. Ten years earlier, when David's dad asked him how committed he was to racing, he had passed up a new Corvette because he wanted the driver's life so badly. But now he began to question his calling. Was racing really right for him?

David sought God's will for his life. "In the ups and downs of having a career in auto racing, I have to ask God for guidance all the time," David said, as he spoke reflectively. He paused and then, in a pensive way, added, "You are on top of the world on some days, and struggling on many others." He stayed positive through this rough patch by reminding himself that he could rely on God and His Word.

Once again, he turned to Jeremiah 29, this time to verse 12 (NASB): "You will call upon Me and come and pray to Me, and I will listen to you."

And then he flipped over to Psalm 32:8 (NASB), "I will instruct you and teach you in the way you should go; I will counsel you with My eye upon you."

The race to find a seat behind the wheel of a NASCAR car was going to be close.

ANSWERED PRAYERS

Talk about a photo finish! At the 11th hour and 59th minute, David's prayers were answered. DAVID RAGAN LANDS LAST AVAILABLE CUP RIDE WITH FRONT ROW, read the headline in *USA Today*. Front Row referred to Front Row Motorsports, a company owned by restaurant entrepreneur Bob Jenkins. When Front Row offered him a ride for the 2012 season, David became a teammate of David Gilliland and Josh Wise, both Christian racers.

But his new ride came with some challenges. Front Row operated on a budget one-third the size of what Roush Fenway Racing worked with each year. Beating the big guys would take a new kind of fight from David and his teammates. Up until 2011, Front Row had never started a race in the front row and had only one Top-10 finish—when Gilliland finished third at the Daytona 500, the race in which David was black-flagged.

Before the 2012 season began, David got to work seeking more sponsorship dollars. He attracted several partners but no primary sponsor. So he kept working—and racing. At the Talladega

Superspeedway, David raced to two Top-10 finishes—a fourth and a seventh. The 2012 season was a mild success, but David felt a foundation had been laid for better things to come. When the season was over, David got married, celebrated another birthday, enjoyed Christmas and New Year's with his family, and then went back to work.

David is considered a multi-tooled driver, meaning he has mechanical skills that can be used around the shop. He can build an engine, a chassis—pretty much anything under the shell. Since he knows how many man-hours go into putting together the cars he drives, he doesn't race as recklessly as some young drivers do. He's known for skirting crashes and not getting caught up in many wrecks, which is why the start of the 2013 season was frustrating for him. His first two races—at Daytona and Phoenix—both ended early with crashes.

David got back to finishing races, but he wasn't placing well. A good goal for a midsized team like Front Row Motorsports is breaking into the Top 20. For the next seven races, David hit the mark just one time. His results were:

- Las Vegas: 31st
- Bristol: 21st
- Fontana: 24th
- Martinsville: 30th
- Fort Worth: 26th
- Kansas: 30th
- Richmond: 20th

The earnings for those seven middle-of-the-pack finishes paid the team $740,032—roughly the same as a Top-5 finish at the Daytona 500. That might sound like good earnings, but it costs a lot of money to follow the NASCAR circus around the country.

After Richmond, the team travelled to Talladega. The 2.66-mile Talladega Superspeedway is often called Daytona's sister track. Slightly longer than Daytona, Talladega is the fastest track on the circuit, so restrictor plates were put on the cars, just as they were at Daytona.

David's father had raced seven times at Talladega before the mandated restrictor plates, with his best finish being 11th in 1984. It was also at Talladega that Ken was involved in a life-threatening accident. Ken crashed hard, and he suffered a serious neck injury as he was pulled from the wreck.

Fortunately, Ken recovered from his injury and was later able to return to racing. But the track still held out fears for the Ragan family. David, as 2012 indicated, had recorded decent results at Talladega, so optimism tiptoed around Front Row Motorsports. David, in true character, faced his fears head on—confident and composed but never brash.

The spring race started as scheduled on May 5. David raced as hard as he could. More than two-thirds of the race in, the rain began to fall, and the race was red-flagged.

Three hours and 46 minutes went by before the rain let up enough to restart the race. Racing resumed on lap 131, but several terrible wrecks soon followed, burying the hopes of many good drivers. David drifted up to the outside to avoid one wreck and down onto the apron to clear the debris of another.

Throughout the race, he and teammate David Gilliland worked the draft brilliantly. Gilliland was in tow for most of the afternoon, and the race ran into the evening, for most of the night, too. When another big wreck occurred on lap 184, the caution came out, meaning the race would end under a green-white-checkered flag.

With two laps to go, teammates David Ragan and David Gilliland were drafting six rows behind the leaders. They found a groove up through the middle and raced their lane toward the front. It was a team effort all the way. From behind, Gilliland's car pushed Ragan's car through the traffic.

On the last lap, David Ragan came up in second place behind leader Carl Edwards, but he was blocked from taking the lead. With only moments to go, David drove to the outside and up the bank, moving slightly to the right of Carl, who maneuvered again to block. But David put a logistical fake on the RFR veteran. Before Carl figured out what was going on, David dove hard to the inside and zipped ahead to take the lead. Gilliland stayed on his bumper the whole way.

With only the front stretch to go, Carl hammered down on the outside of the track to make one final attempt to reclaim the lead. David watched intently from his mirror and cut him off with a block of his own. David then cut back to the inside and created a gap that secured the last seconds of the race and the checkered flag.

At last, David had won.

Gilliland was close behind and took second.

From Victory Lane, David said, "First off, I gotta thank the Lord. Without Him nothing like this is possible."

David didn't know that Vegas bookies had him as a 100-to-1 long shot to win the race. With Almighty God, however, the odds didn't matter because with the Lord, all things are possible.

The next comment David made would be the one that came out in the headlines. "This is a true David-versus-Goliath moment here," he said. Like David of the Bible, David Ragan went out to do battle against bigger and better-funded opponents with confidence and a cause. When the outgunned driver with five smooth stones slayed the field, he gave the press a Bible story to tell NASCAR fans about.

Gilliland marched in step behind David. "Without God none of us would be here and getting to do what we do. So first we start with thanking God," said Gilliland.

MUCH TO BE THANKFUL FOR

Both Davids teamed up to give Front Row Motorsports its first victory and its first one-two finish. Later that night at the press conference, reporters asked David Ragan to expound on his thankfulness and on his use of the David-and-Goliath imagery.

"We certainly have a lot to be thankful for," David said. "We owe what we're doing here today to God and the Lord." David then took the opportunity to talk about his NASCAR Bible study group, saying, "We try to incorporate the Good Word into the commotion of race weekends." About winning at Talladega, he added, "We were in the position today to give God the glory. And I'm thankful for that."

David's unexpected win qualified him for the Sprint Cup All-Star race two weeks later. The 90-lap race was a showcase for the fans, and David started 14th and came across the finish line in 19th. But the significant part of the race was the paint scheme on the hood of David's #34 FRM Ford Fusion.

In 12-inch block lettering, in red on a bright yellow background, were the words BEATS GOLIATH. BRAKES FOR TRAINS. In an ever-so-subtle way, David's message got out: God will use a man to battle a giant, defend a worthy cause, and even (in the case of the biblical David) protect a cherished people.

David Ragan has battled metaphorical giants for most of his racing career. Some he has fought on his own account, but not many. David has battled on behalf of the disabled and of families with Down syndrome children. He has battled the field as part of an underfunded racing team, and battled to credit the Lord when good fortune has come his way.

In the end, if ever there was a portrait of a Philippians 4:6 man on the NASCAR circuit, it's David Ragan. The apostle Paul's words— "Be anxious for nothing, but in everything by prayer and supplication with thanksgiving let your request be made known to God" (NASB)— characterize David well.

David's remains confident in the Lord, and that makes him a great example to follow. If you're facing setbacks in life or had your way blocked by circumstances you can't control, then let David's example of remembering Jeremiah 29:11–12 shine forth.

10

OTHER DRIVERS OF FAITH, YOUNG AND OLD

"What more shall I say? For time will fail me if I tell," wrote the writer of the "Heroes of Faith" chapter, Hebrews 11.

Tell of *what?*

Tell more testimonies of Old Testament men and women who lived by faith.

But then, without pausing, the writer launches into another series of testimonies.

Like that writer, we have a similar conclusion.

What more shall we say about NASCAR drivers who live by faith? There are drivers from the past and the present, Hall of Famers and up-and-comers, veterans and rookies, whose testimonies should be told. NASCAR is stocked with followers of Christ.

What about Jamie McMurray, Ned Jarrett, Morgan Shepherd, Blake Koch, Darrell Waltrip, and others, who by faith in Jesus, do their various NASCAR jobs every season, race after race. They announce races. They visit and preach in churches and cities. They boldly live for Jesus and live out their faith as they fight the good fight of faith.

Let's take a look at a few more NASCAR insiders who live for God.

JAMIE MCMURRAY—A BOLD FINISHER

A few years back, in the gym alongside his personal trainer, Jamie McMurray learned the most valuable lesson in life.

It didn't have anything to do with diet, power lifting, muscle mass, or cardio exercise. The big take away from his six-in-the-morning workouts with his trainer had to do with the power of something far greater. Up until then, Jamie had never viewed God, church, or prayer as being ultimately important. He was what we can call a casual believer, a Christian in name only.

In Jamie's earlier days, he raced or traveled every Sunday—and God was far from his mind. He only hired Aldon Baker, a man of deep faith himself, so he could help Jamie improve his Sunday race results.

Under Baker's tutelage, however, Jamie received an all-inclusive training package. He learned how to stay physically fit so he could become more competitive in NASCAR, and he also learned a few things about the race of faith. As a trainer, Aldon no doubt taught Jamie that diet and exercise are inseparable for healthy living, but he also taught Jamie how faith and prayer are inextricably related—how they are two sides of the same coin.

Jamie began to practice what he learned from Aldon about the importance of growing in Christ. Little by little, Jamie's faith in God grew as his prayer life became more consistent. Morning workouts and daily prayer both required discipline and endurance—and Jamie found the benefits of both.

"Working out has become easier for me," Jamie says. "I don't wake up and say, 'Man, I have to work out today.' " And what about the power of prayer? Jamie doesn't hesitate even for a moment when he says, "I'm a huge believer in prayer."

Prayer gets Jamie through the ups and downs of NASCAR. Jamie says he relies heavily on his faith, especially during the downs. After the 2009 season, he was released from NASCAR powerhouse Roush Fenway Racing. He had married his best friend, Christy Futrell, in July, then only a few months later learned of the cutback at RFR that eliminated his ride. He prayed hard for his life and his racing vocation to get turned around.

Thankfully, Chip Ganassi, the owner Jamie began his NASCAR career with in 2002, hired him back under a one-year contract in 2010. In 2005, Jamie left Ganassi for what looked like greener pastures with RFR, so his return to his former team was truly a second chance. Jamie's gratefulness showed. Today, he is known for being one of the nicest and happiest drivers in the garage.

Jamie also gave thanks to God for the second chance. As Jesus modeled during His own life on earth, Jamie would wake in the morning and "close his door and pray."

On Sunday morning, February 14, 2010, Jamie unavoidably missed church, yet God was still foremost on his mind. He woke up that morning and kneeled beside his couch for prayer. With his hopes running high in anticipation of his eighth Daytona 500 start, Jamie paused, silenced the clamoring voices that besiege a person's mind every day, and asked God to safely guide him around the speedway. He gave thanks for his new team, and, as the writer of the epistle to the Hebrews put it, "drew near with confidence to the throne of grace, to receive mercy and find grace to help in his time of need." Last of all, Jamie boldly requested a strong finish that day at Daytona—a Top 10, if it was God's will.

It was Valentine's Day, and 175,000 fans were in attendance to watch the Daytona 500. The race took more than six hours to complete due to a two-hour, 25-minute red flag delay to repair a pothole. During the delay, Jamie hung out on the pit box with his crew chief and team.

Jamie raced as hard as he could. You only need to lead the last lap of a race in order to win, and, much to his surprise, that's where he and his #1 Bass Pro Shop–sponsored Impala sat with one lap to go. As he approached the checkered flag, he started crying. The race was over, and his childhood dream was fulfilled. As is custom of victors, he burned donuts in the infield, then got out of his car and ran up the track, where he grabbed the checkered flag from the race official. On Jamie's way back to his car, he pointed to the sky, dropped to his knees, and then collapsed on all fours and laid his head on the infield logo.

A few minutes later, when being interviewed in Victory Circle, Jamie broke down in tears, tried to gather his emotions without success, and buried his head in his towel for a minute. Diehard fans called Jamie's win one of the most emotional in the sport's history. "Man, did God ever answer my prayers," he said, wiping his brow.

"Pray . . . more things are wrought by prayer than this world dreams of," Alfred Tennyson wrote. Jamie knows the truth hidden away in Tennyson's sentiment. As the 2010 season moved forward, Jamie won again, this time in Indianapolis, where he raced hard and took the Brickyard 400. After the Daytona 500, Indy's Brickyard 400 is the second most prestigious race on the NASCAR calendar.

But Jamie wasn't done winning yet.

Following the fall race in Richmond, Jamie knew he had not qualified for the Chase for the Sprint Cup yet. There were 10 races to go in the season, and he was in 14th place in the points standings. Only the top 12 drivers in points make the Chase championship, which is akin to the playoff system in major sports in America. Jamie had nine Top-10 finishes and two wins, which gave him a shot at being in the Chase, but things didn't pan out. That was disappointing to him, but he could still keep racing since the last 10 races of the year featured a standard field of 43 racers.

Then, a few weeks later, Jamie lined up in Charlotte at the Bank of America 500. In a total contrast to the close win in Daytona, where Dale Earnhardt Jr. was on his tail, Jamie led the last 21 laps without any real threats behind him.

As the laps wound down and a first-place finish seemed imminent, Jamie reflected back on his win at Daytona as well as his emotions he felt that day. Was that really eight months ago? He and his wife, Christy, were expecting their first child in less than a month. Life was good all around. Except for barely missing the Chase championship, Jamie had enjoyed a dream season that reminded him of his first year back with Ganassi. His dad—his good friend, his fishing buddy, and his best go-kart competition—was watching. Jamie wondered if he would break down in tears again.

Jamie crossed the finish line and made his third Victory Lane appearance of the season. In Charlotte's Victory Lane, standing on the #1 car, rejoicing in his victory, with confetti floating down around him, Jamie jumped off the car and received a bear hug from his father and a long kiss from his wife. Jamie answered one question and talked briefly about a friend. Then, as he had planned during the final laps, he said what he needed to say:

> *I want to take the time to explain something about Daytona and how I was crying in Victory Lane. I don't think I ever really got to explain about why I cried, and what was going on there . . . .*

Articulating every purposefully chosen word and punctuating every sentence with a preacher-like hand gesture, Jamie continued:

> *I had a tough year last year. And I found . . . I found out the power of prayer, and what that can do for you. And so, when you get to Victory Lane, and you get to experience this, it makes you a believer. That is something that is very important to my family and me.*

Jamie looked directly at the audience and finished by saying:

> *That's the stuff I was thinking about. And it made the laps go by really quickly at the end. And so, thanks goes to God, for everything He has blessed my family and me with.*

Jamie has been with the same team since his incredible 2010 season, a season he looks on with awesome affection. He and Christy had their son that November. A few years later, shortly before the 2013 Daytona 500, Jamie wheeled his wife and new daughter out of the hospital and took them home. These were some of the blessings Jamie remains thankful to God for. He has also stayed with his racing team—now called Earnhardt Ganassi Racing—and signed a contract extension, keeping his word that he wouldn't quit on them.

If you don't have a favorite NASCAR driver, Jamie would love to have you on his team and join him in experiencing the power of prayer.

NED JARRETT—STILL BEHIND THE WHEEL

Even though he's in his eighties today, NASCAR legend Ned Jarrett is still licensed to drive.

Good thing, because on a Sunday in October 2010, Ned drove to church with his wife, Martha. Once parked, they walked toward the entrance. Ned lagged behind, and Martha beat him to the church foyer, where the greeter warmly congratulated her on the recent announcement that Ned would be welcomed into the NASCAR Hall of Fame as part of its class of 2011.

Martha's response to the woman who greeted her on Sunday demonstrated the equity Ned had built up over the years as a devoted husband and family man. "Well, that's very nice to say," Martha replied, "but he's been in my Hall of Fame for over 50 years."

Ned had caught up with Martha for that part of the conversation, and when it came time to deliver his Hall of Fame induction speech the following May in Charlotte, North Carolina, he praised his wife for her love and perseverance over the years.

Ned didn't need to drive far for the annual induction ceremony. He lives an hour's drive from Charlotte, near the countryside where he was born in Newton, North Carolina.

When Ned was a boy growing up in Newton, he looked after the family while his father worked tirelessly in the lumberyards. Every Sunday, his folks took him to church because that's what their family did on the Sabbath.

Then one Sunday in 1942, the routine changed slightly. Ned was nine years old and had fallen in love with cars. His dad was keen to this, so that Sunday he let Ned drive the family to church. The boy beamed a huge grin all the way there.

When Ned was a teen, news of a newly constructed speedway dominated the country store table talk. The opening of the Hickory Motor Speedway seemed to have every man in the county bragging about how fast he could drive. The men were mostly farmers and sawmill workers, so Ned kept his desire to drive race cars mostly to himself, but he dreamed of racing, too. His dad caught wind of his desire and, not wanting him to ruin the reputable Jarrett name by racing with the fools and moonshiners the sport attracted, he asked Ned to not be a driver. Ned was allowed to work on cars, his father concluded, but he couldn't drive them.

Ned proceeded to work on race cars, all the while mulling over his father's comment. The young man disagreed with his father's directive, noting that even Jesus became friends with the ruffians of His day. But Ned didn't want to disrespect his father and use the family name without Dad's approval.

One day, however, a driver became ill and couldn't race. The car needed a driver, so Ned jumped into the driver's seat and raced—using the sick driver's name as an alias. He secretly vowed to keep his character intact while being a Christian witness to all those he raced against.

Ned earned respect from the very start. In 1951, he placed 10th in his first amateur race. He ran in more races, using the same alias he'd used when he replaced the sick driver, winning several times. Word eventually got around to Dad, who eventually came around and approved of his son's secret ambition. He even told Ned to get credit for those wins as a Jarrett, not as someone else. Soon after that, Ned earned the nickname "Gentleman Ned" for his gracious demeanor on and off the track.

Ned was an official NASCAR driver from 1953 through 1966, and he won championships in '61 and '65. Winning the title in '65 was especially tricky because after a crash during a June race, Ned continued driving until he collapsed during a pit stop with a broken back. Thirty-six hours after arriving in the ER, Ned walked out in a back brace but with enough strength to climb in a race car 12 hours later and go on to win the season's championship.

In February 1966, eight days before the Daytona 500, Ned was one of President Lyndon Johnson's distinguished guests for the 14th Annual Presidential Prayer Breakfast. Ned heard the president quote from the prophet Isaiah, and the passage hit home:

They that wait upon the Lord shall renew their strength; they shall mount up with wings as eagles; they shall run, and not be weary; and they shall walk, and not faint.

Ned has spent his life waiting upon the Lord. He had witnessed renewed strength during the '65 season.

Midway through the 1966 season, Ned retired from driving without defending his championship. People thought his sudden retirement was bizarre, but he says it was time to be a family man. Remember, he's in the Hall of Fame for that. Good decision, Ned.

After driving professionally, Ned enjoyed a long career in broadcasting. He called races from both the pits and the booth. His shining moment was a partisan call and proud father moment in the booth when he cheered his son, Dale Jarrett, on to victory in the 1993 Daytona 500.

Though the Hall of Famer retired from racing more than 45 years ago, and from broadcasting in 2009, he has not wearied from driving home the message of grace and forgiveness through Jesus Christ. As Ned has grown older, he has developed a plethora of patience and a storehouse of wisdom—both on faith and on NASCAR. Even better, his voice is still heard because he continues to make public appearances as an ambassador for the sport.

What's his message? It hasn't changed.

Love your family.

Love the Lord.

And tell others about the love of Jesus.

MORGAN SHEPHERD—A CLOSE CALL

It's common for NASCAR drivers and enthusiasts—and car aficionados in general—to grow up with a passion for cars derived from their fathers.

Jesse Clay Shepherd played a role in his son Morgan Shepherd's passion for cars, which eventually led to his son's racing career. But it wasn't the usual story in which a father takes his son to spend quality time and the two tinker around the garage together, building an engine, restoring a classic Ford, or going to the races. It was quite the opposite.

"My daddy made moonshine," Morgan says. "Daddy was an old mountain man, and making moonshine was his way of life."

Really? Morgan, who has raced 46 consecutive years in NASCAR, is the only driver around the sport admitting that anymore, though such a declaration used to be commonplace.

Morgan says a lot more than that. He stands willing and ready to tell anyone who'll listen about salvation in Jesus Christ. After years of living under the influence of alcohol, Morgan became a Christian. God changed his life, and in virtually every interview Morgan gives today, he shares openly about having new life in Christ.

Years before Morgan's conversion experience, his father's way of life as an odd-jobber, farmer, and moonshiner also came to an early end. Jesse Clay died in 1954, at age 46, when Morgan was just 12 years old. Morgan was only around his father for part of those years anyhow. He didn't even know his father by sight until he was four years old, when his mother one day said, "Your daddy's coming home."

The Shepherds were a dirt-poor family living in a shack at the end of a rural road in Ferguson, North Carolina. From there, Morgan looked up and saw the man his mother called "your daddy" walking along the dusty driveway. Morgan's father had been in prison after the G-men caught him making moonshine. A couple years later, the federal officers were back searching the property for Shepherd's stills. Sure enough, they found them, and Morgan watched his dad being carried off to do more time.

By then, Morgan understood more about what his father did for a living, and the son vowed he'd never be like his father. That's how Jesse Clay Shepherd influenced his son's career: Morgan promised himself he'd never get stuck making moonshine.

To flee the fate that befell his dad, Morgan started wrenching on a motorbike he bought, hoping to one day become a mechanic—maybe even a race car driver. He became good at taking engines apart and rebuilding them. When he was twelve years old, he bought his first car, an old beat-up Chevy. In a peculiar way, his deceased dad helped with the purchase. "I paid twelve dollars and fifty cents, two flying squirrels, a grey squirrel, and a 20-gauge shotgun for it," Morgan said. "The shotgun was my father's."

But the dream of a better life would have to wait. Morgan was more like his father than he cared to admit. In 1957 in the rural South, the strong taste of moonshine continued to be in demand, and operating a still and distributing its prized liquor tempted cash-strapped boys with the promise of fast money. Morgan fell to the temptation when he was 16, and he and a friend built their first still. "I reckon I followed in my father's footsteps after all," Morgan said. The G-men found Morgan's still and blew it up, but they didn't arrest him because they couldn't link him to the illegal moonshine operation.

Morgan also hauled 'shine for a while. One time, he and his friend arrived at the still early and the batch wasn't ready, so they left, planning to come back later. While speeding through the back roads, they drove into a hornet's nest of law enforcement. Fortunately, Morgan and his friend were hauling empty, but it was a close call. Glad to stay out of jail, Morgan quickly decided to get out of moonshining.

Morgan eventually pushed his way into the sport he'd always dreamed of. For 15 years, he raced hard and lived in the fast lane. He won a ton of races and finished runner-up to the series champ in 1973. Soon, he had most everything he ever dreamed of except for one thing—happiness.

Morgan was miserable. He passed through a series of extreme lows (or what he thought were lows), until he finally hit rock bottom. After a weekend drinking binge at a hotel party, his wife left him. Morgan knew he needed help.

Late at night on February 23, 1975, he was driving down the road when he suddenly broke down in tears. He knew his benders had ruined his marriage and that his lifestyle of girlfriends and hotel parties was purely selfish. He knew he needed a personal relationship with the only One who could save him—Jesus Christ.

"In my home that night," Morgan says, "I fell on my knees and began praying for God to change me. I accepted Jesus Christ as my Lord and Savior. God took the desire for alcohol out of my life."

From then on, everything changed. Morgan kept racing, but this time he had a higher purpose. In 2001 he started his own truck team and named it Victory in Jesus. Year after year, he kept racing, finally living the life he had hoped to live.

In July 2013, Morgan became the oldest driver in NASCAR history to start a Sprint Cup Series race. At 71, he piloted a car for 92 laps before pulling it into the garage with vibration problems.

But Morgan himself is steady as a rock. He still puts on roller skates and sails through the garage, stopping to encourage his friends and share the Lord with them.

To Morgan, winning isn't everything. He describes NASCAR as his mission field. His purpose in hanging around isn't to win races, but to win souls for Jesus. These days, he only gets his car on the track a few races a year, but when he does, his message, painted bold and bright on the hood, says one of two things: "Racing with Jesus" or "Victory in Jesus."

On the back of Morgan's #89 Chevy Impala, in the same bold font: "Racing for Souls."

BLAKE KOCH—THE DRIVER IN PINK

It's Monday night, and Blake Koch (pronounced Cook) and a few of his close NASCAR buddies have just finished a Bible Study.

Blake and his friends have been chilling out this way on their only night around home during the hectic 10-month racing season for a long time. They start the evening with a barbecue for some family time, and then the guys join together for a dose of God's Word.

On this particular night, their wives were still upstairs after the study ended, but the guys were downstairs, relaxing in the coolness of the North Carolina summer evening. Blake was sitting on the curb, and the others were just a few feet to his left on a cast-iron and wood-paneled bench.

Believe it or not, Blake and the boys can keep a rhythm that has nothing to do with engine timing. The guys had brought their instruments down to street level for a jam session. They were hanging out in an open-air veranda, which was softly lit by two street lamps, a green Starbucks sign, and the red lettering of Red Rocks Café. Their music filtered out through Birkdale Village, a throbbing urban community in Huntersville. If the guys were at summer Bible Camp, and not in a buzzing borough, there would be a crackling campfire and wrinkled song sheets. But in the veranda, the guys sat around a Mac laptop with the lyrics on the screen.

Blake, playing his bongo, kept the tempo up for the ragamuffin band. He could play a full drum set, too, but that would have been a little much for this session.

What song was Blake keeping tempo to?

The first cover the guys did was "Rise," a hit by Christian singer Shawn McDonald. The title alone has poignant meaning for Blake, but the rest of the lyrics ("Yes, I will rise out of these ashes") also have profound meaning for this young driver.

As of this writing, Blake is 28 years old and has been around NASCAR for only five years, going back to his 2009 debut in NASCAR'S K&N Pro Series West, which is primarily a driver development league. Before that, he had 18 months of amateur late-model racing experience with a mere 20 stock car races under his belt.

Blake wasn't completely without racing experience when he climbed through his first stock car window—he had 10 years of moto-cross racing to his credit. Growing up around West Palm Beach, Florida, Blake raced motor bikes from the age of nine until he was 19. After a few too many major injuries—the bone-breaking kind—Blake said, "I wanted to set racing aside."

So he enrolled in Northwood University, from which he is now an alumnus. Before he completed his degree, his stepfather bought a race car and asked Blake if he was interested in driving it. The stock car gig seemed to come out of nowhere. Because Blake missed the adrenaline rush from racing fast, he said yes and set his sights on NASCAR.

Stock cars felt like a good fit for Blake. Unlike motorcycles, stock cars put some sheet metal protection around him. At first, though, he didn't love the sport like he thought he would. And then, seemingly out of nowhere, he grew to love the challenge of taking on competitors in the curves and fighting for position on the track.

Then shocking news that came out of nowhere: Blake's mother told him she had breast cancer. The devastating development shook the family and diminished Blake's newfound love for racing. He turned to prayer as his only weapon against the uncontrollable condition. He trusted God, knowing He had control of whatever He willed. Faith sustained Blake as he walked with his mother through the chemotherapy. He even shaved his head in solidarity with his mother after she lost her hair.

While Blake's mother recovered (she eventually went into remission), Blake went into stock car racing with his heart and soul. With his soul already sold out to Christ, Blake made his commitment to have his budding racing career reflect his Christian faith.

His first sponsor fit his purpose perfectly. When he signed with Richard Childress in 2009 as part of the Golden Gate Racing team, his sponsor was GodSpeaks.com, a Christian ministry that focuses on billboard advertising to get the word out about God and to help create a stronger spiritual climate in a city.

Blake grew up in the West Palm Beach area, and he remembers the GodSpeaks.com billboard on Sand Lake Road. The billboard was simply designed—just a black board with white lettering.

The inscription read:

THAT "LOVE THY NEIGHBOR" THING . . . I MEANT THAT.
—GOD

The thought-provoking message was one of nine that popped up in Florida when Blake was a teenager. Since then, the ministry has grown to 10,000 billboards in 200 U.S. cities with more than 70 pithy sayings—some funny, some moving, and some serious—giving millions of drivers something to think about as they drive by.

In 2009, GodSpeaks.com was celebrating 10 years of placing billboards throughout America, so what better way to celebrate any anniversary than to go to the races? The ministry wanted to turn Blake's race car into the fastest billboard on the planet, so a big GodSpeaks .com was painted across his front hood. Billboards don't hide anything, and that fit Blake's style to a T.

In 2011, Blake moved up into a Nationwide Series car owned by Randy and Pat MacDonald, and partly sponsored by his father's Christian ministry, RiseUp.us, which reaches out to America's men with the message, "If you heal the man . . . he will heal his family . . . and the family will heal the nation."

Mark Koch knows personally the healing he promotes. Mark is the movie producer of box office hits such as *Lost in Space*, *Black Dog*, and *The Perfect Game*. After living the Hollywood fast life for many years, God touched him for good in 1997. With his burden lifted, he left behind Hollywood's opulence and trappings to concentrate on healing the wounds he had inflicted on his family.

Could God heal the family?

Absolutely!

Mark Koch believed this, and set a path to reunite with his family. He started by kneeling in remorse during an altar call by a California preacher. A couple months earlier, and a few thousand miles away, in Tampa, Florida, his 12-year-old son Blake had accepted Christ and been baptized while at summer camp. Father and son had been on different courses, but they both found victory in Jesus in 1997.

God's salvation had done a marvelous thing for Mark and Blake. Several years later, in 2011, as two grown men, father and son Mark and Blake Koch decided to team up and do some racing together.

Blake was asked to rise to another challenge in 2011. A familiar one.

His mom had cancer. Again.

The season had barely gotten under way when he learned the hard news. Blake rose to the challenge. This time, his mother's doctors told her she would need a double mastectomy. Blake told his mom, "Let's get it over with and go through this process together."

Blake was true to his word; he stood beside his mom once again. In October 2011, before a Nationwide race, NASCAR honored 300 breast cancer survivors. During the pre-race ceremonies, Blake stood beside his mom, Angie, who was among the courageous women standing in recognition of their battle with cancer.

Like many NASCAR drivers, Blake had to scramble to find

sponsorship in 2012. He thought he had most of the season wrapped up and agreed to make a commercial for one of his prospective sponsors, the Rise Up and Register Campaign, which educates people about the importance of registering to vote in the upcoming presidential election.

ESPN rejected the ad, saying it carried political and religious overtones. But that may have been one of those eye-of-the-beholder situations. Some suspected the real reason was because Blake was so upfront about his faith, reflected by the many links to Christian organizations on his website. Whatever the reason, the Rise Up Campaign decided to stop sponsoring Blake's car since airing commercials during NASCAR races had created such a flap.

On the upside, the kerfuffle provided Blake with a lot of press as well as an opportunity to share his perspective. He told Brian Kilmeade, host of "Fox and Friends," that he would not compromise or deny his beliefs. "I didn't think that my faith in Christ would have an impact on whether or not a sponsor could air a commercial," he said.

Blake is not ashamed to be a Christian. From having Christian ministries sponsor him, to interceding for others in prayer behind closed doors, or playing his bongo drum on a cool Carolina evening, he is faithful to his Lord and Savior.

Be looking for Blake on the NASCAR horizon. As one of his favorite songs goes, he is rising in the ranks every year.

DARRELL WALTRIP—FROM BEING HATED TO BELOVED

"It all comes down to this," Darrell Waltrip said at the close of his NASCAR Hall of Fame induction speech in 2012. "I had a lot of things out of order. I had my priorities all wrong. But I've been blessed; I was given a second chance."

DW, as NASCAR fans and friends affectionately call Darrell, has accepted numerous accolades over his career and been honored in too many ways to mention here. But his prized possession, which he accepted in 1983, was the gift of salvation through the Lord Jesus Christ. Even when DW was accepting high praise for his Hall of Fame career, he made sure he mentioned his greatest achievement—accepting the free gift of eternal life with his cherished Savior.

Darrell, born in 1947, grew up with a strong Christian heritage. His parents, Leroy and Margaret Waltrip, were involved at Crabtree Avenue Baptist Church in Owensboro, Kentucky. Mabel Waltrip, the boy's grandmother, was also a godly example. She read her Bible every morning and night, and whenever Darrell was around, she read God's Word to him, too.

But despite the godly influence growing up, racing came to rule Darrell's life. In fact, racing was his only lifestyle. Church had been lapped several times and was a distant second. He'd already fled Owensboro for Franklin, Tennessee, attempting to leave his reputation for recklessness behind . . . and to escape the watchful eyes of the hometown law. He also drove away from his new wife, Stevie, to clear his way to the track.

Fortunately for Darrell, Stevie was a Southern woman of great faith, and she was devoted to her man from their beginning, and willing to set aside her dreams to follow her husband. They reunited, and once they became a team again, DW found success on the track. Meanwhile, the Waltrips got established in Franklin.

Since the day Stevie moved to Tennessee, Darrell's racing was *their* racing. They made every effort to do it together. Stevie was the first woman allowed into a NASCAR garage. She even served as a crew member so she could stand behind the pit road wall to support her husband.

Even though Darrell did not race alone, he was alone spiritually— an empty jumpsuit. When he burst onto the NASCAR scene in 1972 with his own car and toolbox, he also brought along an ego the size of a speedway. As the victories piled up, he thought he ruled NASCAR because he owned Victory Lane.

In a matter of speaking, Victory Lane was his personal fiefdom. In his first decade of NASCAR, he claimed 51 wins. He was back-to-back Winston Cup Series Champion in 1981 and 1982. He was the alpha male, the top dog who snarled at competitors and at anyone who got close.

What gnawed at his insides, though, was that not many people liked him. Most fans despised Darrell Waltrip, and they booed more than they cheered him. Beer cans, chicken bones, and profanity were thrown at him at every track. Still, Darrell would win. Following victory, he'd cover his miserable state of mind with a smokescreen of words. He'd raise his fist and say, "Bring it on. Nothing bothers me." But then . . .

Wham!

DW's #11 Monte Carlo hit the wall hard during the 1983 Daytona 500. That crash started Darrell on his journey back to church, to a right relationship with the Lord, and to the reality that life was not all about him.

First, paramedics pulled Darrell from that Sunday's wreckage. While he recuperated, he thought about how difficult the year had been. He and Stevie were facing tough, personal issues in their marriage. They wanted desperately to start a family. They had been trying to have a child for years and they grieved one miscarriage. Then, after being under a doctor's care for seven years, Stevie finally got pregnant. "We were beside ourselves with joy," Stevie said. Four months later, however, they were grieving again over a second miscarriage. His life was spinning out of control.

Some close friends invited DW and Stevie to attend their church, which met Wednesday nights in the Hillsboro High School. DW couldn't use his normal excuses for not going—"I race on Sundays" or "I need my rest." Plus, he was moving beyond excuses, realizing his on-the-track success left him feeling hollow.

It was in July—as "hot as Hades," Darrell said—when the pastor, Dr. Cortez Cooper, talked one evening about having a personal relationship with the Lord. Darrell heard the gospel message in a way he had never heard it before, as in the idea that the Christian faith is a daily walk, a regular friendship, and a personal relationship.

After the service, DW, with Stevie right behind him, approached Dr. Cooper. After Dr. Cooper answered his questions, Darrell lowered himself on his knees in the hot hallway of the school. With sweat on his brow and tears on his cheeks, DW accepted Jesus as his Savior.

He started reading the Bible and praying—twin disciplines of his new personal relationship with Christ. He and Stevie prayed together for all parts of their lives. In 1987, after years of infertility, he and Stevie were blessed with the first of their two daughters, and Darrell was able to confidently say, "I want to be the best dad, the best husband, and the best race car driver."

Stevie began taping scripture verses to the dashboard of her husband's race car. Darrell would use caution laps to meditate on the verse his wife had picked for that day. Stevie also wrote out Bible verses for Dale Earnhardt Sr., who, as the story goes, would go searching the pits for Stevie if she hadn't handed him a Bible verse to tape to his dashboard.

The '80s were great years for Darrell on the NASCAR circuit. He won another Winston Cup Series in 1985, the Daytona 500 in 1989, and was honored as NASCAR's "Popular Driver Award" in 1989—quite a turnaround for a driver used to hearing boos and catcalls every time he was introduced. To round out the '80s, he was named NASCAR's "Driver of the Decade."

Darrell continued racing through the 1990s, but it was clear that he was no longer competitive. After the 2000 season, he retired gracefully and quickly moved into the Fox Sports broadcast booth. His role as analyst has allowed him to stay close to the sport he has invested himself in for more than 40 years.

Five years after Darrell accepted Jesus Christ, he made his greatest NASCAR investment. He and Stevie began to join with some Christian friends on racing weekends at the track. At first, it was the Waltrips, Lake and Lisa Speed, and Bobby and Kim Hillin. They called themselves the Racers for Christ. In 1988, Max Helton, a minister from California, wanting to start an outreach to NASCAR drivers and their families, formally joined the couples to launch Motor Racing Outreach.

These days, 36 race weekends a year, 43 drivers and their families have a place to go to church, thanks to Motor Racing Outreach.

In terms of a legacy for Darrell Waltrip, it doesn't get better than that.

GOD'S HALL OF FAME

All of these drivers, and many more, show that God has truly provided professional stock car racing with a crowd of witnesses for His glory. Race fans, as we raise the checkered flag, please read this passage from Hebrews 12:1–2 (NLT):

> *Therefore, since we are surrounded by such a huge crowd of witnesses to the life of faith, let us strip off every weight that slows us down, especially the sin that so easily trips us up. And let us run with endurance the race God has set before us. We do this by keeping our eyes on Jesus, the champion who initiates and perfects our faith.*

APPENDIX

NASCAR HISTORY AT A GLANCE

There is no doubt about the date people began racing automobiles.
It was the day they built the second automobile.
RICHARD PETTY

January 16, 1919—The 18th Amendment of the U.S. Constitution is ratified, prohibiting the manufacture, sale, or transportation of intoxicating liquors (Prohibition Era begins).

October 29, 1929—U.S. Stock Exchange crashes, and the Depression Era begins. A depressed populace seeks survival brewing moonshine.

1930s, '40s, and '50s—Moonshine "trippers" race to outrun Johnny Law and the G-men during the week and then race against one another after church on Sundays.

1934—Bill France arrives in Daytona from Washington, D.C.

1936—France, a mechanic, enters a local car race and takes fifth.

1937—France starts promoting "strictly stock" races.

December 14, 1947—France holds a meeting at the Streamline Hotel in Daytona Beach to organize future stock car racing. NASCAR is born. France takes leadership of NASCAR.

1948–1966—Period of the first-generation stock car.

February 1948—NASCAR runs its first race in Daytona. NASCAR is incorporated.

June 19, 1949—First NASCAR race is held in Charlotte for a prize of $5,000.

1950—NASCAR runs 19 races as the Grand National Series.

February 22, 1959—Daytona International Speedway opens and Lee Petty wins first Daytona 500 in front of 42,000.

January 31, 1960—CBS Sports broadcasts parts of its first live race.

July 16, 1961—ABC Sports features two hours of the Firecracker 250 on its *Wide World of Sports* TV broadcast.

1964—Richard Petty wins the first of seven championships.

1967–1980—Period of the second-generation stock car.

March 24, 1970—Buddy Baker becomes the first driver to break 200 mph.

1971—R.J. Reynolds becomes the series' first major sponsor.

1972—Modern Era of NASCAR begins. Bill France Jr. begins leading NASCAR. Corporate sponsorship begins playing a prominent role. A new points system and more structured schedule are introduced.

February 18, 1979—CBS Sports broadcasts first flag-to-flag NASCAR race, the Daytona 500.

November 18, 1979—Richard Petty wins his seventh championship.

1981–1991—Period of the third-generation stock car.

1982—Anheuser-Busch sponsors NASCAR's second series.

1985—First All-Star exhibition race is held in Charlotte.

1986—NASCAR Winston Cup becomes official name of the premier series.

April 30, 1987—Bill Elliott sets new fastest speed of 212.809 mph at Talladega.

1989—Entire NASCAR Cup Series race is on TV.

1992–2006—Period of the fourth-generation stock car.

November 15, 1992—Richard Petty retires with 200 wins in 35 years.

1994—Dale Earnhardt Sr. wins his seventh NASCAR championship.

1995—NASCAR begins truck racing with sponsor Craftsman. Jeff Gordon wins first of four championships.

1998—NASCAR celebrates its 50th anniversary.

2001—Dale Earnhardt Sr. dies at the Daytona 500. Jeff Gordon wins his fourth championship.

2004—NASCAR's premier series is named after new sponsor, Nextel. NASCAR introduces the Chase, a playoff system to crown a champion. After 26 races, the Top 10 drivers (now the Top 12 drivers) according to points become eligible to compete for season championship.

2007–2012—Period of the fifth-generation stock car, called the "Car of Tomorrow."

2008—NASCAR's premier series takes the name Sprint Cup to reflect the Sprint and Nextel merger of 2005. The Busch series becomes the Nationwide series.

2009—NASCAR's truck series changes title sponsor from Craftsman Tools to Camping World.

May 11, 2010—NASCAR Hall of Fame opens in Charlotte.

November 21, 2010—Jimmie Johnson wins his fifth consecutive championship.

February 20, 2011—Trevor Bayne becomes youngest driver to win the Daytona 500.

2013 —"Generation-6" cars begin their inaugural season.

February 24, 2013—NASCAR celebrates the 55th running of the Daytona 500.

ABOUT THE AUTHORS

Mike Yorkey is the author, co-author, or editor of more than 85 books. He has written about sports all his professional life for a variety of national publications.

Mike has collaborated with Tampa Bay Rays' Ben Zobrist and his wife, Julianna, a Christian music artist, in *Double Play*; Cleveland Browns quarterback Colt McCoy and his father, Brad, in *Growing Up Colt*; San Francisco Giants pitcher Dave Dravecky in *Called Up*; San Diego Chargers placekicker Rolf Benirschke in *Alive & Kicking*; tennis star Michael Chang in *Holding Serve*; and paralyzed Rutgers' defensive tackle Eric LeGrand in *Believe: My Faith and the Tackle That Changed My Life*.

Mike is the author or co-author of seven other books in the *Playing with Purpose* series, including *Playing with Purpose: Inside the Lives and Faith of the NFL's Most Intriguing Personalities*. He is also the co-author of the internationally bestselling *Every Man's Battle* series with Steve Arterburn and Fred Stoker.

Mike's website is www.mikeyorkey.com.

Marcus Brotherton is a journalist and professional writer known internationally for his literary collaborations with high-profile public figures, humanitarians, inspirational leaders, and military personnel. He has authored, co-authored, or edited more than 45 books.

Marcus' notable works include the *New York Times* bestselling *We Who Are Alive and Remain* and the national bestseller *Call of Duty* with Lt. Buck Compton. He last collaborated on *The Real Win*, a men's ministry book with Colt McCoy and Matt Carter.

For more information, visit www.marcusbrotherton.com.

Matt Weeda is a research assistant and historian. He specializes in researching people or stories, present or historical, for lasting truths that today's generations and future generations alike can identify with and embrace. He loves sports and has coached various high school and college teams for the past 15 years.

Matt graduated from Trinity Western University in British Columbia, Canada, with a degree in history. He is a columnist for *ileague.us*, teaches literacy work shops at the Jansen Arts Center, and volunteers as a researcher for the Lynden Pioneer Museum. He has been published in *Sagebrush* journal and researched aircraft tecnicalities for author Marcu Brotherton on the book *Still Lolo*.

Matt blogs at www.matthewnweeda.wordpress.com.

SOURCE MATERIAL

UNDERSTANDING THE THREE NATIONAL SERIES OF NASCAR
"NASCAR consists of three national series . . ." from "About NASCAR," at the NASCAR official website, and available at http://www.nascar.com/en_us/news-media/articles/about-nascar.html

"NASCAR calls the Nationwide Series . . ." from "Careers," at NASCAR official website, and available at http://employment.nascar.com/#/series_racing

THE HISTORY OF NASCAR AT A GLANCE
"There is no doubt about the date people began racing . . ." from *Daytona 500* by Nancy Roe Pimm, Millbrook Press, Minneapolis, 2011, page 13.

1. BOBBY LABONTE: A BROTHERHOOD OF CHAMPIONS
"Stories include such famous brother combos . . ." from *The Great Book of NASCAR Lists* by John Roberts and M.B. Roberts, Running Press, Philadelphia, 2012, pages 133–134.

"This places them sixth on NASCAR's lists of most wins by any brother combo," from *The Great Book of NASCAR Lists* by John Roberts and M.B. Roberts, Running Press, Philadelphia, 2012, pages 133–134.

"[My older brother] showed me what being a champion is all about . . ." from "Labonte Brothers Good at Being Cool: Bobby Watched Terry—and Learned," by the Associated Press, *Toledo* Blade, November 23, 2000, and available at http://news.google.com/

"Goldang, this is so cool . . ." from "Labontes Celebrate Family Day at Atlanta: Terry Takes Title," by Sandra McKee, *The Baltimore Sun*, November 11, 1996, and available at http://articles.baltimoresun.com/1996-11-11/sports/1996316090_1_labonte-brothers-bobby-winning-the-race

"Bobby is not sure what he would be doing if he weren't racing in NASCAR . . ." from Bobby Labonte's official website, retrieved March 2013, and available at http://www.bobbylabonte.com/audio/archive/050404.mp3

"Even Martha Labonte was an active participant . . ." from "From CC Speedway to NASCAR," by Richard Tijerina, *Corpus Christi Caller-Times*, September 26, 2001, and available at http://www.caller2.com/2001/september/26/today/localnew/12738.html

"During those growing-up years, he became his brother's biggest fan . . ." from Bobby Labonte's official website, retrieved March 2013, and available at http://www.bobbylabonte.com/audio/archive/050505.mp3

"He watched his father work on something and then wanted to give it a try himself . . ." from "From CC Speedway to NASCAR," by Richard Tijerina, *Corpus Christi Caller-Times*, September 26, 2001, and available at http://www.caller2.com/2001/september/26/today/localnew/12738.html

"His father also constructed the track Bobby would race on . . ." from Bobby Labonte's official website, retrieved March 2013, and available at http://www.bobbylabonte.com/audio/archive/050505.mp3

"Quarter Midgets of America is the national organization . . ." from Quarter Midgets of America official website, retrieved March 2013, and available at http://www.quartermidgets.org/sport.html

". . . he raced on tracks across his home state of Texas . . ." from Bobby Labonte's official website, retrieved March 2013, and available at http://www.bobbylabonte.com/audio/archive/050505.mp3

". . . two youths who loved fast cars." from "From CC Speedway to NASCAR," by Richard Tijerina, *Corpus Christi Caller-Times*, September

26, 2001, and available at http://www.caller2.com/2001/september/26/today/localnew/12738.html

"I went to Tom Browne Junior High on Friday and was in North Carolina on Saturday . . ." from "From CC Speedway to NASCAR," by Richard Tijerina, *Corpus Christi Caller-Times*, September 26, 2001, and available at http://www.caller2.com/2001/september/26/today/localnew/12738.html

"Bobby enrolled at Trinity High School and excelled . . ." from Bobby Labonte's official website, retrieved March 2013, and available at http://www.bobbylabonte.com/audio/archive/050406.mp3

"Bobby called her 'my rock,'" from "Bobby Labonte: A Driving Faith," by Chad Bonham, *Sports Spectrum*, Fall 2011, and available at http://mydigimag.rrd.com/display_article.php?id=832540

"The time came when raising their children . . ." from Bobby Labonte's official website, retrieved March 2013, and available at http://www.bobbylabonte.com/audio/archive/050628.mp3

"They have made me feel like part of the family . . ." from Bobby Labonte official website, retrieved March 2013, and available at http://www.bobbylabonte.com/news/03_news/030626_contract.shtml

"By winning that race, the Labonte brothers gained . . ." from *The Great Book of NASCAR Lists* by John Roberts and M.B. Roberts, Running Press, Philadelphia, 2012, page 135.

"We'd been building toward this . . ." from "That Trophy, Brother's Role Both Sweet for B. Labonte," by Sandra McKee, *The Baltimore Sun*, November 26, 2000, and available at http://articles.baltimoresun.com/2000-11-26/sports/0011260220_1_bobby-labonte-brothers-petty-family

"On November 7, 2005, Joe Gibbs Racing announced . . ." from "Bobby Labonte to Leave Joe Gibbs Racing After Season," by the Associated Press, *ESPN.com*, November 7, 2005, and available at http://sports.espn.go.com/rpm/news/story?series=wc&id=2216683

"Donna encouraged her husband . . ." from "God's Grace Prevails Through Labonte's Racing Trials," by Lee Warren, *bpsports.net*, November 21, 2009, and available at http://www.bpsports.net/bpsports.asp?ID=6116

"She has cheered him and surprised him . . ." from "Riding with Heart," by Bobby Labonte, in *Chicken Soup for the Soul: NASCAR 101 Stories of Family, Fortitude, and Fast Cars*, ed. Jack Canfield, Mark Victor Hansen, and Cathy Elliot, Chicken Soup for the Soul Publishing, Cos Cob, Connecticut, 2009, pages 91–93.

"Bobby also spent more and more time reading the Bible . . ." from "God's Grace Prevails Through Labonte's Racing Trials," by Lee Warren, *bpsports.net*, November 21, 2009, and available at http://www.bpsports.net/bpsports.asp?ID=6116

"Bobby is really glad it's there because . . ." from Bobby Labonte official website, retrieved March 2013, and available at http://www.bobbylabonte.com/audio/archive/050921.mp3

"It's a chance to get the word out . . ." from "Keeping the Faith: In NASCAR, Lines Blurred Between Racing and Religion," by the Associated Press, *SI.com*, February 10, 2004, and available at http://sportsillustrated.cnn.com/2004/racing/specials/daytona500/2004/02/10/bc.car.racing.religion.ap/index.html

"Bobby is able to say, 'Whatever God wants' . . ." from "God's Grace Prevails Through Labonte's Racing Trials," by Lee Warren, *bpsports.net*, November 21, 2009, and available at http://www.bpsports.net/bpsports.asp?ID=6116

"You know the streak is going to end at some point . . ." from "Bobby Labonte Hoping for Best with JTG Team, Not Sure How Much Longer He Will Race," by Bob Pockrass, *Sporting News.com*, July 5, 2013, and available at http://www.sportingnews.com/nascar/story/2013-07-05/bobby-labonte-retirement-replacement-streak-jtg-daugherty-aj-allmendinger

"That's a question I can't really answer . . ." from "Bobby Labonte Hoping for Best with JTG Team, Not Sure How Much Longer He Will Race," by Bob Pockrass, *Sporting News.com*, July 5, 2013, and available at http://www.sportingnews.com/nascar/story/2013-07-05/bobby-labonte-retirement-replacement-streak-jtg-daugherty-aj-allmendinger

2. MARK MARTIN: FROM BACKWOODS BOY TO LIVING LEGEND

"Mark has the best of his father's traits . . . " from "Mark Martin: Racing's Steady, Consistent, and Complex Superstar," by Larry Cothran, *Stock Car Racing Magazine*, 2002, and available at http://www.stockcarracing.com/featurestories/scrp_0205_winston_cup_driver_mark_martin/viewall.html

"My dad used to prop me up on his lap . . ." from *NASCAR for Dummies* by Mark Martin, Wiley Publishing, Indianapolis, Indiana, 2009, page 15.

"Clyde Martin (Mark's grandfather), at his 100th birthday . . ." from "Clyde Martin: 'Trucking' Through 100 Years of Life," by Lorie Thompson, *The Sun Times*, retrieved April 24, 2013, and available at http://www.reocities.com/motorcity/track/6406/clydemartin.html

"His first race took place in April just four months . . ." from "The Encyclopedia of Arkansas History and Culture" at the Central Arkansas Library System official website, retrieved April 2013, and available at http://www.encyclopediaofarkansas.net/encyclopedia/entry-detail.aspx?entryID=2585

"Mark tested his skills further in 1977 . . ." from *Mark Martin: Small Town Hero, Big League Racer* by Kathy Persinger, Sports Publishing, LLC, Oak Brook, Illinois, 2004, and available at http://books.google.com/books?id=jvO-jDfjdfgC&printsec=copyright#v=onepage&q&f=false

"Is not wisdom found among the aged?" from Job 12:12

"Petty, Earnhardt, and other greats . . ." from "When the Engines No Longer Roar: A Case Study of North Wilkesboro, NC and the North Wilkesboro Speedway," by Andrew J. Baker, *North Wilkesboro Speedway*, 2005, and available at http://www.savethespeedway.net/index.php/track-history

". . . young racers, older veterans, car owners . . ." from "When the Engines No Longer Roar: A Case Study of North Wilkesboro, NC and the North Wilkesboro Speedway," by Andrew J. Baker, *North Wilkesboro Speedway*, 2005, and available at http://www.savethespeedway.net/index.php/track-history

"Any guesses as to where the first season's champion . . ." from *The Earnhardts: A Biography* by Gerry Souter, ABC-CLIO, LLC, Santa Barbara, 2009, and available at http://books.google.com/books

"The retail giant had its humble beginnings . . ." from "About Lowe's," at Lowe's company website, and available at http://media.lowes.com/about-lowes/

"In 2004, the Roush Racing Team . . ." from "When the Engines No Longer Roar: A Case Study of North Wilkesboro, NC and the North Wilkesboro Speedway," by Andrew J. Baker, *North Wilkesboro Speedway*, 2005, and available at http://www.savethespeedway.net/index.php/track-history

"When I was twelve Richard Petty was my favorite . . ." from Mark Martin's twitter feed on April 26, 2013, and available at https://twitter.com/55MarkMartin

"He told ESPN journalist David Newton . . ." from "Martin Wouldn't Change His Tough Days," by David Newton, *ESPN.com*, October 20, 2009, and available at http://sports.espn.go.com/rpm/nascar/cup/columns/story?columnist=newton_david&id=4559324

"Mark's cocky side also ignored Waltrip's attempt . . ." from "Martin Wouldn't Change His Tough Days," by David Newton, *ESPN.com*, October 20, 2009, and available at http://sports.espn.go.com/rpm/nascar/cup/columns/story?columnist=newton_david&id=4559324

"Mark's answer to his situation was . . ." from "Martin Wouldn't Change His Tough Days," by David Newton, *ESPN.com*, October 20, 2009, and available at http://sports.espn.go.com/rpm/nascar/cup/columns/story?columnist=newton_david&id=4559324

"If '82 wasn't humiliating enough . . ." from "Martin Wouldn't Change His Tough Days," by David Newton, *ESPN.com*, October 20, 2009, and available at http://sports.espn.go.com/rpm/nascar/cup/columns/story?columnist=newton_david&id=4559324

"Overall, he had a low level commitment to God . . ." from "Mark Martin's Christian Testimony," by Victor Lee, and available at http://www.go2mro.com/testimonies/markmartin.php

"But Mark says he wasn't really seeking spiritual growth either . . ." from "Mark Martin: Racing's Steady, Consistent, and Complex Superstar," by Larry Cothran, *Stock Car Racing Magazine*, 2002, and available at http://www.stockcarracing.com/featurestories/scrp_0205_winston_cup_driver_mark_martin/viewall.html

"On this visit, his sister Glenda introduced Arlene . . ." from "Passion Drives NASCAR's Mark Martin," by Becki Moore, *In Arkansas.com*, July 1, 2008, and available at http://www.inarkansas.com/390/passion-drives-nascars-mark-martin

"We're talking heavy drinking, late at night . . ." from "Martin Wouldn't Change His Tough Days," by David Newton, *ESPN.com*, October 20, 2009, and available at http://sports.espn.go.com/rpm/nascar/cup/columns/story?columnist=newton_david&id=4559324

"Later in the season when word got around . . ." from "Martin Wouldn't Change His Tough Days," by David Newton, *ESPN.com*, October 20, 2009, and available at http://sports.espn.go.com/rpm/nascar/cup/columns/story?columnist=newton_david&id=4559324

". . . the boozing had to stop . . ." from "Martin Wouldn't Change His Tough Days," by David Newton, *ESPN.com*, October 20, 2009, and available at http://sports.espn.go.com/rpm/nascar/cup/columns/story?columnist=newton_david&id=4559324

"That meant I had a ride in NASCAR," from "7 Days—Mark Martin," YouTube video by BMM248, October 28, 2012, and available at http://www.youtube.com/watch?v=JzksfXnb5G8

"What happened over the next 19 seasons . . ." from *Mark Martin: The Racer's Racer* by Jerry F. Boone, PRIMEDIA, St. Paul, Minnesota, 2006, http://www.amazon.com/Mark-Martin-Racers-Racing-Motorbooks/dp/B007K52IPI

"He says, "'The cool thing about the Bible . . .'" from "Mark Martin: Racing's Steady, Consistent, and Complex Superstar," by Larry Cothran, *Stock Car Racing Magazine*, 2002, and available at http://www.stockcarracing.com/featurestories/scrp_0205_winston_cup_driver_mark_martin/viewall.html

"He was my hero. He was a man's man, with everything that represents . . ." from "Mark Martin: Racing's Steady, Consistent, and Complex Superstar," by Larry Cothran, *Stock Car Racing Magazine*, 2002, and available at http://www.stockcarracing.com/featurestories/scrp_0205_winston_cup_driver_mark_martin/viewall.html

"I don't see myself running Cup races when I'm fifty-something . . . " from "Can't Let Go," by Ryan Mcgee, *ESPN.com*, updated: April 15, 2009, and available at http://sports.espn.go.com/espnmag/story?id=3476170

"His grandfather, Clyde Martin, once tried . . ." from "Clyde Martin: 'Trucking' Through 100 Years of Life," by Lorie Thompson, *The Sun Times*, retrieved April 24, 2013, and available at http://www.reocities.com/motorcity/track/6406/clydemartin.html

3. MICHAEL MCDOWELL: ALWAYS AIMING HIGHER

"Reagan became the first sitting President to witness a NASCAR race . . ." from *The Reagan Diaries* by Douglas Brinkley, HarperCollins, 2007, page 253.

"Reagan in '84 . . ." from *The Reagan Diaries* by Douglas Brinkley, HarperCollins, 2007, page 277.

"When Michael was old enough to begin competitive racing . . ." from "Biography" at Michael McDowell's official website, retrieved April 2013, and available at http://mmcdowell.com/bio/

"His very first day at the kart track . . ." from "Michael McDowell—Building Blocks," by Don Hamilton, John Hill, *Stock Car Racing Magazine*, February 2009, and available at http://www.stockcarracing.com/featurestories/scrp_0803_michael_mcdowell/viewall.html

"Karting was a way of life for my family and I . . ." from Michael McDowell's official website biography, retrieved April 2013, and available at http://mmcdowell.com/bio/

"Michael's family even took on a venture of buying and selling karts . . ." from "Michael McDowell—Building Blocks," by Don Hamilton, John Hill, *Stock Car Racing Magazine*, February 2009, and available at http://www.stockcarracing.com/featurestories/scrp_0803_michael_mcdowell/viewall.html

"Though his parents would keep cheering him on . . ." from "Anything but a Dream—A NASCAR Driver's Story of Perseverance," by Joe Michael Feldpaush, *Finish a Winner*, April 4, 2012, and available at http://finishawinner.com/stories

"So he sat down and wrote his first sponsorship proposal at age twelve . . ." from "Local Kid Makes Good . . . Fast," by Jon Shafer, *Bimmerfest*, September 7, 2005, and available at http://www. bimmerfest.com/forums/showthread.php?t=110692

"He took other random jobs as well . . ." from "Anything but a Dream—A NASCAR Driver's Story of Perseverance," by Joe Michael Feldpaush, *Finish a Winner*, April 4, 2012, and available at http://finishawinner.com/stories

"Michael wasn't religious growing up . . ." from "A Conversation with NASCAR Driver Michael McDowell," by Chad Bonham, *Beliefnet*, August 15, 2011, and available at http://features.beliefnet.com/inspiringathletes/2011/08/a-conversation-with-nascar-driver-michael-mcdowell.html

"Jami's family would end up having a huge impact . . ." from "Michael McDowell's Christian Testimony," by Michael McDowell, *Motor Racing Outreach*, retrieved April 2013, and available at http://www.go2mro.com/testimonies/michaelmcdowell.php

"In California he met Greg Bell . . . Bill Mayer . . ." from "Michael McDowell—Building Blocks," by Don Hamilton, John Hill, *Stock Car Racing Magazine*, February 2009, and available at http://www.stockcarracing.com/featurestories/scrp_0803_michael_mcdowell/viewall.html

"Following Huber's unlikely and bizarre death . . ." from "Michael McDowell's Christian Testimony," by Michael McDowell, *Motor Racing Outreach*, and available at http://www.go2mro.com/testimonies/michaelmcdowell.php

"Michael was listening the day of Ron's memorial service . . ." from "Michael McDowell's Christian Testimony," by Michael McDowell, *Motor Racing Outreach*, and available at http://www.go2mro.com/testimonies/michaelmcdowell.php

"Driving education courses at Bondurant . . ." from author research, April 2013, and available at www.bondurant.com

"Rob, a racing enthusiast and successful businessman . . ." from "Michael McDowell—Building Blocks," by Don Hamilton, John Hill, *Stock Car Racing Magazine*, February 2009, and available at http://www.stockcarracing.com/featurestories/scrp_0803_michael_mcdowell/viewall.html

"I have been focusing my whole career to get to this point . . ." from "Rocketsports Champ Car Team Replaces American with American," by A. Skyler, *Paddock Talk*, October 14, 2005, and available at http://archive.paddocktalk.com/story-22772.html

"Sadly, during the off-season that year, Michael lost his mother to cancer . . ." from "Tracy Lynn McDowell Obituary," *The Arizona Republic*, January 11, 2006, and available at http://www.legacy.com/obituaries/azcentral/obituary.aspx?n=tracy-lynn-mcdowell&pid=16291257#fbLoggedOut

"I want to do well . . ." from "McDowell's Dream to Come True," by Mark Armijo, *The Arizona Republic*, March 3, 2008, and available at http://www.azcentral.com/sports/speed/articles/2008/03/03/20080303nascar.html

"I have dedicated myself . . . 100 years . . ." from "Rocketsports Champ Car Team Replaces American with American," by A. Skyler, *Paddock Talk*, October 14, 2005, and available at http://archive.paddocktalk.com/story-22772.html

"But after the race, he got lambasted . . ." from "McDowell Takes First Step Recovering After Horrific Crash," by Gary Graves, *USA Today*, April 5, 2008, http://usatoday30.usatoday.com/sports/motor/nascar/2008-04-05-mcdowell_N.htm

"Something is not right, I'm going to run another lap . . ." from "McDowell Takes First Step Recovering After Horrific Crash," by Gary Graves, *USA Today*, April 5, 2008, http://usatoday30.usatoday.com/sports/motor/nascar/2008-04-05-mcdowell_N.htm

"Jami, Michael's wife, felt her stomach drop . . ." from " 'McFlippin' Michael McDowell," by Michael McDowell, April 6, 2008, and available at http://mmcdowell.blogspot.com

"Fearful of losing his Sprint Cup ride . . ." from "Michael McDowell Interview After Crash @ Texas Qualifying," YouTube video by mylocalamerica, April 5, 2008, and available at https://www.youtube.com/watch?v= ktw7fGhmU9M

"When a close friend of his asked him later . . ." from "NASCAR Driver Michael McDowell—Interview on Daystar," YouTube video by Daystar TV, April 21, 2011, and available at http://www.youtube.com/watch?v=9AeQh5Nhdfk

"A distant third or fourth . . ." from "NASCAR Driver Michael McDowell—Interview on Daystar," YouTube video by Daystar TV, April 21, 2011, and available at http://www.youtube.com/watch?v=9AeQh5Nhdfk

"After the 2010 season, Michael felt his career was stuck in neutral . . ." from "NASCAR Driver McDowell Gains Perspective in the Arms of Orphans," by Lee Warren, *The Christian Post*, May, 22, 2011, and available at http://www.christianpost.com/news /nascar-driver-mcdowell-gains-perspective-in-the-arms-of-orphans-50353/

"As exciting as that was, it was an extremely emotional . . ." from "NASCAR Driver McDowell Gains Perspective in the Arms of Orphans," by Lee Warren, *The Christian Post*, May, 22, 2011, and available at http://www.christianpost.com/news /nascar-driver-mcdowell-gains-perspective-in-the-arms-of-orphans-50353/

"Then in 2013 Michael called it quits . . ." from "After Bible Study, NASCAR Driver Takes 30-day Break from Twitter and Facebook," by Jeff Gluck, *USA Today*, January 10, 2013, and available at http://www.businessinsider.com/after-bible-study-nascar-driver-takes-30-break-from-twitter-and-facebook-2013-1

"I wanna thank Jesus, first and foremost . . ." from "Michael McDowell Daytona," YouTube video by Tom Patton, February 24, 2013, and available at http://www.youtube.com/watch?v=Sg1EqeGx87I

4. DAVID REUTIMANN: A BUILDER RELYING ON FAITH

". . . it was one of his proudest moments ever," from "Conversation: David and Buzzie Reutimann," by Dave Rodman, at *NASCAR.COM*, 2007, and available at http://sports.dir.groups.yahoo.com/group/NascarNUTs/ message/85229

"In 1925, he moved to Zephyrhills . . ." from "The Reutimanns: A History of Racing," by Brant James, *Tampa Bay Times*, February 18, 2005, and available at http://www.sptimes.com/2005/02/18/Sports/The_Reutimanns__ A_his.shtml

"Of course, the joke is that David's mother . . ." from "Conversation: David and Buzzie Reutimann," by Dave Rodman, at *NASCAR.COM*, 2007, and available at http://sports.dir.groups.yahoo.com/group/Nascar NUTs/ message/85229

". . . his racing bloodlines . . ." from "The Reutimanns: A History of Racing," by Brant James, *Tampa Bay Times*, February 18, 2005, and available at http://www.sptimes.com/2005/02/18/Sports/The_Reutimanns__ A_his.shtml

"David wanted only to be like Buzzie Reutimann . . ." from "A Conversation with NASCAR Driver David Reutimann," by Chad Bonham, at *Beliefnet*, and available at http://blog.beliefnet.com/inspiringathletes/2012/03/a-conversation-with-nascar-driver-david-reutimann.html

"Lisa worked at a local realty office . . ." from "Reutimann Enjoying a Truckload of Success," by Brant James, *St. Petersburg Times*, November 19, 2004, and available at http://www.sptimes.com/2004/11/19/Sports/Reutimann_enjoying_a_.shtml

"At times as a young racer . . ." from "A Dynamic Father-Son Duo," by David Newton, *ESPN.COM*, 2011, and available at http://sports.espn.go.com/rpm/nascar/cup/columns/story?columnist=newton_david&id=6664398&campaign=rss&source=RPMHeadlines

"Maybe he was too old for elite level racing . . ." from "NASCAR's Reutimann: Faith-Driven," by Lee Warren, at *BPSports.net*, April 2, 2007, and available at http://www.bpsports.net/bpsports.asp?ID=5552

"And his sheer racing ability . . ." from "Conversation: David and Buzzie Reutimann," by Dave Rodman, *NASCAR.COM*, 2007, and available at http://sports.dir.groups.yahoo.com/group/NascarNUTs/message/85229

"At the end of the conversation . . ." from "NASCAR Nextel Cup Driver David Reutimann," YouTube video by Bryan Lacey, October 9, 2012, and available at https://www. youtube.com/watch?v=JqLTvE0sLVk

"God had a plan . . ." from "NASCAR's Reutimann: Faith-Driven," by Lee Warren, at *BPSports.net*, April 2, 2007, and available at http://www.bpsports.net/bpsports.asp?ID=5552

"The other thing he did was pray . . ." from "Tears Flow as Reutimann Slips into Daytona 500," by Brant James, *Tampa Bay Times*, February 16, 2007, and available at http://www.sptimes.com/2007/02/16/Sports/Tears_ flow_as_Reutima.shtml

"I am no expert on scripture, and I am probably as big a mess-up as anyone . . ." from the David Reutimann 2013 Edition of Motor Racing Outreach's Driver Testimony Card.

"David may not be an expert on scripture, but he knows it is the guide for his life . . ." from "A Conversation with NASCAR Driver David Reutimann," by Chad Bonham, at *Beliefnet*, and available at http://blog.beliefnet.com/inspiringathletes/2012/03/a-conversation-with-nascar-driver-david-reutimann.html

"The road back went through a bully at his school . . ." from "NASCAR's Reutimann: Faith-Driven," by Lee Warren, at *BPSports.net*, April 2, 2007, and available at http://www.bpsports.net/bpsports.asp?ID=5552

". . . g-force impact during the crash was one of the hardest ever recorded . . ." from "Reutimann's Crash Among Hardest Ever Recorded," by Marty Smith, *ESPN.com*, March 5, 2007, and available at http://sports.espn.go.com/rpm/news/story?seriesId=2&id= 2780606

"Though David admits a victory in a rain-shortened race . . ." from "NASCAR: David Reutimann Career at Crossroads but Relies on Faith for the Future," by Luke Krmpotick, at *BleacherReport.com*, November 1, 2011, and available at http://bleacherreport.com/articles/920184-nascar-michael-reutimann-has-big-plans-but-relies-on-faith-for-the-future

"David wouldn't be with MWR in 2012 . . ." from "Michael Waltrip Won't Bring David Reutimann Back in 2012," by Chad Leistikow, *USA TODAY*, November 3, 2011, and available at http://usatoday30.usatoday.com/sports/motor/ nascar/story/2011-11-03/david-reuitmann-wont-return-with-waltrip-in-2012/51062990/1

"Nine times out of ten, faith was really the only thing that was constant . . ." from "NASCAR: David Reutimann Career at Crossroads but Relies on Faith for the Future," by Luke Krmpotick, at *BleacherReport.com*, November 1, 2011, and available at http://bleacherreport.com/articles/920184-nascar-michael-reutimann-has-big-plans-but-relies-on-faith-for-the-future

"David, cut from the same cloth, made for a good fit . . ." from "Reutimann Finds Ride with Tommy Baldwin Racing," by Dave Rodman, *NASCAR.COM*, January 3, 2012, and available at http://www.nascar.com/en_us/news-media/ articles/2012/01/03/dreutimann-tommy-baldwin-racing-2012.html?eref=/ news/headlines/cup

"Now he was back in a building role with the one-year-old BK team . . ." from "Team Preview: BK Racing," by John Singler at *Motor Racing Network*, February 2, 2013, and available at http://www.

motorracingnetwork.com/Race-Series/NASCAR-Sprint-Cup/News/
Articles/2013/02/Team-Preview-BK-Racing.aspx

"He once said . . ." from "Conversation: David and Buzzie Reutimann,"
by Dave Rodman, *NASCAR.COM,* 2007, and available at http://sports.
dir.groups.yahoo.com/group/NascarNUTs/ message/85229

5: TREVOR BAYNE: REACHING HIS BIG DREAM

"The kid just might be the next big deal . . ." from "Trevor Bayne, Wood
Brothers Post Race Daytona 500 News Conference Part 1," YouTube
video by Greg Engle, February 23, 2011, and available at https://www.
youtube.com/watch?v=xOuzankDuXA

"On the starting grid five hours earlier . . ." from "2011 Daytona 500,"
YouTube video by NascarAllOut, March 15, 2011, and available at
https://www.youtube.com/watch?v=tHWs8AhIBFw

"I bet 1991 even makes you feel a little bit old . . ." from "Trevor
Bayne, Wood Brothers Post Race Daytona 500 News Conference Part
1," YouTube video by Greg Engle, February 23, 2011, and available at
https://www.youtube.com/watch?v=xOuzankDuXA

"Trevor smiled ear-to-ear, laughed . . ." from "Trevor Bayne, Wood
Brothers Post Race Daytona 500 News Conference Part 4," YouTube
video by Greg Engle, February 23, 2011, and available at https://www.
youtube.com/watch?v=ZVL0P__MZIo

"His parents, Rocky and Stephanie Bayne, raised Trevor . . ." from
"Life in the NASCAR Fast Land: Knoxville's Baynes Adjusting to
Son's Sudden Success," by Andrew Gribble, *Knoxnews.com,* 2011, and
available at http://www.knoxnews.com/news/2011/mar/18/trevor-
bayne-knoxville-family/

"In middle school, God first . . ." from "Trevor Bayne: Testimony at Lumpkin Campground Part 1," YouTube video by dvillecw1, July 27, 2012, and available at https://www.youtube.com/watch?v=AMU7ouUFfz0

"As a two-year-old he rumbled around in a battery-powered jeep . . ." from "Success Finds NASCAR Prodigy Trevor Bayne Ahead of Schedule," by John Romano, *Tampa Bay Times*, February 20, 2011, and available at http://www.tampabay.com/sports/ autoracing/success-finds-nasca

"At home later that evening . . ." from "Trevor Bayne: Testimony at Lumpkin Campground Part 1," YouTube video by dvillecw1, July 27, 2012, and available at https://www.youtube.com/watch?v=AMU7ouUFfz0

"With his parents support, he left his family . . ." from "Success Finds NASCAR Prodigy Trevor Bayne Ahead of Schedule," by John Romano, *Tampa Bay Times*, February 20, 2011, and available at http://www.tampabay.com/sports/autoracing/success-finds-nasca

"After a team signs a developmental driver, one of two things happens . . ." from *NASCAR for Dummies,* by Mark Martin, Wiley Publishing, Indianapolis, Indiana, 2009, page 50.

"The ten-year-old boy stood in his living room and cried . . ." from "Trevor Bayne: Testimony at Lumpkin Campground Part 1," YouTube video by dvillecw1, July 27, 2012, and available at https://www.youtube.com/watch?v=AMU7ouUFfz0

"The farm-turned-speedway was the nation's first . . ." from Thompson Speedway official website, and available at http://www.thompsonspeedway.com/track_history.htm

"Then one day, Trevor was out wakeboarding . . ." from "Trevor Bayne: Testimony at Lumpkin Campground Part 1," YouTube video by dvillecw1, July 27, 2012, and available at https://www.youtube.com/watch?v=AMU7ouUFfz0

"They'd made the trip annually since Trevor had been nine . . ." from "Life in the NASCAR Fast Land: Knoxville's Baynes Adjusting to Son's Sudden Success," by Andrew Gribble, *Knoxnews.com*, 2011, and available at http://www.knoxnews.com/news/2011/mar/18/trevor-bayne-knoxville-family/

"He says he journeyed away from being in the Word . . ." from "Trevor Bayne: Testimony at Lumpkin Campground Part 1," YouTube video by dvillecw1, July 27, 2012, and available at https://www.youtube.com/watch?v=AMU7ouUFfz0

"You will love this kid . . ." from "Trevor Bayne Brings Flair to Cup," by Lee Spencer, *FoxSports.com*, 2011, and available at http://msn.foxsports.com/nascar/story/Trevor-Bayne-Wood-brothers-show-family-side-of-NASCAR-in-Daytona-500-celebration-022111#!fTVAD

"Trevor passed 140 times during the race . . ." from "Trevor Bayne to Run 17 Cup Races for Wood Brothers," *Skirts and Scuffs*, 2011, and available at http://www.skirtsandscuffs.com/2011/01/trevor-bayne-to-run-17-cup-races-for.html

". . . join a weeklong mission trip to Mexico . . ." from "Daytona 500 Winner, Trevor Bayne, Affirms His Support of Back2Back," by Lonnie Clouse, *Back2Back Ministries*, February 21, 2011, and available at, http://back2back.org/2011/02/daytona-500-winner-bayne-affirms-his-support-of-back2back/

"There are a lot of foundations and ministries . . ." from "Trevor Bayne, Wood Brothers Post Race Daytona 500 News Conference Part 5," YouTube video by Greg Engle, February 23, 2011, and available at https://www.youtube.com/watch?feature=endscreen&NR=1&v=wxSMf7JYUsQ

"Trevor took part in the Bible studies . . ." from "Daytona 500 Winner, Trevor Bayne, Affirms His Support of Back2Back," by Lonnie Clouse, *Back2Back Ministries*, February 21, 2011, and available at http://back2back.org/2011/02/daytona-500-winner-bayne-affirms-his-support-of-back2back/

"He was just serving the orphans around him out of the joy . . ." from "Daytona 500 Winner, Trevor Bayne, Affirms His Support of Back2Back," by Lonnie Clouse, *Back2Back Ministries*, February 21, 2011, and available at http://back2back.org/2011/02/daytona-500-winner-bayne-affirms-his-support-of-back2back/

"And the guys made quite an impression . . ." from "Daytona 500 Winner's Race for Faith," by Eric Marrapodi, *CNN Belief Blog*, February 21, 2011, and available at http://religion.blogs.cnn.com/2011/02/21/daytona-500-winners-race-for-faith/

"One day, Trevor and fellow driver Michael McDowell . . ." from author interview with Lonnie Clouse on May 16, 2013

"Lonnie told him he had an open invitation . . ." from "Daytona 500 Winner, Trevor Bayne, Affirms His Support of Back2Back," by Lonnie Clouse, *Back2Back Ministries*, February 21, 2011, and available at http://back2back.org/2011/02/daytona-500-winner-bayne-affirms-his-support-of-back2back/

"Two days before the start of the season . . ." from "Daytona 500 Winner, Trevor Bayne, Affirms His Support of Back2Back," by Lonnie Clouse, *Back2Back Ministries*, February 21, 2011 and available at http://back2back.org/2011/02/daytona-500-winner-bayne-affirms-his-support-of-back2back/

"He's come on strong; he's got a great personality . . ." from "2011 Daytona 500," YouTube video by NascarAllOut, March 15, 2011, and available at https://www.youtube.com/watch?v=tHWs8AhIBFw
"Many of NASCAR's most dramatic scenes . . ." from "2011 Daytona 500 Part 1 of 18 (Intro/Starting Grid)," YouTube video by Buggy1Boy, February 24, 2011, and available at https://www.youtube.com/watch?v=EF2WSCYKgY4

"In the " '60s and " '70s NASCAR fans came . . ." from "The Woodchopper: Glen Wood," by Deb Williams, *Legends: The Official Hall of Fame Yearbook*, 2012, pages 50–59.

"Are you kidding me . . ." from "2011 Daytona 500 Part 17 of 18 (Finish/Trevor Bayne Wins)," YouTube video by Buggy1Boy, February 24, 2011, and available at https://www.youtube.com/watch?v=M7mX8yYV7zc

"The year before Trevor was just a kid watching . . ." from "Success Finds NASCAR Prodigy Trevor Bayne Ahead of Schedule," by John Romano, *Tampa Bay Times*, February 20, 2011, and available at http://www.tampabay.com/sports/autoracing/success-finds-nasca

"Finding Christ. He is the reason I'm here . . ." from "Trevor Bayne, Wood Brothers Post Race Daytona 500 News Conference Part 4," YouTube video by Greg Engle, February 23, 2011, and available at https://www.youtube.com/watch?v=ZVL0P__MZIo

"Trevor's assessment at the time . . ." from "Daytona 500 Champ Trevor Bayne Reflects on His Illness," by Al Pearce, *Autoweek.com*, May 26, 2011, and available at http://www.autoweek.com/article/20110526/nascar/110529849

"Every day he asked the doctors how long . . ." from "Daytona 500 Winner Trevor Bayne Turns to Faith in Adversity," by Bruce Martin, *SI.com*, June 28, 2011, and available at http://sportsillustrated.cnn.com/2011/writers/bruce_martin/06/28/trevorbayne/index.html

"But that was far from what happened . . ." from "One Year Later, Trevor Bayne Still Searching for Stability," by Nate Ryan, *USA Today.com*, February 23, 2012, and available at http://usatoday30.usatoday.com/sports/motor/nascar/story/2012-02-22/Trevor-Bayne-still-searching-for-stability/53214712/1

"I should have got married a long time ago . . ." from "Bayne Gets Win in Iowa Nationwide Race," by the Associated Press, *Floridatoday.com*, June 11, 2013, and available at http://www.floridatoday.com/viewart/20130610/SPORTS03/306100021/Bayne-gets-win-Iowa-Nationwide-race

"During the call, Trevor cried, and as Lonnie . . ." from "Daytona 500 Winner, Trevor Bayne, Affirms His Support of Back2Back," by Lonnie Clouse, *Back2Back Ministries*, February 21, 2011, and available at http://back2back.org/2011/02/daytona-500-winner-bayne-affirms-his-support-of-back2back/

6: JUSTIN ALLGAIER: THE TRIUMPH OF THE "LITTLE GATOR"

"Follow Jesus, Not Me . . ." from "A Day at the Race with NASCAR Driver Justin Allgaier," by Marcia Martinez, *Little Falls Times.com*, July 28, 2010, and available at http://www.littlefallstimes.com/archive/x1026041966/A-day-at-the-races-with-NASCAR-driver-Justin-Allgaier?zc_p=0#axzz2XCGXpxGr

"His inspiration for sharing his faith . . ." from *Chicken Soup for the Soul: Billy Graham & Me: 101 Inspiring Personal Stories from Presidents, Pastors, Performers, and Other People Who Knew Him Well*, by Steve Posner, Amy Newmark, Chicken Soup for the Soul Publishing, 2013, pages 22–23.

"But if there were one thing this twenty-seven-year-old driver could change . . ." from "Justin Allgaier Answers Bonus Questions on NASCAR Race Hub," YouTube video by Valli Hilaire, November 4, 2010, and available at http://www.youtube.com/watch?v=JZO0X_c1u2s
"One day, young Justin was hanging out . . ." from "Inside the Helmet of Justin Allgaier," by Amanda Ebersole, *Skirts and Scuffs*, 2011, and available at http://www.skirtsandscuffs.com/2011/05/inside-helmet-of-justin-allgaier.html

"Riverton's claim to fame was that in 1831 . . ." from *Abraham Lincoln: The Prairie Years—I* by Carl Sandburg, Scribner's, New York, 1926, page 132.

"Earlier that day, his mother was looking . . ." from "Illinois Man Driving AG Message for Brandt," by Cindy Ladage, *Farm World*, January 20, 2012, and available at http://www.farmworldonline.com/news/ArchiveArticle.asp?newsid=13933

"We watched him race, and I fell in love with it . . ." from "NASCAR Nationwide Series Driver Justin Allgaier on Starting Young, Marrying His Childhood Sweetheart, and Dealing with the Dangers of Stock Car Racing," by Chad Bonham, *Beliefnet.com*, June 4, 2011, and available at http://blog.beliefnet.com/inspiringathletes/2011/06/nascar-nationwide-series-driver-justin-allgaier-on-starting-young-marrying-his-childhood-sweetheart-and-dealing-with-the-dangers-of-stock-car-racing.html

"By the time he was twelve, he had racked up . . ." from "Justin Allgaier Biography" at Turner Scott Motorsports official website, and available at www.turnerscottmotorsports.com/drivers/show/4197-justin-allgaier/

"Schrader soon became a mentor for Justin . . ." from "Home Again: Justin Allgaier," Vimeo video by Justin Burnett, and available at http://vimeo.com/59532650

"Riverton Christian Church was Justin's home church . . ." from "NASCAR Nationwide . . . Stock Car Racing," by Chad Bonham, *Beliefnet.com*, June 4, 2011, and available at http://blog.beliefnet.com/inspiringathletes/2011/06/nascar-nationwide-series-driver-justin-allgaier-on-starting-young-marrying-his-childhood-sweetheart-and-dealing-with-the-dangers-of-stock-car-racing.html

". . . the benefit of the Lord's Word . . ." from "Justin Allgaier's Testimony Card" distributed by Motor Racing Outreach Ministry, and available at, http://www.go2mro.com/testimonies/justinallgaier.php

"His longtime friends say his fame hasn't changed him . . ." from "Home Again: Justin Allgaier," Vimeo video by Justin Burnett, and available at http://vimeo.com/59532650

"After meeting Ashley at the game . . ." from "Ashley and Justin Allgaier: A Love Story," by Amanda Ebersole, *Skirts and Scuffs*, September 3, 2011, and available at http://www.skirtsandscuffs.com/2011/09/ashley-and-justin-allgaier-love-story.html

"We'd had our eye on Justin for some time . . ." from "Drivers, Start Your Engines," by Catrina McCulley Wagner, *Illinois Country Living*, April 2009, and available at http://icl.coop/icl/archive/archive/04_09/feature.php

"Great competitor . . ." from "Justin Allgaier Wins the Raybestos Rookie of the Year Award, NASCAR Banquet," YouTube video by gibbysgarage, December 30, 2009, and available at https://www.youtube.com/watch?v=QtdwIMAKzFo

"Thanks goes to God . . ." from "2010 Scott's Turf Builder 300 at Bristol Part 15 of 15 (Post Race)," YouTube video by Buggy1Boy, March 25, 2010, and available at https://www.youtube.com/watch?NR=1&feature=endscreen&v=5ai9tHqGBls

"Bristol holds special meaning for Justin . . ." from "Justin Allgaier: Bristol as a Fan, Racing for Penske, His First Win and More," YouTube video by ThunderValley, July 27, 2010, and available at https://www.youtube.com/watch?v=0NjD7U6jCF0

"Penske announced the news to Justin . . ." from "Justin Allgaier Looks For New Opportunity After Loss of Sponsorship at Penske," by Ashley McCubbin, *Bleacher Report*, October 19, 2010, and available at http://bleacherreport.com/articles/495869-justin-allgaier-looks-for-new-opportunity-after-loss-of-sponsorship-at-penske

"Additionally, Rick Brandt, CEO . . ." from "Illinois Man Driving AG Message for Brandt," by Cindy Ladage, *Farm World*, January 20, 2012, and available at http://www.farmworldonline.com/news/ArchiveArticle.asp?newsid=13933

"Veteran NASCAR racer Mark Martin gives . . ." from *NASCAR for Dummies* by Mark Martin, Wiley Publishing, Indianapolis, Indiana, 2009, page 286.

"*USA Today* reporter Jeff Gluck, expert . . ." from "12 Questions with Justin Allgaier," by Jeff Gluck, *USA Today*, June 5, 2013, and available at http://www.usatoday.com/story/sports/nascar/2013/03/06/justin-allgaier-turner-scott-motorsports-nascar/1967801/

"Justin mustered the strength after the race . . ." from "NASCAR Nationwide 2011: Road America Bucyrus 200 (Full Race)," YouTube video by NARLtv, March 27, 2012, and available at https://www.youtube.com/watch?v=4YqO5UYDvzo

"Number one, I'm first and foremost, a Christian . . ." from "12 Questions with Justin Allgaier," by Jeff Gluck, *USA Today*, June 5, 2013, and available at http://www.usatoday.com/story/sports/nascar/2013/03/06/justin-allgaier-turner-scott-motorsports-nascar/1967801/

". . . raised by a father who said he could raise the best . . ." from "Home Again: Justin Allgaier," Vimeo video by Justin Burnett, and available at http://vimeo.com/59532650

"Awesome, awesome, awesome! God's great . . ." from "2012 NAPA Autoparts 200: Justin Allgaier Wins," YouTube video by nascarvideoarchive, August 18, 2012, and available at https://www.youtube.com/watch?v=khYnbBeXcPI

"Instead of spending all their time lying on the beach . . ." from "Justin Allgaier Diary: All Around the World . . . and Then On the Top of NASCAR's," *Frontstretch*, date unpublished, and available at http://www.frontstretch.com/drivers/42528/

"There have been times when I was ready to give up . . ." from "Inside the Helmet of Justin Allgaier," by Amanda Ebersole, *Skirts and Scuffs*, and available at http://www.skirtsandscuffs.com/2011/05/inside-helmet-of-justin-allgaier.html

"They were with family and friends . . ." from "Additional Family Member in the Making! Welcome 'Baby Gator,' " at *Racetires.com*, February 19, 2013, and available at http://www.racetires.com/2013/02/20/additional-family-member-in-the-making-welcome-baby-gator/

"Growing up, I've faced quite a bit of intimidation . . ." from "Walking Away with a Story to Tell," by Justin Allgaier for the I Am Second ministry

7. JEFF GORDON: THE GREATEST DRIVER OF THIS ERA

"It was no accident that Jeff was a racing demon . . ." from "A Sudden Star," by Ed Hinton, *Sports Illustrated*, 1997, and available at http://sportsillustrated.cnn.com/features/1997/nascar/nsgord.html

"As a boy, Jeff was more drawn to the San Francisco side of the bay . . ." from *The Great Book of NASCAR Lists* by John Roberts and M.B. Roberts, Running Press, Philadelphia, 2012, page 204.

"As the boy began to learn the art of controlling a machine . . ." from "Biography" at Jeff Gordon official website, and available at http://jeffgordon.com/aboutjeff/

"A year later, the first-grader won 35 main events . . ." from "Biography" at Jeff Gordon official website, and available at http://jeffgordon.com/aboutjeff/

"When you're a kid, you need to be a learner . . ." from "A Sudden Star," by Ed Hinton, *Sports Illustrated*, 1997, and available at http://sportsillustrated.cnn.com/features/1997/nascar/nsgord.html

"But Jeff and his family appealed to the insurance . . ." from "Biography" at Jeff Gordon official website, and available at http://jeffgordon.com/aboutjeff/

"In 1986, with Jeff still four years away . . ." from "A Sudden Star," by Ed Hinton, *Sports Illustrated*, 1997, and available at http://sportsillustrated.cnn.com/features/1997/nascar/nsgord.html

"Jeff also began receiving national attention . . ." from *Then Junior Said to Jeff*, by David Poole and Jim McLaurin, Triumph Books, Chicago, 2006, page 225.

"Larry insisted that Jeff really needed to try and drive stock cars . . ." from "Jeff Gordon—No Boundaries," by Bruce Martin, *Stock Car Racing*, February 2009, and available at http://www.stockcarracing.com/youngracers/scrp_0203_jeff_gordon/viewall.html

"But Baker's most famous pupil . . ." from "Buck Baker," by Cary Estes, *Legends: The Official Hall of Fame Yearbook*, 2013, page 24.
"He exclaimed to his mom . . ." from "Buck Baker," by Cary Estes, *Legends: The Official Hall of Fame Yearbook*, 2013, page 24.

"The next thing he did was call his stepdad . . ." from *Then Junior Said to Jeff* by David Poole and Jim McLaurin, Triumph Books, Chicago, 2006, page 225.

Hendrick muttered, "That guy's tail is gonna bust loose . . ." from *Then Junior Said to Jeff* by David Poole and Jim McLaurin, Triumph Books, Chicago, 2006, page 224.

"Hendrick told his general manager . . ." from "A Sudden Star," by Ed Hinton, *Sports Illustrated*, 1997, and available at http://sportsillustrated.cnn.com/features/1997/nascar/nsgord.html

"Of that day, Jeff said, 'I pretty much felt out of place' . . ." from "Race of Ages: Jeff Gordon's First, Richard Petty's Last and a Championship to Boot," by Jay Busbee, *Sports Yahoo.com*, 2012, and available at http://sports.yahoo.com/news/nascar--race-of-ages--gordon-s-first--petty-s-last-and-a-championship-on-the-line-to-boot.html

"Jeff didn't grow up going to church . . ." from "Jeff Gordon's Problem," by a staff reporter at *Stock Car Racing Magazine*, March 1996, and available at http://books.google.com/books

"I started paying more attention . . ." from "A Talk with Jeff Gordon," by Dave Caldwell, *Beliefnet.com*, 2001, and available at http://www. beliefnet.com/Faiths/Christianity/2001/08/A-Talk-With-Jeff-Gordon. aspx

"He accepted Christ that night . . ." from "Interview of Bobby Hillin, Jr. by Kyle Rote, Jr." and available at http://soamc.org/tfh/FILES/ Christian%20Testimonies/Bobby%20Hillin%20Jr.%20NASCAR,%20 On%20the%20Right%20Track/

"Jeff also got to know Darrell Waltrip . . ." from "Speed Racer," by Chad Bonham, *Charisma Magazine*, 2011, and available at http:// www.charismamag.com/blogs/1430-j15/0311-magazine-articles/ features/12846-speed-racer

"He was a big influence on me . . ." from "A Talk with Jeff Gordon," by Dave Caldwell, *Beliefnet.com*, 2001, and available at http://www. beliefnet.com/Faiths/Christianity/2001/08/A-Talk-With-Jeff-Gordon. aspx

"In 1994, he committed his life to Christ . . ." from "A Talk with Jeff Gordon," by Dave Caldwell, *Beliefnet.com*, 2001, and available at http:// www.beliefnet.com/Faiths/Christianity/2001/08/A-Talk-With-Jeff-Gordon.aspx

"I told her she was crazy," from "Jeff Gordon's Problem," by a staff reporter at *Stock Car Racing Magazine*, March 1996, and available at http://books.google.com/books

"The "Boo-Birds" showed up . . ." from *Jeff Gordon: Racing Back to the Front—My Memoir* by Jeff Gordon and Steve Eubanks, Atria Books, New York, 2003, page xxviii.

"Then he led the group in a short prayer . . ." from *Jeff Gordon: Racing Back to the Front—My Memoir*, by Jeff Gordon and Steve Eubanks, Atria Books, New York, 2003, page xv.

"Bring it to the house . . . " from *Jeff Gordon: Racing Back to the Front—My Memoir* by Jeff Gordon and Steve Eubanks, Atria Books, New York, 2003, page xxvii.

"It doesn't matter what level of talent . . ." from "God and Nascar," by Alice Rhee, *NBCNews.com*, May 2005, and available at http://www. nbcnews.com/id/7286393/ns/msnbc/t/god-nascar/#.UeAx2RaTNmA

"Racing is important to me . . ." from "Jeff Gordon and His Faith," YouTube video by AIAUSA, June 11, 2007, and available at https://www. youtube.com/watch?v=iKt_IEGWbuM

". . . it's estimated that 75 percent . . ." from "These 9 Athletes Make More Endorsing Products than Playing Sports," by Tony Manfred, *Business Insider* (website), July 16, 2012, and available at http://www. businessinsider.com/athlete-endorsement-money-2012-7?op=1

"Jeff established his foundation in hopes . . ." from "Jeff Gordon Foundation" at Jeff Gordon official website, and available at http:// jeffgordon.com/aboutjeff/foundation.php

8. MICHAEL WALTRIP: TIMING IS EVERYTHING

"God's season is the best season . . ." from *The Riches of Bunyan* by John Bunyan, Barbour Publishing, Uhrichsville, Ohio, 1998, page 189.

"I believe in God. I believe in Jesus . . ." from "Waltrip Wins Season-Opening Truck Series Race," by Gary Graves, *USA Today.com*, February 19, 2011, and available at http://usatoday30.usatoday.com/sports/ motor/nascar/2011-02-18-truck-series-daytona_N.htm

"As I grew up, I learned more about the Bible . . ." from "Michael Waltrip's Christian Testimony," by Michael Waltrip, *Motor Racing Outreach*, retrieved July 2013, and available at http://www.go2mro.com/testimonies/michaelwaltrip.php

"At the time, Leroy worked at the Pepsi bottling plant . . ." from *In the Blink of an Eye: Dale, Daytona, and the Day that Changed Everything* by Michael Waltrip and Ellis Henican, Hyperion, New York, 2011, page 10.

"Man, that killed me . . ." from *In the Blink of an Eye: Dale, Daytona, and the Day that Changed Everything* by Michael Waltrip and Ellis Henican, Hyperion, New York, 2011, page 12.

". . . Michael decided he wanted to be a race car driver too . . ." from "The Plan," by Michael Waltrip, in *Chicken Soup for the Soul: NASCAR; 101 Stories of Family, Fortitude, and Fast Cars*, ed. Jack Canfield, Mark Victor Hansen, and Cathy Elliot, Chicken Soup for the Soul Publishing, Cos Cob, Connecticut, 2009, pages 94–97.

"Every month . . ." from *In the Blink of an Eye: Dale, Daytona, and the Day that Changed Everything* by Michael Waltrip and Ellis Henican, Hyperion, New York, 2011, page 12.

"Occasionally, on Sundays, his mom would drive . . ." from "Michael Waltrip Steered His Own Way to NASCAR Success," by Mike Graham, *Courierpress.com*, February 2012, and available at http://www.courierpress.com/news/2012/feb/22/ev_23waltrip/?print=1

"You're wasting your time, Mikey . . ." from *In the Blink of an Eye: Dale, Daytona, and the Day that Changed Everything* by Michael Waltrip and Ellis Henican, Hyperion, New York, 2011, page 21.

"Michael's first race in Bobby's kart..." from *In the Blink of an Eye: Dale, Daytona, and the Day that Changed Everything* by Michael Waltrip and Ellis Henican, Hyperion, New York, 2011, page 27.

"My first big win on my first night out . . ." from *In the Blink of an Eye: Dale, Daytona, and the Day that Changed Everything* by Michael Waltrip and Ellis Henican, Hyperion, New York, 2011, page 33.

"The persistence and dedication paid off . . ." from Michael Waltrip Racing official website, retrieved May 2013, and available at http://www.michaelwaltripracing.com/teams/team-owners/michael-waltrip

"I really didn't have any opportunities to race much . . ." from "The Plan," by Michael Waltrip, in *Chicken Soup for the Soul: NASCAR; 101 Stories of Family, Fortitude, and Fast Cars*, ed. Jack Canfield, Mark Victor Hansen, and Cathy Elliot, Chicken Soup for the Soul Publishing, Cos Cob, Connecticut, 2009, page 95.

"If you want to be a Winston Cup driver . . ." from "The Plan," by Michael Waltrip, in *Chicken Soup for the Soul: NASCAR; 101 Stories of Family, Fortitude, and Fast Cars*, ed. Jack Canfield, Mark Victor Hansen, and Cathy Elliot, Chicken Soup for the Soul Publishing, Cos Cob, Connecticut, 2009, page 96.

"A plan is important..." from "The Plan," by Michael Waltrip, in *Chicken Soup for the Soul: NASCAR; 101 Stories of Family, Fortitude, and Fast Cars*, ed. Jack Canfield, Mark Victor Hansen, and Cathy Elliot, Chicken Soup for the Soul Publishing, Cos Cob, Connecticut, 2009, page 97.

"I walked up there, and the car was gone..." from "Michael Waltrip Crash Bristol 1990," YouTube video by TheRealJoseyWales, July 25, 2006, and available at http://www.youtube.com/watch?v=QVlj7F8OJCY

"Life was more precious to the both of them . . ." from "Biography: Michael Waltrip," by Kellyanne Lynch, at *Mikey Power.com*, February

2003, and available at http://www.mikeypower.com/mbio.html

"And since Michael's debut race had been at the super speedway . . ." from *In the Blink of an Eye: Dale, Daytona, and the Day that Changed Everything* by Michael Waltrip and Ellis Henican, Hyperion, New York, 2011, page 77.

"I'm building my Mom and Daddy a house!" from "1996 Winston Select All Star Race: Part 7 of 8," YouTube video by Michael McIntyre, November 30, 2012, and available at https://www.youtube.com/watch?v=73UG0IwAeMA

"Michael had wanted his parents to move . . ." from *In the Blink of an Eye: Dale, Daytona, and the Day that Changed Everything* by Michael Waltrip and Ellis Henican, Hyperion, New York, 2011, page 83.

"But I still ain't won a race have I? . . . " from "1996 Winston Select All Star Race: Part 7 of 8," YouTube video by Michael McIntyre, November 30, 2012, and available at https://www.youtube.com/watch?v=73UG0IwAeMA

"That second place finish looked good on paper . . ." from *In the Blink of an Eye: Dale, Daytona, and the Day that Changed Everything* by Michael Waltrip and Ellis Henican, Hyperion, New York, 2011, page 87.

"As a boy, Michael felt that he didn't have a very close . . ." from *In the Blink of an Eye: Dale, Daytona, and the Day that Changed Everything* by Michael Waltrip and Ellis Henican, Hyperion, New York, 2011, page 13.

"Why? Why, God? Why couldn't you let me win this one for Dad? . . ." from *In the Blink of an Eye: Dale, Daytona, and the Day that Changed Everything* by Michael Waltrip and Ellis Henican, Hyperion, New York, 2011, page 87.

"I hate when I question God's grace and mercy . . ." from *In the Blink of an Eye: Dale, Daytona, and the Day that Changed Everything* by Michael

Waltrip and Ellis Henican, Hyperion, New York, 2011, page 88.
"Thank you, God, for allowing my dad to enjoy this win . . ." from *In the Blink of an Eye: Dale, Daytona, and the Day that Changed Everything* by Michael Waltrip and Ellis Henican, Hyperion, New York, 2011, page 91.

"His three-year battle with cancer ended . . ." from *In the Blink of an Eye: Dale, Daytona, and the Day that Changed Everything* by Michael Waltrip and Ellis Henican, Hyperion, New York, 2011, page 99.

"I want to win, but my life doesn't hinge . . ." from "Biography: Michael Waltrip," by Kellyanne Lynch, at *Mikey Power.com*, February 2003, and available at http://www.mikeypower.com/mbio.html

"After the 2000 season ended, Earnhardt . . ." from "Waltrip Still Haunted by 'That Day,' " by Ed Hinton, *ESPN.com*, February 2011, and available at http://m.espn.go.com/rpm/nascar/story? storyId=6125753&wjb=&pg=3

"Michael prayed and hoped everything would work out . . ." from *In the Blink of an Eye: Dale, Daytona, and the Day that Changed Everything* by Michael Waltrip and Ellis Henican, Hyperion, New York, 2011, page 105.

"Come on man! That a boy! You got 'em Mikey!" from "2001 Daytona 500 Last Lap & Post Race," YouTube video by RRaquello, August 2, 2009, and available at https://www.youtube.com/watch?v=rIGR07z5bpI

"Thank God. Thank my Daddy. I love him so much . . ." from "2001 Daytona 500 Last Lap & Post Race," YouTube video by RRaquello, August 2, 2009, and available at https://www.youtube.com/watch?v=rIGR07z5bpI

"Momma, I love you. Momma, I wish you were here . . ." from "2001 Daytona 500 Last Lap & Post Race," YouTube video by RRaquello, August 2, 2009, and available at https://www.youtube.com/watch?v=rIGR07z5bpI

"Human beings aren't designed to go through . . ." from "Michael Waltrip: Dale Earnhardt Died Trying to Win the Daytona 500, Not Trying to Block," by Mike Bianchi, *The Orlando Sentinel*, February 15. 2011, and available at http://articles.orlandosentinel.com/2011-02-15/sports/os-bianchi-earnhardt-waltrip-0214-20110213_1_dei-race-michael-waltrip-race-car

"This book is a man emotionally naked . . ." from C.S. Lewis, *The Complete C.S. Lewis Signature Classics*, by C.S. Lewis, Harper One, New York, 2002, page 654.

"Dale is dead . . ." from *In the Blink of an Eye: Dale, Daytona, and the Day that Changed Everything* by Michael Waltrip and Ellis Henican, Hyperion, New York, 2011, page 172.

"With Buffy's help, Michael began his mission with a letter . . ." from "Letter to Fans, February 22, 2001" by Michael and Buffy Waltrip, retrieved on July 13, 2013, and available at http://www.motorsport.com/nascar-cup/news/michael-and-buffy-waltrip-letter-to-fans-and-nascar-community/

". . . the verse from 1 Corinthians 15:22 that would later . . ." from *In the Blink of an Eye: Dale, Daytona, and the Day that Changed Everything* by Michael Waltrip and Ellis Henican, Hyperion, New York, 2011, page 193.

"His inability to let go of the past would change his life . . ." from "Waltrip Still Haunted by 'That Day,'" by Ed Hinton, *ESPN.com*, February 2011, and available at http://m.espn.go.com/rpm/nascar/story?storyId=6125753&wjb=&pg=3

"I prayed for it to rain. I prayed for God to forgive me . . ." from "Biography: Michael Waltrip," by Kellyanne Lynch, at *Mikey Power.com*, February 2003, and available at http://www.mikeypower.com/mbio.html

"I wanted to have a team like Dale's . . ." from *In the Blink of an Eye: Dale, Daytona, and the Day that Changed Everything* by Michael Waltrip and Ellis Henican, Hyperion, New York, 2011, page 210.

"I've got a big race shop and a couple . . ." from "Waltrip Still Haunted by 'That Day,'" by Ed Hinton, *ESPN.com*, February 2011, and available at http://m.espn.go.com/rpm/nascar/story?storyId=6125753&wjb=&pg=3

"What followed was a wreck of a man . . ." from "Decade Later, Waltrip Deals with a Crash at Daytona," by George Vecsey, *NY Times.com*, February 16, 2011, and available at http://www.nytimes.com/2011/02/17/sports/17vecsey.html?_r=0

9. DAVID RAGAN: DRIVEN BY FAITH AND ACTION

"David was the second child . . ." from "Adam Ragan Is His NASCAR Driving Brothers' Biggest Fan," by Ed Grisamore, February 2013, and available at http://www.davidragan.com/news_article.cfm/i/380

"Once, when the brothers were still in day care . . ." from "Adam Ragan Feature," Vimeo video by Joel Maydek, June 14, 2013, and available at http://vimeo.com/68405808

"And today, down at the David Ragan Ford . . ." from "Adam Ragan Is His NASCAR Driving Brothers' Biggest Fan," by Ed Grisamore, February 2013, and available at http://www.davidragan.com/news_article.cfm/i/380

"Family is everything! . . ." from authors' interview with David Ragan

"That's how God has used Adam, as a teacher . . ." from authors' interview with David Zachariah Glover, July 29, 2013

"So when I'm thrown a curve, I look . . ." from authors' interview with David Ragan

"We've had family, we've had community . . ." from "Adam Ragan Feature," Vimeo video by Joel Maydek, June 14, 2013, and available at http://vimeo.com/68405808

"David said God ultimately gets the glory . . ." from "NASCAR Driver David Ragan on His Foundation of Faith," by Chad Bonham, *Beliefnet.com*, July 2011, and available at http://blog.beliefnet.com/inspiringathletes/2011/07/nascar-driver-david-ragan-on-his-foundation-of-faith.html

"If you wanna forget this racing deal . . ." from "David Ragan—Home Town Heroes," YouTube video by DrewWRagan, May 28, 2008, and available at https://www.youtube.com/watch?v=b0RoqFo8gmQ

"Good things come to good people . . ." from "David Ragan—Home Town Heroes," YouTube video by DrewWRagan, May 28, 2008, and available at https://www.youtube.com/watch?v=b0RoqFo8gmQ

"David caught a big break in 2005 when he took . . ." from "David Ragan Biography," at David Ragan's official website, retrieved June 2013, and available at http://www.davidragan.com/biography.cfm

"We were just slow . . ." from "David Ragan Gives Notice That He's on Right Track," by Carlos Mendez, *Star Telegram*, July 2011, and available at http://www.star-telegram.com/2011/07/13/v-print/3220183/david-ragan-gives-notice-that.html

"Over the years, delivery routes have strategically . . ." from "Left-Hand-Turn Elimination," by Joel Lovell, *New York Times.com*, December 2007, and available at http://www.nytimes.com/2007/12/09/magazine/09left-handturn.html?_r=0

"Now is the time to fight for every spot . . ." from "David Ragan Gives Notice that He's on Right Track," by Carlos Mendez, *Star Telegram*, July 2011, and available at http://www.star-telegram.com/2011/07/13/v-print/3220183/david-ragan-gives-notice-that.html

"He was raised to be " 'a good guy . . .' " from "David Ragan Interview: Daytona 500 Setback Tough to Forget," by Jeff Gluck, *SBNation.com*, March 2011, and available at http://www.sbnation.com/nascar/2011/3/3/2027148/david-ragan-nascar-news-roush-fenway-racing-2011

"We had a shot to finish in the top three or four . . ." from "Drivers React to Sunday's Martinsville Results: Good, Bad, and Ugly," by Jeff Gluck, *SB Nation.com*, April 2011, and available at http://www.sbnation.com/nascar/2011/4/3/2089105/martinsville-nascar-matt-kenseth-marcos-ambrose-martin-truex-paul-menard-2011

"David, you get up and count your blessings . . ." from "David Ragan—Home Town Heroes," YouTube video by DrewWRagan, May 28, 2008, and available at https://www.youtube.com/watch?v=b0RoqFo8gmQ

"Welcome to Victory Lane, my friend . . ." from "David Ragan Wins 2011 Coke Zero 400 at Daytona," YouTube video by Darth Ridiculous1, July 2, 2011, and available at http://www.youtube.com/watch?v=MQOg4RvVpeU

"But now he began to question his calling . . ." from "NASCAR Driver David Ragan on His Foundation of Faith," by Chad Bonham, *Beliefnet.com*, July 2011, and available at http://blog.beliefnet.com/inspiringathletes/2011/07/nascar-driver-david-ragan-on-his-foundation-of-faith.html

"In the ups and downs of having a career . . ." from authors' interview with David Ragan

"David Ragan Lands Last Available Cup Ride . . ." from "David Ragan Lands Last Available Cup Ride with Front Row," by Chad Leistikow, *USA Today.com*, January 2012, and available at http://usatoday30. usatoday.com/sports/motor/nascar/story/2012-01-16/David-Ragan-lands-last-available-Cup-ride-with-Front-Row/52595270/1

"First off, I gotta thank the Lord . . ." from "David Ragan Wins Talladega Aarons 499 and Gives Glory to God!," YouTube video by tfake91, May 6, 2013, and available at https://www.youtube.com/watch?v=BlMz4c85y08

"This is a true David-versus-Goliath moment here . . ." from "David Ragan Wins Talladega Aarons 499 and Gives Glory to God!," YouTube video by tfake91, May 6, 2013, and available at https://www.youtube.com/watch?v=BlMz4c85y08

"Without God none of us would be here and getting . . ." from "David Ragan Wins Talladega Aarons 499 and Gives Glory to God!," YouTube video by tfake91, May 6, 2013, and available at https://www.youtube.com/watch?v=BlMz4c85y08

"We certainly have a lot to be thankful for . . ." from "NASCAR Sprint Cup Post Race from Talladega May 5, 2013: David Ragan," YouTube video by Greg Engle, May 6, 2013, and available at https://www.youtube.com/watch?v=LINrSq1XEMg

"Beats Goliath. Brakes for Trains" from "2013 NASCAR Sprint All-Star Race Paint Schemes," at *Jayski.com*, retrieved July 2013, and available at http://www.jayski.com/news/schemes/story/_/page/2013-NASCAR-Sprint-All-Star-Race-Paint-Schemes

10. OTHER DRIVERS OF FAITH, YOUNG AND OLD

"Up until then, Jamie had never viewed God . . ." from "Son's Birth Culminates Quite a Year for Jamie McMurray," by Dustin Long, *Carroll County Times*, December 3, 2010, and available at http://www. carrollcountytimes.com/mobile/article_9fb00578-fee8-11df-9cf8-001cc4c03286.html

"Working out has become easier for me . . ." from "Jamie McMurray's Training Program," by Brittany Risher, *Men's Health*, retrieved July 2013, and available at http://www.menshealth.com/fitness/jamie-mcmurrays-training-program

"I'm a huge believer in prayer . . ." from "Speed Victory Lane: Jamie McMurray," YouTube video by edwards99rules, February 14, 2010, and available at http://www.youtube.com/watch?v=iCnMn4-Dm-s

"He woke up that morning and kneeled beside . . ." from "Speed Victory Lane: Jamie McMurray," YouTube video by edwards99rules, February 14, 2010, and available at http://www.youtube.com/watch?v=iCnMn4-Dm-s

"Man, did God ever answer my prayers . . ." from "Speed Victory Lane: Jamie McMurray," YouTube video by edwards99rules, February 14, 2010, and available at http://www.youtube.com/watch?v=iCnMn4-Dm-s

"I want to take the time to explain something . . ." from "2010 Bank of America 500: Jamie McMurray in Victory Lane," YouTube video by pacmancucumber1783, October 17, 2010, and available at http://www. youtube.com/watch?v=0wvlt-VHAcI

"Well, that's very nice to say . . ." from "Ned Jarrett Never Rode Alone," Vimeo video by the Lutheran Hour Ministries, "Profiles: Beyond the Spotlight with Chris Schneider," retrieved August 2013, and available at http://vimeo.com/56814152

"They *took* us; they didn't *send* us," from "Ned Jarrett Never Rode Alone," Vimeo video by the Lutheran Hour Ministries, "Profiles: Beyond the Spotlight with Chris Schneider," retrieved August 2013, and available at http://vimeo.com/56814152

"Then one Sunday in 1942 . . ." from "Ned Jarrett Was a Racing Legend by Any Name," by Jason Stein, *Newsday.com*, January 8, 2013, and available at http://www.newsday.com/classifieds/cars/ned-jarrett-was-a-racing-legend-by-any-name-1.4419977

"Ned was allowed to work on cars . . ." from "Ned Jarrett Never Rode Alone," Vimeo video by the Lutheran Hour Ministries, "Profiles: Beyond the Spotlight with Chris Schneider," retrieved August 2013, and available at http://vimeo.com/56814152

"In February 1966, eight days before . . ." from "Ned Jarrett Chief's Guest" by the Associated Press, *The Sumter Daily Item*, February 17, 1966, and available at http://news.google.com/

"They that wait upon the Lord shall renew their strength . . ." from Isaiah 40:31

"My daddy made moonshine . . ." from "Morgan Shepherd: Last Call from Wilkes County," May 8, 1996, from *Motorsports.com*, retrieved August 5, 2013, and available at www.motorsports.com/nascar-cup/news/morgan-shepherd-interview/

"Your daddy's coming home . . ." from "Morgan Shepherd: Last Call from Wilkes County," May 8, 1996, from *Motorsports.com*, retrieved August 5, 2013, and available at www.motorsports.com/nascar-cup/news/morgan-shepherd-interview/

"I paid twelve dollars and fifty cents . . ." from "Morgan Shepherd: Last Call from Wilkes County," May 8, 1996, from *Motorsports.com*, retrieved August 5, 2013, and available at www.motorsports.com/nascar-cup/news/morgan-shepherd-interview/

"In my home that night . . ." from "Morgan Shepherd's Christian Testimony," by Morgan Shepherd, from the Motor Racing Outreach official website, retrieved August 2013, and available at http://www.go2mro.com/testimonies/morganshepherd.php

"Before that, he had 18 months of amateur . . ." from "Biography" at Blake Koch's official website, retrieved July 2013, and available at http://www.blakekoch.com/index.php?bio

"I wanted to set racing aside," from "A Conversation with NASCAR Driver Blake Koch," by Chad Bonham, *Beliefnet.com*, retrieved July 2013, and available at http://blog.beliefnet.com/inspiringathletes/2011/10/a-conversation-with-nascar-driver-blake-koch.html

"Faith sustained Blake as he walked with . . ." from "A Conversation with NASCAR Driver Blake Koch," by Chad Bonham, *Beliefnet.com*, retrieved July 2013, and available at http://blog.beliefnet.com/inspiringathletes/2011/10/a-conversation-with-nascar-driver-blake-koch.html

"If you heal the man . . . he will heal . . ." from "Homepage" at Rise Up official website, retrieved July 2013, and available at http://www.rizeup.us/contact_us.html

"After living the Hollywood fast life . . ." from "Mark Koch: Hollywood's Comeback Kid," video by CBN Entertainment Podcast, retrieved July 2013, and available at http://www.cbn.com/tv/1414129722001

"A couple months earlier . . ." from "GodSpeaks.com Blake Koch," by Bill Sullivan, Dec 1, 2009, and available at http://goodnewsfl.org/godspeaks-com_blake_koch/

"Let's get it over with and go . . ." from "A Conversation with NASCAR Driver Blake Koch," by Chad Bonham, *Beliefnet.com*, retrieved July 2013, and available at http://blog.beliefnet.com/inspiringathletes/2011/10/a-conversation-with-nascar-driver-blake-koch.html

"I didn't think that my faith in Christ . . ." from "Blake Koch.com Blog" at Blake Koch official website, retrieved July 2013, and available at http://www.blakekoch.com/index.php?blog&action=view&post_id=4

"It all comes down to this . . ." from "NASCAR Hall of Fame Induction Ceremony," YouTube video by EdwinTV9, February 20, 2012, and available at https://www.youtube.com/watch?v=vCbfpauObLI

". . . grew up with a strong Christian heritage . . ." from "Waltrip Helping Lead Revival Among NASCAR Race Drivers," by the Associated Press, *Times-News*, June 14, 1992, and available at http://news.google.com/newspapers

"Bring it on. Nothing bothers me . . ." from "Darrell Waltrip's Film," at the I Am Second website, retrieved August 2013, and available at http://www.iamsecond.com/seconds/darrell-waltrip/

"We were beside ourselves with joy . . ." from *What Southern Women Know About Faith* by Ronda Rich, Zondervan, Grand Rapids, 2009, page 15.

"I race on Sundays . . ." from "Lord, This Is Car #17," by Dave Caldwell, *Beliefnet.com*, 2004, and available at http://www.beliefnet.com/Entertainment/Books/2004/09/Lord-This-Is-Car-17.aspx

"The Christian faith is a daily walk . . ." from *Sundays Will Never Be the Same* by Darrell Waltrip and Nate Larkin, Free Press, New York, 2012, page 119.

"I want to be the best dad, the best husband . . ." from "Waltrip Helping Lead Revival Among NASCAR Race Drivers," by the Associated Press, in *Times-News*, June 14, 1992, and available at http://news.google.com/newspapers